Alexander Balloch Grosart

Representative Nonconformists :

With the Message of Their Life-Work for To-Day

Alexander Balloch Grosart

Representative Nonconformists :
With the Message of Their Life-Work for To-Day

ISBN/EAN: 9783337053796

Printed in Europe, USA, Canada, Australia, Japan

Cover: Foto ©Thomas Meinert / pixelio.de

More available books at **www.hansebooks.com**

# Representative Nonconformists:

WITH THE MESSAGE OF THEIR LIFE-WORK FOR TO-DAY.

I. JOHN HOWE: *Intellectual Sanctity.*
II. RICHARD BAXTER: *Seraphic Fervour*
III. SAMUEL RUTHERFORD: *Devout Affe......*
IV. MATTHEW HENRY: *Sanctified Common-Sense.*

BY THE REV.

ALEXANDER B. GROSART,
LL.D. (EDIN.), F.S.A. (SCOT.),

ST. GEORGE'S PRESBYTERIAN CHURCH, BLACKBURN, LANCASHIRE;
AUTHOR OF "THE PRINCE OF LIGHT AND PRINCE OF DARKNESS IN CONFLICT," "JESUS, MIGHTY TO SAVE," "SMALL SINS," "THE LAMBS ALL SAFE," "HELPER OF JOY," "THE KEY-BEARER," "JOINING THE CHURCH," "HYMNS," ETC.; EDITOR OF "FULLER WORTHIES' LIBRARY," "CHERTSEY WORTHIES' LIBRARY," ETC.

London:
HODDER AND STOUGHTON,
27, PATERNOSTER ROW.

MDCCCLXXIX.

THE SPRING LECTURE

OF THE

PRESBYTERIAN CHURCH OF ENGLAND

FOR 1879.

Delivered in the College, Guildford Street, London.

INTRODUCTION.

IN his funeral sermon for DR. WILLIAM BATES, JOHN HOWE—the greatest of our four REPRESENTATIVE NONCONFORMISTS—in his splendid summing-up, announces his purpose thus:—"The little I shall say of him shall be, not by way of history, but of character."*

This admirably expresses my own *motif* in these Lectures. I trust that in my Lives of DR. RICHARD SIBBES, THOMAS BROOKS, and many other of the Puritan Divines, as well as in my FULLER WORTHIES' LIBRARY and CHERTSEY WORTHIES' LIBRARY—to name

---

* Works, vol. vi., p. 294.

only these—sufficient proofs have been given that when called for I have not grudged any expenditure of pains or research or toil, towards getting at the facts of the Lives in hand, or elucidatory of the Works.

But in the present case it does not at all come within my province to tell the external story of any of my Worthies. I assume that the Life itself is in each case less or more familiar to my Readers. This is surely not unreasonable, seeing that there are readily accessible such authorities as these:—

(α) JOHN HOWE.—Life by HENRY ROGERS, author of "The Eclipse of Faith," etc., etc., 1 vol. 8vo., 1863 (also original edition): Calamy: Hunt: Dr. James Hamilton: Christophers, etc., etc.

(β) RICHARD BAXTER.—Life by WILLIAM ORME (editor of "Practical Works"), 1 large vol., 8vo, 1830: Reliquiæ

Baxterianæ (folio) and numerous Memoirs, Essays, etc., etc.

(γ) SAMUEL RUTHERFORD.—Life by Thomson in his "Letters," 2 vol. cr. 8vo, 1836: by Dr. Andrew A. Bonar, prefixed to "Letters," 2 vols. 8vo, 1863: Wodrow: McCrie, etc., etc.

(δ) MATTHEW HENRY.—Life by SIR J. B. WILLIAMS, Knt., and numerous others introductory to editions of the "Commentary," and of his miscellaneous works.

Besides these, there are the equally accessible Histories of the LATER PURITANS and Nonconformists, in which all our quaternion fill considerable space.

From these and kindred sources any one seeking to master the facts of the several Lives, or who wishes critically to determine their historical-literary, literary-historical place among leading Nonconformists and in relation to Churchmen, will have himself to blame if he do not draw ample materials, as well for their Biography as for their part in the chief movements of their time.

My present commission (as my choice) is wholly different. As addressing in the first instance young men—students and others—and my fellow-ministers and fellow-workers, my main design is from SELECTED CHARACTERISTICS of the Life and Life-work of these Representative Nonconformists to incite and quicken to higher and nobler service of The Master in our day and generation. This being so, I am perfectly at ease under the foreshadow of blame, on the ground that what is wanted is presentation of facts and letting them make their own impression. One naturally answers, 'Wanted by whom?' Equally at ease am I in anticipation of being charged with 'improving' Howe and Baxter, Rutherford and Henry—as the old Divines called their reading of lessons from special events and circumstances. TO DRAW SUCH LESSONS and to drive them home into heart and conscience *is* my purpose and endeavour. In order to this I am—necessarily as I think—discoursive and discursive. If any one choose to fling stones at me as 'didactic,' 'hortatory,' 'moralizing,' and so on: so be it. I shall not like the stone-flinging, but shall bear it.

I believe the didactic and hortatory to be effective in their own place. I believe them both to be urgently demanded to-day. For the loss is that except here and there, FACTS and CHARACTERISTICS if simply told do not leave the impression which they might and ought. A bullet will not strike or kill without gunpowder and fire. I cherish a hope that in these Lectures there is some pointblank shot and some magnetic force. So far as I know my own heart, my *animus* is not polemical, but if possible to do some good in the way of practical stimulus, of rousing, of winning to study and re-study, and to emulation of these Worthies among our forefathers. And so I turn to our four Representative Nonconformists.*

---

* It is deemed well to explain that most of the illustrative quotations throughout, were not read but reserved for the printed book, from the limited time available.

CONTENTS.

INTRODUCTION—Quotation—*motif* of the Lectures—'character' not external story—accessible authorities—'improving,' etc. —intentionally hortatory and didactic—practical usefulness in stirring to higher service . . . *Pages* v. *to* x.

I. JOHN HOWE:

Intellectual Sanctity.

Inevitable impression—portraits—incident at Whitehall—appointed domestic chaplain to Cromwell—'noble presence' —advantage of—description of Dr. Bates—heredity— meanly-housed souls—noble form and falsehood—Shakespeare quotations—the Platonism of Spenser and Milton— quotations from—A FIRST PRESENT-DAY TRUTH AND DUTY —Christians to-day urged to fashion and transfigure their very look—evils of the opposite—Whittier—Andrew Fuller— Dr. Robert S. Candlish—Howe a fellow-disciple with John Smith, Dr. Henry More, Dr. Ralph Cudworth— expression of face a beatitude—of grace not of birth— Phineas Fletcher—George Herbert—an over-looked incident—controversy with Thomas Larkham, of Tavistock— rash, ill-informed, pestiferous zeal, hot of temper—heart-change—controlling grace—contrast of "bitter words" to and of Larkham with after-words—Stillingfleet—Psalm cxli. 5—A SECOND PRESENT-DAY TRUTH—'conversion' a reality and universal need—Christ unique (note)—modern Scientists unscientific and uncritical herein—A THIRD PRE-

SENT-DAY TRUTH—the every-day life of Howe—"notional knowledge" worthless—faith transforms the character—beliefs must enter into the life—"Meditation"—Intuition—Ratiocination—intellectual sanctity to be striven for—be "partakers of Divine nature"—the wonder and glory of man's destiny to be 'like God'—character makes a minister's 'preaching' his power—A FOURTH PRESENT-DAY TRUTH—habitual reverence—Milton's word-portrait of President Bradshaw—a living message to the Scientists of to-day—quotations from Howe—awe and its opposite—"petulant and irreverent liberty"—spurious reverence—Socinus and what can only be known by the Scriptures—sarcasm—the "Divine simplicity," misconceptions of—Tennyson's cry for "more reverence"—Dr. Darwin—Tyndall—Huxley—a "rectified frontier"—large ideas of the legitimate sphere of 'hard thinking'—A FIFTH PRESENT-DAY TRUTH—right and lawful to THINK and even speculate—A SIXTH PRESENT-DAY TRUTH—impassioned appeal for Christ-like lives—the most attractive of all evidence—rebuke of Atheists—"higher criticism"—just disdain—A SEVENTH PRESENT-DAY TRUTH—exalted conception of man—argument from what man is, being a Christian, to what God *is*—the problem—'was,' not 'is'—'is' or 'was'—restitution—quotations from Howe—Christianity recognizes and addresses our reason, conscience, moral nature, and counts on capacities of response—great passages from Howe on the ruined temple of man's soul, and the fitness of God's departure from it—summary—man re-made in God's image—man, though fallen, responsive to truth and grace—AN EIGHTH PRESENT-DAY TRUTH—'application' and appeal after argument or exposition—quotation from the "Redeemer's Tears wept over Lost Souls"—revival of this coveted—points 'left out' in Life and Work—Robert Hall's estimate of Howe for himself "as a minister"—our confirmation—Rev. S. W. Christophers—the "good man"—Edward Young. . . *Pages* 1 *to* 105.

II. RICHARD BAXTER:

Seraphic Fervour.

Epithets of Bede and Hooker—the '*holy* Baxter'—Essayist—Orme—Coleridge—Howe—Calamy—Macaulay—Tulloch—Trench—FIRST PRESENT-DAY TRUTH AND DUTY—THE VOLUME OF HIS BEING, AND PRODIGIOUS VITALITY—Grainger—physical, intellectual, moral, spiritual—ubiquity and 'uncanny' omnipresence—Society for Propagation of the Gospel—the Slave Trade—Sir James Stephen and Brougham—tireless energy—Burns—writings—enormous difference—heir-looms—APPEAL TO MINISTERS AND OTHERS NOW—SERAPHIC FERVOUR—'liturgical'—modern fastidiousness—horror of vulgarity—ultra-refinement—A SECOND PRESENT-DAY TRUTH AND DUTY—SOUGHT THE GOOD OF 'THE COMMON PEOPLE'—preaching and books—creator of popular Christian literature—contrast with George Herbert—remarkable quotation from Sir James Stephen—successive 'practical' books—their value as literature—style—Archbishop Trench—A THIRD PRESENT-DAY TRUTH—FAITH IN THE HUMAN CONSCIENCE—Savonarola—Whitfield—no academical training—Sir James Stephen—addressed the conscience—needed to-day—to be combined with sympathy—the tenderness and humanity of Baxter—quotations—Dr. Bates—Orme—declarative preaching—urgent want of to-day—not 'informing' merely, but 'transforming'—scholarship—revision of Authorized Version—results—quotations exemplifying Baxter's preaching—A FOURTH PRESENT-DAY TRUTH AND DUTY—THE USE MADE OF THE ENGLISH BIBLE BY BAXTER—a tribute to the English Bible—a lustrous story—A FIFTH PRESENT-DAY TRUTH—SCHISM of the Church of England in its attitude toward Nonconformists—John Howe—'meetings'—actual results—longing for a change—"Valediction," poem by Baxter. . . *Pages* 107 *to* 193.

III. SAMUEL RUTHERFORD:

Devout Affection.

Rutherford not a "household word" like the others—by-ways not high-ways of history and literature—one small "bush burning but not consumed"—the Letters, Rotterdam, 1664—other writings—characterized—controversial writings condemned for their bitterness and narrowness—JOHN GOODWIN—BUCKLE—JOHN MILTON—PROFESSOR MASSON—at Westminster Assembly—widened views and estimates—FREEDOM OF CONSCIENCE—imperfect enunciations of it—DR. ANDREW A. BONAR—an edition more perfect—Cromwell—the Letters' popularity far and near—BAXTER—LOVE—TOPLADY—ROMAINE—HERVEY—RICHARD CECIL—WILBERFORCE—THOMAS CHALMERS—ERSKINE OF LINLATHEN—a possible misuse of the Letters—Song of Solomon—enfeebling the moral nature—PRESENT-DAY TRUTHS AND DUTIES—I. THE LORD JESUS AS A LIVING PERSON IS ALL IN ALL—the Person not the Book—'bodily presence'—'personal reign'—Napoleon—II. THE SECOND APPEARING OF THE LORD JESUS IS LONGED FOR—the 'blessed hope'—its certainty—but not as millenarians teach—criticism of Dr. Bonar—III. THE WORK OF CHRIST IS PUT IN THE FOREGROUND—no mere 'asides'—central—'imputed righteousness'—correction of prevalent mistakes—righteousness.—IV. PERSONAL HOLINESS IS STRENUOUSLY AIMED AT AND SPIRITUAL DECLENSION MOURNED—human and divine side—"take more pains"—imperfect realization of Rutherford—spiritual decay—lamentation over the state of the Church and world—protest—V. CONSOLATION TO THE AFFLICTED IS RICH AND FULL—Fetched from the Bible—personal experience—consolation not spiritual coddling—the Letters broadly regarded—their message for to-day—THE POWER AND INFLUENCE OF LETTER-WRITING—ancient and modern Letters—the New Testament Letters—opportunities—occasions—"go and do likewise"—H. T. White—Adelaide Procter. *Pages* 195 *to* 262.

IV. MATTHEW HENRY:

Sanctified Common-Sense.

Philip Henry—of 'The Ejected'—Thomas Baker—Matthew Henry a 'child of many prayers'—the 'Flight into Egypt' —home-training—education—at Gray's Inn—theology—invited to preach at Nantwich by Mr. Illidge—at Chester— settlement there—activity—exposition of the entire Bible— removal to London—annual visit to Chester—death:—his 'Commentary' his supreme achievement—minor writings —NO COMMENTARY HAS HAD SUCH A LARGE AND SUSTAINED CIRCULATION—Trapp—Clarke—Scott—Gill—a living sale—its significance and value—THE CIRCULATION IS RELIGIOUS NOT LITERARY—its spiritual character its attraction—a grandmother—Kinross-shire—a 'good man' there—multiply by the aggregate—at the bottom of the Revival under Wesley and Whitfield—kept the 'lamp alive' when Presbyterianism lapsed into Arianism—*the* one available Commentary on the whole Bible—ITS FINE CATHOLICITY—no sectarianism or controversies—willing to be held for 'old-fashioned'—the central controlling thing. SANCTIFIED COMMON-SENSE, 18th and 16-17th centuries—most uncommon of all sense—John Foster on Henry—speaking *of* him now speaks *for* himself—EXAMPLES OF SANCTIFIED COMMON-SENSE — quotations — secular employments—earthly and heavenly—communion with God and duties—temptation— "no child"—complaints *to* God not *of* God—communion and prayer—Abraham's sin, imitated by Isaac—"curious questions"—infirmities—family-differences—over-strictness at home—constancy and obstinacy—over-doing—design of Holy Scripture—explaining everything—robes of service— the Church—"A String of Pearls" of quotations from the Commentary—another "String of Pearls"—other characteristics, with illustrative quotations— I. Brevity and Wisdom —II. Pungency and Ingenuity—III. Savouriness and Quaint felicities of wording—mere gleanings—any other from a different standpoint find as many more—the place of the

Commentary among forces in the religious life of England, and elsewhere—Hunt—Lecky—the Author's intention to supplement 'learned' commentaries—Bp. Patrick—Pool—prayerfulness—"Homer nods" (foot-note).
Pages 263 *to* 346.

CONCLUSION—many other equally illustrious REPRESENTATIVE NONCONFORMISTS—why Presbyterians selected—closing remarks—practical appeals for a higher life and nobler service—longing for union—ultimate triumph
Pages 346 *to* 357.

APPENDIX A.: SPENSER'S Hymn . *Pages* 358 *to* 360.

APPENDIX B.: THOMAS LARKHAM and HOWE; and notice of an earlier controversy hitherto overlooked.
Pages 361 *to* 376.

APPENDIX C.: Opponents of Rutherford . *Page* 377 *to* 380.

JOHN HOWE:
Intellectual Sanctity.

"Do not suffer yourselves to be insensibly seized by a mean and sordid sloth. Set your thoughts awake with vigorous diligence, give not out before you have well begun. Resolve, since you have a thinking power about you, you will use it to this most necessary purpose; and hold your thoughts to it. See that your minds do not presently tire and flag; that you be rationally, peremptorily, and soberly obstinate in this pursuit; yield not to be diverted. Disdain, having minds that can reach up to the Great Original and Author of all things, that they should be confined to this dirty earth, or only to things low and mean."—*The Living Temple*, Pt. II., c. iii.

"Let such as have not been used to think of anything more than what they could see with their eyes, and to whom reasoning only seems difficult because they have not tried what they can do in it, but use their thoughts a little; and by moving them a few easy steps, they will soon find themselves as sure of this as that they see, or hear, or understand, or are anything."—*Ibid.*, Pt. I., c. ii.

JOHN HOWE, M.A.,

FELLOW OF MAGDALEN COLLEGE, OXFORD.

Born at Loughborough, Leicestershire, May 17, 1630 : *Died at London, April* 2, 1705 : *Buried in Parish Church, All-Hallows, Bread Street.*

THE inevitable impression left on a capable, "considering,"* and modest reader of the Life and Works of JOHN HOWE is, that he must have been a man of exceptionally noble presence, and of co-equal intellect.

I wish, in the outset, TO ACCENTUATE THE FORMER. I have gone over and over to the

---

* "Considering"—a favourite word with Howe, *e.g.*, "The continual mixture of good and evil in this present state of things . . . does naturally prompt a *considering* mind to the belief and hope of another" (Works, by Rogers, vol. i., p. 13). "The supposal of a not unusual *asyndeton*, would, without the help of magic, have relieved a *considering* reader" (*Ibid.*, vol. v., p. 169), *et frequenter.*

Williams' Library to study and re-study his portrait there; while at home I have found myself similarly drawn to Sir Peter Lely's equally authentic one, as engraved by F. Holl for Hewlett.* I never have been thus occupied without enrichment, or without a deepened sense of his greatness and sanctity. It actualizes to me—next to Milton's—the world-known saying of "the human face divine." HENRY ROGERS—his amplest Biographer—thus puts it :—

"Howe's external appearance was such as served to exhibit to the greatest advantage his rare intellectual and moral endowments. His stature was lofty, his aspect commanding, and his manner an impressive union of ease and dignity. His countenance—the expression of which is at once so sublime and so lovely, so full both of majesty of thought and purity of feeling—is best understood by the portrait. It is (to use the language of Gregory Nyssa in reference to Basil) βλέμμα τῷ τόνῳ τῆς ψυχῆς ἐντεινόμενον, 'a countenance attuned to harmony with the mind.'"†

CALAMY, who knew him well, tells us that—

---

* Works, 3 vols., 8vo. (Tegg).
† Life, by Rogers, p. 318.

"As to his person, he was very tall and exceeding graceful. He had a good presence, and a piercing but pleasant eye; and there was that in his looks and carriage, that discovered that he had something within that was uncommonly great, and tended to excite veneration." *

That the living face was an arrestive one, is proved by the well-known, and happily, well-authenticated incident, whereby he became the Domestic Chaplain of OLIVER CROMWELL: "one of those trifling incidents, as men are wont to consider them, but on which Divine Providence seems to delight in suspending the most important events." † His already-quoted Biographer—following Calamy—thus narrates it:—

"At the close of 1656, or in the beginning of 1657, some important business brought him to London. On the last Sabbath of his stay there (and it is worthy of remark that he had already been detained beyond the period he had assigned for his return), curiosity led him to the Chapel at Whitehall. The name of the preacher who attracted him thither is unknown. Cromwell was present; and as 'he generally had his eyes everywhere' (an expression of Calamy's) the noble and

---

* *Ibid.*   † *Ibid.*, p. 37.

expressive physiognomy of Howe soon fell under his notice. Nor was this to be wondered at; an observer of human nature, far less sagacious than Oliver Cromwell, might have discerned in the lineaments of Howe's face, the indications of no common character. As soon as service was concluded, a message was despatched to inform Howe that the Protector desired to speak with him. If surprised at such an extraordinary summons, he must have been still more surprised to hear the Protector (who had already concluded from his appearance that he was a minister) request him to 'preach at Whitehall Chapel on the following Lord's Day.' Howe, whose modesty recoiled from a proposal which other and more ambitious men would have exulted to embrace, endeavoured to excuse himself. Cromwell, with that peremptoriness which ever characterized him, told him 'that it was in vain to think of excusing himself, for that he would take no denial.' Howe, who did not know much of the arts of a courtier, and probably would have disdained to practise them, pleaded with much simplicity, that 'he had despatched all the matters which had brought him to London, that he was now anxious to return home, and that he could not be detained longer without serious inconvenience.' 'Why,' rejoined the pertinacious Oliver, 'what great injury are you likely to sustain by tarrying a little longer?' To this Howe—who, in the spirit of a true pastor, considered the welfare of his flock far more important than the favour of the Protector, their esteem as the highest honour, and their love as his most grateful reward—replied, that his people were very kind to him; that they would be uneasy at his protracted absence;

that they would think he neglected them, and that he but little valued their esteem and affection.' 'Well,' said Cromwell, 'I will write to them myself, and will undertake the task of procuring them a suitable substitute.' This he actually did; and Howe, being thus relieved from his scruples, or rather not knowing how to persist in opposing the wishes of one whose requests, like those of kings, were little less than commands, consented to the Protector's proposal. But after he had preached one, Cromwell in the same manner insisted upon a second and third sermon, and prevailed by the same pertinacity as before; and at length, after much private conversation, told him that 'nothing would serve him but Howe must remove to London, and become his domestic chaplain, and that he would take care that the people at Torrington should be supplied to their satisfaction.' Howe exerted himself to the utmost to escape such an unwelcome honour; but Cromwell, who, as Calamy truly observes, 'could not bear to be contradicted after he had once got the power into his hands,' would listen to no denial. At length, therefore, Howe, who was assured that he would have the means of doing great service to religion in the Protector's household, the whole arrangements of which were to be submitted to himself and a reverend colleague, was induced to consent. He accordingly removed with his family to Whitehall, where some of his children were born."*

* Life, as before, pp. 37-40. *In loco* Rogers effectively disposes of Palmer's blundering account—afterwards cancelled by himself—in the "Nonconf. Memorial," *s.n.*

This incident is suggestive in many ways; and one would greatly wish to recover the letter that Cromwell wrote to Torrington.* I give it, however, mainly to confirm our opening remark on Howe's noble presence.

It was unquestionably an immense advantage to him to have such a temple for his soul. His own fine words of another at once admirably enforce the advantage, and unconsciously describe himself. In the celebrated funeral sermon for silver-tongued DR. BATES, he thus introduces his 'character':—

"First, to take notice of, what must with every one come first in view; namely, his *self-recommending aspect*, composed of gravity and pleasantness, with the graceful mien and comeliness of his person. That was said upon no slight consideration of the nature of man, from unbribed common estimate, that whatever a man's virtuous endowment be, it is the more taking and acceptable as coming *e pulchro corpore*, 'from a handsome well-formed body.' God had designed him to circumstances and a station not obscure in the world, and had accordingly formed him with advantage,

---

* Several such letters of Cromwell are preserved. See Carlyle, *s.n.*

so that his exterior and first aspectable part, might draw respect. And though the treasure to be lodged there, was to be put into an earthen vessel, yet even that was wrought *meliore luto,* of finer or more accurately-figured and better-turned clay. He was to stand before kings. . . . His concern lay not only with mean men, though he could tell also how to condescend to the meanest. His aspect and deportment was not austere, but both decently grave and amiable, such as might command at once both reverence and love; and was herein not a lying, but the true picture of his mind. I may to this purpose borrow his own words concerning one . . . whose fragrant memory will long survive the age he lived in. . . . Of him the Doctor says, 'A constant serenity reigned in his countenance, the visible sign of the Divine calm in his heart; the peace of God that passes all understanding.' . . . Of whom could this have been more fitly said than, *mutato nomine,* of Dr. Bates? How rarely should we see a countenance so constant and so faithful an index of an undisturbed, composed mind! Through that, if we looked into this, how rich furniture of the inner man should we perceive and admire!"*

I have dwelt thus at length and lingeringly, on "the first aspectable part" of Howe, because I find in it A LIVING MESSAGE FOR US TO-DAY.

---

* Works, as before, vol. vi., p. 294-5.

First of all, in the fact that John Howe inherited his "noble presence"—from his illustrious and venerable father, and in all probability a long ancestry—I am summoned to remember that we inherit and transmit form and feature. We cannot sunder a man from his ancestry. There is a vast deal more of suggestion than some apprehend, in the Scriptural expression, "received by tradition (inherited) from your fathers" (1 Peter i. 18). Even in such a thing as this of noble (and equally of ignoble) presence, there is a strange, mysterious heredity and "visiting" to the third and fourth generation; and a "shewing of mercy" more transcendent still. Parents would do well to ponder this.

Further: over-against the "noble presence" of Howe, I do not forget that some of the noblest souls have been meanly housed. It is the tenant that has 'enfamoused' the house. What would a valuator name for some of England's supremest 'mighties'' and worthies' houses, viewed simply as brick and mortar?

The shekinah is the glory. Take for example the house inhabited by the soul that the world calls Socrates: what have you? A bald head, flat nose, fleshy lips, a stout and rather ungainly figure. Or, take Paul. I do not know, but I imagine for myself the writer of "Fought the good fight" as a little hook-nosed, gray, old man, with no look of majesty, but the reverse, as he dips his pen in the ink-bottle and writes that grand letter, ere he dies, to "Timothy, my dearly beloved son." That is the man of whom his detractors said, "His bodily presence is weak, and his speech contemptible." Those who have no "bodily presence" may gratefully recall this.

Once more: I must indicate—without dwelling on it—that noble presence or form may be associated with falsehood and baseness. Beside homely Socrates stands Alcibiades, with the form and beauty of an Apollo, admiring the good, but hopelessly following the bad. Shakespeare knew man,—as scarcely another ever has done,—and does not he say?—

> "O what may man within him hide,
> Though angel on the outward side."—
> *Measure for Measure*, iii. 2.

And again—

> "The devil can cite Scripture for his purpose :
> ... O what a goodly outside falsehood hath."—
> *Merchant of Venice*, i. 3.

This must never be forgotten, else we shall be deceived manifoldly and sorrowfully.

Beyond these elements and details, I must broaden-out a more fundamental thing still, in (to return on quoted words) "the constant serenity that reigned in his countenance, the visible sign of the Divine calm in his breast; the peace of God that passes all understanding."

I am heretic enough to believe in the Platonism of Spenser and Milton. I regard it not as idle Pleasures of Imagination, but as a subtle reality that to a measureless extent we hold in our own keeping and fashioning this body of ours and its immortal inhabitant. "So"—to select one consummate stanza from as dulcet a piece of music as our language possesses—Spenser's Hymn in Honour of Beauty :—

" ——So every spirit, as it is most pure
And hath in it the more of heavenly light,
So it the fairer bodie doth procure
To habit in, and is more fairely dight
With chearefull grace and amiable sight:
For of the soule the bodie forme doth take;
For soule is forme, and doth the bodie make."*

Similarly Milton in Comus, tells how "oft converse with heavenly habitants" will

"Begin to cast a beam on th' outward shape,
The unpolluted temple of the mind,
And turns it by degrees to the soul's essence
Till all be made immortal."

I know of none whose pictured face so exquisitely and perfectly and grandly fulfils the "fine phrenzy" of the earlier and later poet. I add grandly, because with surpassing loveliness there is a majesty that beauty alone does not express. I do not tarry to discuss either the fact or the speculation. MY PURPOSE IS A PRACTICAL ONE. I would urge that while only a comparatively elect few are dowered with such a presence as cannot escape men's notice,

---

* See Appendix A. for full quotation.

but, whether alone or in the street, magnet-like draws attention, and compels another and another look, and the question, 'Who is that?' we yet have all something—more than we think—to do with the fashioning and tempering and mellowing (so to say) of our face. That is—as I take it—the soul informs and transforms feature and expression, until whatever the soul comes to be—by God's grace—these reflect and interpret it. It is no common beatitude when by our very face—its look and light—we bring sunshine and purity and something of a celestial air with us. Contrariwise, how very many ministers of the Gospel—in all the Churches—and private Christians, by their "vinegar aspect," their austere, rigid, PROFESSIONAL bearing, or by a religious simper and artificial, reedy, whining voice, repell hearts that are yearning to unburden themselves! How very many have so hardened their facial muscles and the hang of their lips, into sour, or peevish, or irritable and sanctimonious expression, and de-naturalized their tones and mode of speaking and intercourse with their fellow-men, that unreality is stamped on them! Age and care corrugate the brow and place crow-feet about the eyes, and pinch and tan soon enough and surely enough, without our co-operation. So that we ought to conserve this body of ours, so "fearfully and wonderfully made," and bring out, not obliterate; beautify, not deform; ennoble, not demean ourselves. I like to call up two grandmothers who, in a serene old age —well-nigh the completed century—had ruddy apple-cheeks and a light of hope that paled your mythical saint's mythical nimbus. Let there be within the heart the peace, the calm, the joy, the "good hope" that belong to us as we are Christians,—when behind the (mere) name, Christ by His Spirit has re-made us after His own likeness,—and let us strenuously and vigilantly watch against artificiality, and our very face shall be wrought into conformity. WHITTIER, of America, in a delightful little poem has painted for us just such a face:—

> " Sweet promptings unto kindest deeds
> Were in her very look;
> We read her face, as one who reads
> A true and holy book."

It is told of ANDREW FULLER—who certainly was as plain and un-intellectual-looking as almost any of like eminence—that in the pulpit a light of unearthly glory seemed sometimes to suffuse and make beautiful his rugged and homely features as he pleaded in prayer with God for men and with men for God in his great sermons. I was told at Kettering that the little children ran across the streets to catch his benignant look or to feel the soft pressure of his great hands on their young heads.

I myself can testify that the slight, not to say deformed, body of Dr. Robert Candlish dilitated into grandeur and his face flashed as with inward brightness—as though some invisible star burned within,—when with bearing-down and incomparable power, he expounded and applied some deep saying of his beloved Lord or some subtle argument of St. Paul. Thus roused and lifted above himself, that quaint and almost weird face, with its alp of forehead and elf-locks, wore to me a strange pathetic beauty, as the great preacher—and I never have heard a greater—in passion sprung of compassion—after marvellous penetrativeness of insight and argument, drove home Divine warning and Divine remonstrance, and wistfully entreated his fellow-men to be "reconciled" to God in Christ.

The soul therefore, I reiterate, can and does transform and transfigure the face into a resemblance of itself; and I must hold it obligatory on us to verify the line that

"Soul is forme, and doth the bodie make."

The whole facts of his Life, and the entire teaching of his Works, will satisfy any one who takes the (well-spent) pains to master them, that John Howe was not the "inward friend" (his own words) merely, but a fellow-disciple with JOHN SMITH, and DR. HENRY

MORE, and DR. RALPH CUDWORTH; and that he deliberately and devoutly aimed at restoring in himself the lost harmony between body and soul, and to incarnate—if I may dare to appropriate the stupendously-appropriated word —his Christianity in his look and every-day life.

Granted, that most of us can only follow such as John Howe with far-off footstep; none the less is it duty and privilege to follow. Do any demur to the possibility of attainment whereby the inward "Divine calm," peace, holiness, joy, are made visible and readable? I have within my personal knowledge not a few who in relatively humble spheres thus demonstrate the reality of that better and richer change than the poet's sea-change, wrought in the face by sanctity of character; and the longer I live, and the more I observe, the profounder is my conviction that a serene, beaming, happy face is a witness for Christ and Christianity far beyond spoken words. On the other hand, I am persuaded—

and I risk repetition to emphasise it—that many good ministers of the Gospel and private Christians little know the damage they do by the expression they have suffered their face to assume, and the *tone* they have allowed their voice to take in speaking of religion. Do let us, at whatever cost, get rid of everything that can be pronounced PROFESSIONAL.

I have the more readily and fully stated and illustrated this, because the ultimate serenity and "beauty of holiness," and "delighting in God," and "patience in expectation of future blessedness" in John Howe, were the OUTCOME OF DISCIPLINE—BODILY, INTELLECTUAL, MORAL, AND SPIRITUAL—OF GRACE, NOT OF NATURE, OF GRADUAL HARD-CONTESTED CONQUEST AND ATTAINMENT, NOT OF BIRTH OR NATIVE TEMPERAMENT. This still further makes the life and character of John Howe bear a living message for us to-day; and I must therefore dwell on it.

It has been my privilege to make this good in the case of two worthies of England, concerning whom anything of struggle or antagonism with the Spirit of God had not before been suspected. I refer to PHINEAS FLETCHER, the poet of "The Purple Island" and "Locustæ"; and GEORGE HERBERT, the "sweet singer" of "The Temple." As I show in their Memoirs incontestably, these ultimately meek, sweet, gentle, most meet followers — in the language of THOMAS DEKKER—of Him,

"The first true Gentleman that ever breathed,"

had many and many "spiritual conflicts" before they laid down their weapons of rebellion and yielded their wills to their Divine Lord's (as He Himself in Gethsemane).*

It has been my good fortune similarly to discover an incident in the early ministerial life of John Howe, that goes to establish the

---

* Fuller Worthies' Library edition of the Poems of Phineas Fletcher, 4 vols., vol. i.; and the same of George Herbert, and also in the Aldine edition of the Poems.

same conflict and victory in him. Seeing that neither Calamy, nor Hunt, nor Rogers, nor Dr. James Hamilton, nor Christophers, nor any of his biographers, chanced to be aware of this incident, it seems expedient to re-tell it. It turned up in a very unlikely place, to wit, in the "Diary of the Rev. Thomas Larkham, M.A., Vicar of Tavistock"*
—a saintly and notable man in various ways. Turning to page twenty-three of this little book, these entries are found:—

"Jan. 16 [1656], being the day of the eclipse of the sun, Mr. John Howe, minister of Great Torrington, had been to preach here at Tavistock: who most fiercely lashed at me in his sermon about the improper obedience of such as were truly gracious. I wrote to him that I would make good what I had preached the next lecture day, etc.; against which time there was great riding and sending to gather the ministers of the county together, in hope that I should have been swallowed up." "Jan. 23.—I preached upon the same text Mr. Howe preached on the week before; and after sermon a conference in the parish church;

---

* Privately printed (50 copies) by Rev. William Lewis (1871).

and in the afternoon among the ministers in private. I acknowledge thankfully God's hand over me. We all parted lovingly at the last."

The excellent editor of the 'Diary' was unable to shed any light on these entries; but on reading them I recalled a curious mention of the incident by Larkham in his very remarkable quarto on "The Attributes of God Unfolded and Applied" [1656],—one of the rarest of later Puritan books. Summarily—for I must not venture to give it here in full—the matter in debate was whether the Lord spoke in human though un-sinning weakness in His prayer, "If it be possible let this cup pass from Me," as Larkham maintained, or whether He so prayed of His Divine nature. The lecturer vindicates his position super-abundantly, and easily convicts Howe "and the brethren" of unripe scholarship, and of unacquaintance with the *consensus* of theological and philological opinion. But the element of the debate with which we have now to do is its spirit on Howe's side. Larkham having thus vindicated his interpretation turns on Howe, as one of his young neighbour ministers—"I am bold to say young," he intercalates, "because I had a gown on my back and Universitie degrees before he could read English long"—and in tart sharp phrase rebukes his "ignorance and malice" in the "mightie dust" that ¡"in divers places" of the county he had raised, charging him with "blasphemie," and "inveigling many credulous ministers" into a belief that he had taught that "Christ at that time had not a jot of grace," which he uncompromisingly avouches was "a lewd and loud ly." He further speaks with much more of the *fortiter* than the *suaviter* of Howe's "unworthy carriage," and retorts on his "odd divinity" and foolish claim to be of "the mighty doctors," and his "forward and peremptory" presumption, instead of 'tarrying at Jericho until his beard were grown.' Then follow keen *hits* at his "superabundant knowledge" (or pride rather), and pestiferous "prattle," and unworthy "wandering up and down to reproach, and backbite, and defame, and abuse brethren and neighbours." He adds :—"I am told my neighbour will answer me if I write, etc. I had rather he would have saved me the trouble of this unpleasing task, by seeing his faultiness and acknowledging his errours."*

The narrative from which I have fetched these "bitter words" must be read no doubt *cum grano salis;* for it is plain the scholarly old Puritan was roused, and held a drastic and vehement pen. But after every deduction, we have in this incident MATTER-OF-FACT. For Thomas Larkham was a true, devout, consecrate "minister of the Gospel," with a conscience sensitive and tender as an inviolate child's; and we have "line upon line" and testimony upon testimony to prove that he was of the most choice and chosen men of his century —a man of God who in Old England and New England alike,—for he was one of the

---

* See Appendix B., for the full Narrative, and notice of Larkham; also of an earlier controversy.

persecuted fugitives to New England—in prosperity and adversity, and cruel and wanton persecution for his Nonconformity—remained faithful to his Lord. I believe him, therefore, to have been incapable of the slightest deviation from the truth. I accredit his narrative as if on oath. Thus sanctioned, the incident is to my mind extremely significant. At first it may be it will give a shock to find such accusing and contemptuous and nevertheless righteous words spoken to and of John Howe. But the shock will be beneficial if the occasion of it be rightly regarded and turned to right account. Larkham was right and sound theologically, and Howe ill-informed and rash-spoken and evilly precipitate and mistaken in his zeal, I must hold; and PROLONGED AS WAS THE "RIDING UP AND DOWN" AND ENGAGING OF OTHERS IN OPPOSITION TO LARKHAM, IT CANNOT BE THOUGHT OF AS A *SPURT*, BUT DECLARATIVE OF CHARACTER. Consequently the incident reveals that John Howe, in what he grew to be, was made, not born; that he was debtor to grace; that naturally he was imperious, "fierce," touched of pride and the meaner thing vanity, arrogant and impetuous of temper, and so was subdued, over-mastered, only by the subduings and over-masterings and sanctifying grace of The Spirit.

For my own part, I am free to confess that just as with Bible worthies, I like this *humanizing* of John Howe infinitely better than the "faultless monster" of his Biographers' unbroken eulogy. It is satisfying to know that Howe did not 'stand' to his hasty and shallow fault-finding. This is evidenced by his absolute silence throughout his numerous writings on it. It is noteworthy also that he himself had to pass through a like ordeal with Larkham, when, but for the chivalrous defence of Andrew Marvell, he had been covered with obloquy in the controversy concerning God's prescience of the sins of men.

How deep and controlling was the change that passed over Howe's entire temper and conduct appears by his after-calm, his large charity, his gracious thinking of the very best of his opponents, and the hard arguments in soft words of his many controversial books.

I know not that in the language there is a finer example of self-mastery than his treatise-letter "written out of the country to a person of quality in the City who took offence at the late sermon of Dr. Stillingfleet, Dean of St. Paul's, before the Lord Mayor." Stillingfleet had turned his back upon himself, and forgetful of his "Irenicum" had abused the Nonconformists with a vulgar ribaldry that might well have turned milk of human kindness to gall, and stung Howe into use of his tremendous gift of sarcasm. His every feeling was outraged; but he did not answer the fool according to his folly. It will do us good to read and re-read this 'Letter.' I must here make room for a specimen of it, as follows :—

"For the qualifying of your own *too great resentment and offence*, I would have you consider how good reason you have to believe that this blow came only from the (somewhat misgoverned) hand of a pious and good man. Be it far from you to imagine otherwise. If you think he was to blame for intimating suspicions of their sincerity whom he opposes, make not yourself equally blameable by admitting hereupon any concerning his: which would argue a mean narrow spirit, and a most unwarrantable fondness of a party, as if all true religion and godliness was bound up in it.

"And if it look unlovely in your eyes to see one of so much avowed latitude and enlargedness of mind, and capable upon that account of being the more universally serviceable to the Christian Church, forsaking that comprehensive interest, so far as to be engulfed into a party upon a private and distinct basis, consider what effect the same thing would have in yourself. And never make his difference with you in this matter a reason to yourself of a hard judgment concerning him; who can, you must consider, differ no more from us than we do from him.

"Believe him, in the substance of what he said, to speak according to his present judgment. Think how gradually and insensibly men's judgments alter, and are formed by their converse, that his circumstances have made it necessary to him to converse most for a long time, with those who are fully of that mind which he here discovers; that his own real worth must have drawn into his acquaintance the best and most valuable of them, and such for whom he might not only have a kindness, but a reverence; and who, therefore, must have the same power and influence upon him, to conform his sentiments to their own.

"We ourselves do not know, had we been by our circumstances led to associate and converse mostly with men of another judgment, what our own would have been. And they that are wont to discover most confidence of themselves, do usually discover most ignorance of the nature of man, and how little they consider the power of external objects and inducements to draw men's minds this way or that. Nor, indeed, as to matters of this nature, can any man be confident that the grace of God shall certainly incline him to be of this or another opinion in future in these matters; because we find those that we have reason to believe have great assistance of Divine grace are divided about them, and go not all one way."*

One must go back on an old Psalm for fit words to describe conduct of controversy in this manner :—" Let the righteous smite me it shall be a kindness : and let him reprove me; it shall be an excellent oil, which shall not break my head : for yet my prayer also shall be in their calamities" (Psalm cxli. 5).

It is pleasing to learn that Stillingfleet— like Tillotson, Archbishop of Canterbury,

---

* Works, as before, vol. v., pp. 250-251.

later—was deeply touched with his opponent's considerateness and gentleness. Except Robert Hall under the dissecting-knife of John Foster there is no such thorough exposure of the inconsequential reasoning and blind prejudices and unscholarly forgetfulness of another, as Howe's 'Letter' on Stillingfleet's unhappy Sermon. But throughout, and throughout his controversial writings, he never for a moment forgets that he is a Christian gentleman. This could not be affirmed earlier, or in relation to Larkham.

I think that this revelation concerning John Howe speaks to us to-day personally, and more widely. Personally, it ought to be a priceless incentive to us that he who early "spake unadvisedly" and harshly and persistently of a Father in Christ, became—and, as it would seem, from the date of the incident—"meek and lowly," judicially calm and charitable. We have in the ultimate character of John Howe, through long years to a ripe old age (seventy-six years) a type, as

I have named him, of INTELLECTUAL SANCTITY. That is, we have in him a brain of no ordinary mass and power, a large, strong, forceful nature, with "holiness to the Lord" inscribed on every faculty and acquirement. I put stress on this; and I LOOK MORE WIDELY, AS I HAVE INDICATED. For the phenomenon presented in John Howe is something very different in kind, and not mere degree, from that change in conversion that takes place in a man who has debased and polluted himself. Such a man's conversion—and I prefer the plain old word—is a lifting of him, as it were, from the Prodigal's swine-troughs, is a cleansing of flesh and spirit comparable with the most absolute cleansing that we can conceive. There is joy in heaven over one such sinner. "God forbid" that I should seek to lessen either the blessedness or the wonder or the love of it. But it is of the last importance that we keep a firm grasp of the Biblical teaching that conversion is a necessity of EVERY MAN.

John Howe at once confirms and exemplifies this. It needed that The Spirit of God should go in and down to the roots of his being; it needed that his imperial intellect and lofty self-consciousness should be laid hold of and 'changed'; it needed that he should surrender himself to the keeping of the all-holy and hallowing One. Conversion out of fleshly dominion ("publicans and harlots") may in the first thought be more palpable and demonstrative, more convincing of preterhuman interference; but conversion from intellectual sovereignty to sanctity, and to humility when before the 'spirit' was haughty, vain, unsubdued, is more precious and carries profounder insignia.

Hence that perspective of message for to-day that I have asserted in all this. I must affirm as against all who ignore or mock or deny the fundamental facts on which the doctrines of the Bible rest in this matter of UNIVERSALLY-NEEDED CONVERSION, that it is alike unscientific and uncritical to so deal with the myriad-fold experience and attestation of men like John Howe. Here at least is no fanatic or (so-called) vulgar enthusiast, or raw, uneducated, untrained man. Here is a man of admittedly supreme intellectual *calibre*, a scholar of both Universities—as poor Robert Greene pathetically wrote himself—of ripe and rich culture, of commanding position and influence, lettered and travelled, and the familiar associate of the highest in highest contemporary circles; and he is the first to admit that whatever he had of self-rule, of government of will and "passions" and affections, of tranquillity of heart, of serenity of conscience, of ability to live out his Christianity, he dated from that spiritual experience which is named conversion. Multiply such testimony by millions; and does it not proclaim that Scientism to be a paradox of self-contradiction which puts out of court such facts and experience and testimony? For if one set of facts and experiences is to be held as verified and incontestable because the five senses (or some of them) attest them, why flout this other set of facts and experiences, verified equally by something higher and subtler than mere sense, and illustrated by after-lives; which after-lives are in correspondence with the revelation and teaching of the Bible. Human nature is a wider thing than your sectarian Scientist knows; and it argues to my mind a shallow philosophy that depreciates or ignores everything outside of what the ten fingers can touch. Assuming that God is, it is an inevitable corollary that He has access to these natures of ours—corporeal, mental, spiritual—that in Howe's phrase, He is "conversable with man"—and it is the wisest philosophy that accepts the facts of Christian experience freely as it accepts other facts. I do not in all this ask your Scientist, or moral or metaphysical philosopher, to become a theologian. I am quite aware that modern "science" (whatever intellectual faculties it may call into exercise) rests on its own proper basis, which is that of sense. "Science"—in our present use of the word—I know, receives nothing which does not rest ultimately on the evidence of the senses, and "knows" only the "natural." It cannot take cognizance, I remember, of the spiritual. It knows nothing *qua* science of the spiritual. It does not know God. It will never by all its "searching" with the most deft and delicate instruments, come upon that awful, mysterious ESSENCE. What we expect from science (with reference to the soul and this matter of "conversion") is just what we expect of a blind man in the matter of colour; do not let a blind man deny colour, and do not let a scientific man deny, much less mock at, conversion because it is inappreciable by his five senses. Says the Scientist, surrounded by his retorts, and microscopes, and spectrum-analysis prisms and so forth, "I have never come upon *spirit*; *ergo* I do not believe in spirit." We answer—"Quite so; and you never will come on spirit." "Canst thou by *searching* find out God?" (Job xi. 7), comes to be with your Scientist=Who can by touching, tasting, smelling, find Him out? till you have exhausted all that can be done by the noblest of the senses or any scientific extension of the senses. I take my stand on the transformation that took place in John Howe. I say there is a Fact as real and actual as any in all your science; and I must demand that such a fact be not ignored, but accepted and fairly dealt with.*

I have now to notice another element of Howe's ultimate character, that seems to me of vital interest for us to-day. We have gone back on the laying of the foundation; we have now to see how the superstructure was raised. Theoretically, perhaps all professing Christians avouch that their 'knowledge' of Divine truth is to be reduced to practice, *i.e.*, THAT WE ARE INFORMED THAT WE MAY BE TRANSFORMED.

---

* *En passant*—in a mere sentence as being aside from our main inquiry—it is of the *unique* things in Jesus Christ that nowhere is 'conversion' affirmed or implied in Him. That which is the centre of the lives of His servants—*e.g.* Paul—is left out in His life. This is in accord with His claims as "God manifest in the flesh," but in discord if you hold Him to be Man only. So we contrast with Paul's and others' urgent requests for the prayers of friends on their behalf, the absolute absence in Christ of any such request.

But how all too many practically treat the Christ-like life as a beautiful but impossible ideal. It is to the praise of John Howe that with all his humility and lowliness, he regarded his Christianity as of worth to him only in the measure that it went to make him day by day a truer, nobler, holier, more serviceable man.

No one can study either his Life or Works without feeling that he habitually lived as under the great Taskmaster's eye. He 'walked,' He 'communed' with God. His 'meditation' and 'contemplation' were irradiated with the light of the "comprehensive and all-pervading excellence" that is in God and that God is. His visions of 'Virtue' had the purity of Plato, but superadded the holiness of the Holy One, the One Holy. His gaze up to the face of Christ was that he might be transformed "by the Spirit of the Lord." His "delighting in God" was his highest intellectual pleasure. It was also his intensest passion to be "like God," to be made a "partaker of Divine nature" (as the Bible fearlessly tells us we may: 2 Peter

i. 4). Few soared so high in speculation within Bible-laid limits. Fewer "went out and in" among his fellow-men with so penetrative a practical influence on his life of the truths he discovered and of the graces he received. All that went to his daily life, whether of bright or dark, of joy or suffering, of "good hope" or fear, brought so many summonses for expansion and maturing of his own CHARACTER. He had no rest until lost instincts were restored. He compacted graces into habits. He coveted to be on this hither side what might take the impress of immortality. What we pursue in other paths he pursued steadily, systematically, prayerfully, with the one end in view of attaining that moral and spiritual beauty and sanctity which the Gospel of Jesus Christ is designed to create. Enlarged and touched with his own grandeur is his conception of the Christian life. It was a sorrow to him wherever he fell short of it. He mourned in "secret places" over any jarring note in the music that body and soul in harmonious unison ought to give out.

Trebonius uncovered in the presence of his schoolboys in consideration of possibilities: I bare my head before the actualities of attainment, the INTELLECTUAL SANCTITY of John Howe.

I would now briefly illustrate this from his Works. In his "Treatise on Delighting in God" he thus speaks of faith:—

"Faith is a part of homage paid to the authority of the great God, which is to be estimated sincere according as it answers the end for which the things to be believed were revealed. That end is not to beget only the nature of those things, as truths that are to be lodged in the mind, and go no further,—as if they were to be understood true only that they might be so understood; but that the person might accordingly have his spirit formed, and might shape the course of his whole conversation; therefore is it called 'the obedience of faith;' and the same word which is wont to be rendered 'unbelief' signifies disobedience, obstinacy, unpersuadableness; being from a theme which (as is known) signifies *to persuade*. So that this homage is then truly given to the eternal God, when His revelation is complied with and submitted to, according to the true intent and purpose of it; which that it may be, requires that His Spirit urge the soul with His authority, and overpowers it into an awful subjection thereto; the soul being so disjointed by the apostasy, that its own faculties keep not (in reference to the things of

God) their natural order to one another, further than as a holy rectitude is renewed in them by the Holy Ghost. Therefore is it necessary that the enlightening communication which He transmits into it be not only so clear as to scatter the darkness that beclouded the mind, but so penetrating as to strike and pierce the heart, to dissolve and relax its stiff and frozen organs, and render it capable of a new mould and frame. In order whereto, 'God, Who,' at first, 'commanded the light to shine out of darkness,' is said to have 'shined into the hearts' of them He renews, 'to give the light of the knowledge of the glory of God in the face of Jesus Christ' (2 Cor. iv. 6)."*

Again: in discussing the "revolving in one's own mind the notions that belong to religion, without either the experience or the design and expectation of having the heart and conversation formed according to them," he thus vividly warns such :—

"The more any one doth only notionally know in the matters of religion, so as that the temper of his spirit remains altogether unsuitable and opposite to the design and tendency of the things known, the more he hath lying ready to come in judgment against him; and if, therefore, he count the thing excellent which he knows, and only please himself with his own knowledge of them, it is but like case as if a man should be much delighted

---

* Works, as before, vol. ii., pp. 27-8.

to behold his own condemnation written in a fair and beautiful hand; or, as if he should be pleased with the glittering of that sword which is directed against his own head, and must be the present instrument of death to him: and so little pleasant is the case of such a person in itself, who thus satisfies his own curiosity with the concernments of eternal life and death, that any serious person would tremble on his behalf, at that wherein he takes pleasure, and apprehend just horror in that state of the case where he draws matter of delight."*

Once more: in the "Living Temple" he is discussing imagined 'manifestations' of God in order to convince the gainsayers, and shewing that they would lead to "a constant and comfortless restraint from any free and ingenuous access to God or conversation with Him—wherein the very life of religion consists," and he thus proceeds:—

"And then, to what purpose doth the discovery and acknowledgment of the Deity serve? insomuch as it is never to be thought that the existence of God is a thing to be known only that it may be known: but that the end it serves for is religion—a complacential and cheerful adoration of Him, and application of ourselves, with at once both dutiful and pleasant affections towards Him."†

---

* *Ibid.*, p. 125.
† *Ibid.*, vol. iii., p. 152.

Of 'Meditation' he thus writes:—

"Solemnly set yourselves at chosen times to think on God. Meditation is of itself a distinct duty, and must have a considerable time allowed it among the other exercises of the Christian life. It challenges a just share and part in the time of our lives; and He in whom we are to place our delight is, you know, the prime and chief object of this holy work. Is it reasonable, that He who is our life and our all should never be thought on, but now and then, as it were by chance and on the bye? 'My meditation of Him shall be sweet.' Doth not that imply that it was with the Psalmist a designed thing to meditate on God,—that it was a stated course? Whereas it was become customary and usual to him, by ordinary practice, to appoint times for meditating on God, his well-known exercise (which is supposed), he promises himself satisfaction and solace of soul therein. Let your eyes herein, therefore, 'prevent the night-watches.' Reckon you have neglected one of the most important businesses of the day if you have omitted this, and that to such omissions you owe your little delight in God. Wherein, therefore, are you to repay yourselves, but by redeeming this great neglect?"*

Deeper still is his ever-recurring 'magnifying' of the rapture of intellectual-spiritual thought of God and with God, and his fore-

---

* *Ibid.*, vol. ii., p. 227.

feeling of intuition. I can but now glean a few scattered sentences on this—*e.g.* of the "Act of vision or intuition itself."

"How great the pleasure will be that accrues to the beloved from the sight of God's face is very much to be estimated from the nature of the act, as well as the excellency of the object. Inasmuch as every vital act is pleasant, the most perfect act of the noblest faculty of the soul must needs be attended with highest pleasure. IT IS A PLEASURE THAT MOST NEARLY IMITATES DIVINE PLEASURE. And everything is more perfect, AS IT MORE NEARLY APPROACHES DIVINE PERFECTIONS."*

Then he characteristically ascends to the very "third heaven," and expatiates as though already "out of the body," on intuitional as distinguished from ratiocinative knowledge :—

"Here is no need of a busy search, a tiresome indagation,—the difficulty whereof makes the more slothful rather trust than try—a chaining together of consequences. The soul hath its clothing, its vestment of light, upon as cheap terms as the lilies theirs; doth 'neither toil nor spin' for it; and yet Solomon, 'in all the glory' of his famed wisdom, was not arrayed like it. This knowledge saves the expense of study ; is instantaneous, not succes-

---

* *Ibid.*, vol. i., p. 93.

sive. The soul now sees more, at one view, in a moment, than before in a lifetime; as a man hath a speedier and more grateful prospect of a pleasant country, by placing himself in some commodious station that commands the whole region, than by travelling through it. It is no pains to look upon what offers itself to my eye. Where there is a continued series of consequences, that be naturally connected, the soul pleasingly observes the continuity; but views the whole length of the line at once (so far as its limited capacity can extend), and needs not discuss every particle severally in this series of truths, and proceed *gradatim* from the knowledge of one truth to another; in which case only one at once would be present to its view. It sees things that are connected, not because they are so: as a man conveniently placed in some eminent station, may possibly see, at one view, all the successive parts of a gliding stream: but he that sits by the water's side, not changing his place, sees the same parts, only because they succeed; and those that pass make way for them that follow, to come under his eye."*

Again: "Now, when the grace of God supervenes, [it] doth exalt and sublimate nature." †
And deeper:—" Surely it is of equal necessity to the soul's blessedness, to partake the glory of God, as to behold it; as well to have the Divine

---

* *Ibid.*, pp. 95-6.
† *Ibid.*, Funeral Sermon for Bates, vol. vi.

likeness impressed upon it, as represented to it."*
Then searchingly and culminatingly- -

"It [the soul] must therefore be 'all glorious within,' have the Divine nature more perfectly communicated, the likeness of God transfused and wrought into it. This is the blessed work begun in regeneration; but how far it is from being perfected, we may soon find by considering how far short we are of being satisfied in our present state, even in the contemplation of the highest and most excellent objects. How tasteless to our souls are the thoughts of God! How little pleasure do we take in viewing over His glorious attributes, the most acknowledged and adorable excellences of His being! And whereunto can we impute it but to this, that our spirits are not yet sufficiently con-naturalized to them? Their likeness is not enough deeply enstamped on our souls. Nor will this be 'till we awake;' when we see better we shall become better: 'when He appears we shall be like Him, for we shall see Him as He is.' But do we indeed pretend to such an expectation? Can we think what God is, and what we are in our present state, and not confess these words to carry with them an amazing sound, 'we shall be like Him'? How great a hope is this! How strange an errand hath the Gospel into the world! How admirable a design—to transform men and make them like God! Were the dust of the earth turned into stars in the firmament, were the most stupendous poetical transformations assured realities, what could equal the

---
* *Ibid.*, vol. i., p. 61.

greatness and the wonder of this mighty change? Yea, and doth not the expectation of it seem as presumptuous as the issue itself would be strange? Is it not an overbold desire? too daring a thought? a thing unlawful to be affected, as it seems to be attained. . . . It is a matter therefore that requires some disquisition and explication."*

Across well-nigh two hundred years I would have John Howe's INTELLECTUAL SANCTITY

---

* *Ibid.*, vol. i., p. 62. With all this aspiration and anticipative joy Howe held in highest honour ratiocination. Thus he says: "To the altogether unlearned it will hardly be conceivable, and to the learned it need not be told, how high a gratification this employment of his reason naturally yields to the mind of a man; when the harmonious contexture of truths with truths, the apt coincidence, the secret links and junctures of coherent notions are clearly discerned; when effects are traced up to their causes; properties lodged in their native subjects; things sifted to their principles. What a pleasure is it, when a man shall apprehend himself regularly led on, though but by a slender thread of discourse, through the labyrinths of nature; when still new discoveries are successfully made, every further enquiry ending in a further prospect, and every new scene of things entertaining the mind with a fresh delight!"— *Ibid.*, p. 94.

stir us: I would have his holy indignation with mere "notional knowledge" and orthodoxy of creed apart from the Divine life, be as a fire in our bones to startle us into a recognition that mere 'knowledge' severed from being, mere scholarliness, mere culture, will not suffice beneath the eyes of fire. I would have us emulate his strenuous as robust sequestering of himself daily for thought and meditation, not mere book-reading; I would have us breathe this ampler air and ascend to those serener regions of principles and to God Himself; above all, I would press upon all who preach, or who teach others, to seek a deepening sense of their own personal need of what is preached and taught; a sense of need like hunger for our necessary food (Job xxiii. 12), and of humiliation and sorrow in so far as we find ourselves failing to work into the substance of our ordinary lives the knowledge we have attained and the insight that has been given, and sadness of heart that only fitfully there comes on us the joy, the delight—a joy with something of passion in it ("My soul *breaketh* for the longing which it hath unto Thy judgments at all times":) in the word which we preach and teach that once we had. We sing, "Oh for a closer walk with God." Let us get that. We pray, "Make us like unto Thyself." Let us wrestle for that. We are summoned to "adorn" the doctrine. We are charged to "commend" Christ.

I shall not have recalled the beautiful exemplar of John Howe in vain, if but readers here and there, lay it to heart and seek to REPRODUCE THEIR CHRISTIAN KNOWLEDGE IN THEIR DAILY LIVES. Faith, belief may be extremely orthodox or sound; but if it do not ennoble, purify, sanctify, as St. James says, "Can *that* faith save him?" Our religion must compact itself into habits, and not disperse itself in mere impulses and sporadic emotion; must replace in the soul its primary instincts, whereby it becomes as natural to hate sin as to shrink from pain; must, to be true and worthy, bring us into daily, hourly, continuous communion with God; must, in short, become 'Habitual Godliness.'

I feel constrained to add here, that in the CHARACTER which John Howe by self-discipline and the grace of God exhibited before the world,—consistent not merely with itself, but with the great Law of Life,—must be sought the secret of his power in the pulpit. I am growingly convinced that—with CHARACTER *i.e.*, with a consistent life to back it—a minister's preaching is his power. There is in our day a great deal of talkee-talkee in useless (so-called) visitation, and 'nice' funny platform speeches devout '*havering*' (to use a Scotch expressive word), etc., etc. I wish to lead back thought to the POWER of one who like John Howe stands up in his pulpit and tells out what he has meditated and prayed over, and when he speaks what he knows and testifies what he has seen. It is treason to truth and the God of truth for a moment to stand in doubt of the power, undecaying and unspent, of such preaching.

Passing now onward, I would notice another specific characteristic of Howe that appears to me of surpassing value for us to-day. I refer to his HABITUAL REVERENCE. I think of him always as reproducing later that immortal portrait—more grandly taken than any even in Clarendon—by Milton of President Bradshaw in his "Second Defence of the People of England." I turn to it and read a portion :—

"At last, when he was entreated by the Parliament to preside on the trial of the King, he did not refuse the dangerous office. To a profound knowledge of the Law, he added the most comprehensive views, the most generous sentiments, manners the most obliging and the most pure. Hence he discharged that office with a propriety almost without a parallel; he inspired both respect and awe; and, though menaced by the daggers of so many assassins, he conducted himself with so much consistency and gravity, with so much presence of mind and so much dignity of demeanour, that he seems to have been purposely destined by Providence for that part which he so nobly acted on the theatre of the world. And his glory is as much exalted above that of all other tyrannicides, as it is both more humane, more just, and more strikingly grand, judicially to condemn a tyrant, than to put him to death without a trial. In other respects there was no forbidding austerity, no moroseness in his manner; he was courteous and benign; but the good character which he then sustained, he with perfect consistency still sustains, SO THAT YOU WOULD SUPPOSE THAT NOT ONLY THEN, BUT IN EVERY FUTURE PERIOD OF HIS LIFE, HE WAS SITTING IN JUDGMENT UPON THE KING."

The entire facts of Howe's life, and the entire tone (so to say) of his writings, impress the Reader with his never-ceasing sense of the Divine Presence, and of the awe and reverence due to Him in discussing anything appertaining to His Being, Nature, Word, or Works. His extraordinary treatise (for it is a treatise and *facile princeps* before all others) on the Trinity, and that on "The Reasonableness of God's Prescience of the Sins of Men with the Wisdom and Sincerity of His Counsels, Exhortations, and whatsoever other means He uses to prevent them," demonstrate that his intellect *qua* intellect was of the highest order, and that it was congenial to him to 'intermeddle' with at once the most exalted and the deepest and most abstract problems. They show that he had metaphysical affinities and aptitudes of an almost unique type. He inevitably soars to the high-*est* region of principles; but it is not merely to "consider" (his favourite word), but to worship. The darkness from excess of light is sacred, venerable to him; for he knows The Presence behind it. He equally descends into the deepest depths; but his plummets are the "written Word" and his own many-sided consciousness. In height or depth he remembers before Whom he is. Hence to him a wayside flower or an insect partakes of its Creator's awfulness.

I think that in this John Howe's character and Works bring AN URGENT MESSAGE FOR TO-DAY; a message that it were good if our Scientists laid to heart. Here is an example of how he addressed such, and nothing could be more prescient for present-day use. He is confuting the "over-bold and adventurous intruders into the deep and most profound *arcana* of the Divine nature," more especially that baseless "simplicity" ascribed to God's nature whereby "Trinity" is pronounced unscientific, unphilosophical, and impossible. He has all respect for genuine "observing" and lowly-minded "science and philosophy," but a fine scorn for hasty, evil-tongued, presumptuous dogmatists, be their names however famous and their authority within certain lines, however weighty. And so he writes thus:—

"It would be an over-officious and too meanly servile religiousness, to be awed by the sophistry of presumptuous scholastic wits into a subscription to their confident determinations concerning the being of God; that such and such things are necessary or impossible thereto, beyond what the plain undisguised reason of things or His own express Word do evince. To imagine a sacredness in their rash conclusions, so as to be afraid of searching into them or of examining whether they have any firm and solid ground or bottom; to allow the Schools the making of our Bible or the forming of our Creed, WHO LICENCE AND EVEN SPORT THEMSELVES TO PHILOSOPHIZE UPON THE NATURE OF GOD WITH AS PETULANT AND IRREVERENT A LIBERTY AS THEY WOULD UPON A WORM OR ANY OF THE MEANEST INSECTS,—while yet they can pronounce little with certainty even concerning *that*,—hath nothing in it either of the Christian or the man. It will become as well as concern us, to disencumber our minds, and release them from the entanglements of these unproved dictates, whatsoever authority they may have acquired only by having been long and commonly taken for granted. The more reverence we have of God, the less we are to have for such men as have themselves expressed little."*

Further :—

"I only wish these things might be considered and discussed with less confidence and peremptory determination; WITH A GREATER AWE OF WHAT IS DIVINE AND SACRED; and that we may more confine ourselves to the plain word of Scripture on this matter, and be content therewith. I generally blame it on the Socinians, who appear otherwise rational and considering men, that they seemed to have formed their belief of *things not possible to be known but by the Scriptures*, without them; and then think they are, by all imaginable arts and they care not what violence (as Socinus himself hath in effect confessed), to mould and form them according to their preconceived sense. Common modesty and civility, we would have thought, should have made Schlictingius abstain from prefacing and continuing that as a running title to a long chapter: *Articulus Evangelicorum de Trinitate cum sensu communi pugnat;* engrossing common sense to himself and his party, and reproaching the generality of Christians, as not understanding common sense! They should

* *Ibid.*, vol. v., pp. 83-4.

take upon them less, and not vaunt, as if they were the men, and wisdom must die with them."*

More specifically :—

"I believe few would have thought [this author] to see the less clearly, if he had been content to see for himself, not for mankind ; and if he had not talked at that rate as if he carried the eyes of all the world in his pocket, they would have been less apt to think he carried his own there. Nor had his performance, in this writing of his, lost anything of real value, if in a discourse upon so grave a subject [as the Trinity of the Godhead] some *lepidities* had been left out, as that of *Dulcinea del Toboso*, etc."†

Finally here, with passionate emotion :—

"I judge human, and even all created, minds very incompetent judges of the Divine simplicity. We know not what the Divine nature may include consistently with its own perfection, nor what it must, as necessary thereto. Our eye is no judge of corporeal simplicity. In darkness it discerns nothing but simplicity, without distinction of things : in now dusky light the whole horizon appears most simple, and everywhere like itself : in lighter light we perceive great varieties, and much greater if a microscope assist our eye. But of all the aërial people that replenish the region (except rare ap-

---

* *Ibid.*, vol. v., p. 112.
† *Ibid.*, pp. 112, 113.

pearances to very few), we see none. Here want not objects, but a finer eye. It is much at this rate with our minds on beholding the spiritual sphere of beings, most of all the uncreated, which is remotest and farthest above out of our sight. We behold simplicity: and what do we make of that? vast undistinguishable vacuity; sad, immense solitude: only this at first view! If we draw nearer and fix our eye, we think we apprehend somewhat, but dubiously hallucinate; as the self-cured blind man did, when he thought he saw men like trees. But if a voice which we acknowledge Divine, speak to us out of the profound abyss, and tell us of grateful varieties and distinctions in it; good God! shall we not believe it? or shall we say we clearly see *that* or not, which only *we* do not see? This seems like omewhat worse than blindness!"*

Surely I do not err in pronouncing all this as vital for us to-day? I re-address them to the Scientists of our time. Their awelessness, their utter lack of recognition of reverence as a factor of human nature, their glib and flippant talk with no slightest touch of wonder, no sense of mystery, no suspicion of limits and boundaries to human capacity, no concession of possibilities and realities that you cannot

---

* *Ibid.*, p. 120.

pronounce on through the five senses, no word of veneration for the Book that as a mere book stands in the van of all literatures, no trust of universal Christian experience and testimony, —is a pain to those of us who welcome all genuine, patient, non-generalizing observation, as holding it sure that Christianity and the Bible have nothing to fear from anything that can be shown *to be*. That it *is* suffices to make us accept it——and wait.

Apart altogether from dogmatic beliefs, it is to impoverish human nature to rob it of reverence; it is to vulgarize it to fashion it into that awelessness that walks and smirks and chatters in a cathedral as in the common street; it is worse than Wordsworth's "botanizing on a mother's grave:" for your Agnostic, having killed God, has not a tear or pang for so stupendous a tragedy as 'God dead,' and botanizes on His awful grave. Indeed I fancy that he goes a stage beyond the 'botanizing,' and puts the dead God's crown on his own slant-browed head, and sits down as if it were the most natural thing in the world, on his vacant throne. But need I guard myself by saying that it is not Science (in its true sense) that is atheistic—only "The Fool"? The Laureate's demand needs to sink into the national heart :—

> "Let knowledge grow from more to more,
>   But MORE OF REVERENCE in us dwell;
> That mind and soul, according well,
>   May make one music as before."
>   —*In Memoriam :* Introduction.

I venture to say that such scientific observation of the habits of animals, birds, insects, and flowers as that of DR. CHARLES DARWIN— slowly and with long patience and beautiful modesty carried on through a lifetime, and tentatively put on record—is priceless to me. I do not pronounce on his theory of Evolution; but I can pronounce on the wealth of inestimable data being accumulated by him, and on his spirit. I nowhere meet in his books the mock, the scoff, the sneer, the shallow gibes on Christianity of Tyndall and, though not so flagrantly and with neutralizing admissions,

Huxley. It is an outrage on MANKIND to so jeer and ridicule what has gone to build up the wisest, truest, noblest, holiest men and women of our race, and achieved such results through THE BOOK as makes this nineteenth century the magnificent heritage it is. The humility, the modesty, the reverence, the awe, the sense of being ever in the shadow of God, present all through Howe's Life and Works, I should like to find in present-day controversies, whether religious or scientific. We theologians and Christians have been imperiously warned off scientific ground. We refuse; for we, too, as men of education and culture, have the *apparatus* and the "five senses" with which Scientists work: while Scientists *qua* Scientists —*i.e.*, in so far as they are non-Christian—have not our *apparatus* and our—as we believe— divinely restored nature and access to God. It is about time that there were rectification of frontier ("a scientific frontier") far nearer and in far more momentous regions than Afghanistan— a rectification that shall shut the Scientist's mouth on what he does not know, and write folly and sectarianism on that "science" that limits evidence to sense, and turns metaphysic and all philosophy into physiology—anatomizing a gut-string in search of Mozart's Requiem in it —and that pursues investigation with aweless and reverenceless dogmatism.

That John Howe, while thus filled with awe and reverence for all awful and reverend, had no narrow conception of the sphere within which it is right and lawful to THINK and even speculate, all his Works attest. With him not Ignorance, but ripest Knowledge is the mother of devotion. THIS IS A FIFTH PRESENT-DAY TRUTH. Let one great passage in "The Living Temple" establish this:—

"But though it would be both an ungrateful and insignificant labour, and as talking to the wind, to discourse of religion with persons that have abjured all seriousness and that cannot endure to think; and would be like fighting with a storm, to contend against the blasphemy and outrage of insolent mockers of whatever is sacred and divine; and were too much a debasing of religion to retort sarcasms with men not capable of being talked with in any other than such (that is, their own) language:

yet it wants neither its use nor pleasure to the most composed minds, and that are most exempt from wavering herein, to view the frame of their religion, as it aptly and even naturally rises and grows up from its very foundations ; to contemplate its first principles, which they may in the meantime find no present cause or inclination to dispute. They will know how to consider its most fundamental grounds, not with doubt or suspicion, but with admiration and delight ; and can, with a calm and silent pleasure, enjoy the repose and rest of a quiet and well-assured mind,—rejoicing and contented to know to themselves, when others refuse to partake with them in this joy,—and feel all firm and stable under them whereupon either the practice or the hopes of their religion do depend.

"And there may be also many others, of good and pious inclinations, that have never yet applied themselves to consider the principal and most fundamental grounds of religion, so as to be able to give or discern any tolerable reason of them. For either the sluggishness of their own temper may have indisposed them to any more painful and laborious exercise of their minds, and made them to be content with the easier course of taking everything upon trust and imitating the example of others; or they have been unhappily misinformed that it consists not with the reverence due to religion, to search into the grounds of it : yea, and may have laid this for one of its main grounds, that no exercise of reason may have any place about it : or perhaps, having never tried, they apprehend a greater difficulty in coming to a clear and certain resolution herein than indeed there is. Now such need to be excited to set their own thoughts a-work this way, and to be assisted herein. They should therefore consider who gave them the understandings which they fear to use? and can they use them to better purpose or with more gratitude to Him who made them intelligent, and not brute creatures, than in labouring to know, that they may also by a reasonable service, worship and adore their Maker? Are they not to use their very senses about the matters of religion? 'For the invisible things of God, even His eternal power and Godhead, are clearly seen,' etc. And their faith comes by hearing. But what? Are these more sacred and divine, and more akin to religion, than their reason and judgment, without which also their sense can be of no use to them herein? Or is it the best way of making use of what God has revealed of Himself by whatsoever means, not to *understand* what He hath revealed? It is most true indeed, that when we once come clearly to be informed that God hath revealed this or that thing, we are then readily to subject (and not oppose) our feeble reasonings to His plain revelation ; and it were a most insolent and uncreaturely arrogance, to contend or not yield Him the cause, though things have to us seemed otherwise. But it were as inexcusable negligence not to make use of our understandings to the best advantage ; that we may both know that such a revelation is Divine, and what it signifies after we know whence it is. And any one that considers, will soon see it were very unseasonable, at least, to allege the written Divine revelation as the ground of his religion, till he have gone lower, and foreknown some things (by-and-by to be insisted on) as preparatory and fundamental to the knowledge of this." *

Let us not be afraid then to THINK and KNOW everything thinkable and knowable.

Another present-day truth and duty is Howe's WISTFUL AND IMPORTUNATE PLEADING WITH MEN THAT THEY SHALL SO BE AND DO THAT THE WORLD SHALL BE COMPELLED TO PAY HOMAGE TO CHRISTIANITY. For combined eloquence and weight of thought, clear-cut reasoning and insight, there are few continuous passages so memorable as his rebuke of Atheists on the one hand, and appeal, on the other, to Christians to be nobly Christian. I dare not withhold it, though it be long :—

"To these, the discussion of the notion we have proposed to consider, will be thought a beating the air, an endeavour to give consistency to a shadow; and if their reason and power could as well serve their purpose as their anger and scorn, they would soon tear up the holy ground on which a temple is set, and wholly subvert the sacred frame.

* *Ibid.*, vol. iii., pp. 25-7.

"I speak of such as deny the existence of the ever blessed Deity, or (if they are not arrived to that express and formed misbelief) whose hearts are inclined and ready to determine, even against their misgiving and more suspicious minds, 'there is no God;' who, if they cannot as yet believe, do wish there were none; and so strongly, as in a great degree to prepare them for that belief: that would fain banish Him, not only out of all their thoughts, but the world too; and to whom it is so far from being a grateful sound, that 'the tabernacle of God is with men on earth,' that they grudge to allow Him a place in heaven; at least, if they are willing to admit the existence of any God at all, do say to Him, 'Depart from us;' and would have Him so confined to heaven, that He and they may have nothing to do with one another; and do therefore rack their impious wits to serve their hypothesis either way; that under its protection they may securely indulge themselves in a course, upon which they find the apprehension of a God interesting Himself in human affairs would have a very unfavourable and threatening aspect.

"They are therefore constrained to take great pains with themselves, to discipline and chastise their minds and understandings to that tameness and patience, as contentedly to suffer the razing out of their most natural impressions and sentiments. And they reckon they have arrived to a very heroical perfection, when they can pass a scoff upon anything that carries the least signification with it of the fear of God; and can be able to laugh at the weak and squeamish folly of those softer and effeminate minds, that will trouble themselves with any thoughts or cares how to please and propitiate a Deity: and doubt not but they have made all safe, and effectually done their business, when they have learned to put the ignominious titles of frenzy and folly upon devotion, in whatsoever dress or garb; to cry 'canting' to any serious mention of the name of God, and break a bold, adventurous jest upon any of the most sacred mysteries or decent and awful solemnities of religion.

"These content not themselves to encounter this or that sect, but mankind; and reckon it too mean and inglorious an achievement to overturn one sort of temple or another; but would 'down with them' all, even 'to the ground.'

"And they are in the reason and justice to pardon the emulation which they provoke, of vieing with them as to the universality of their design; and not regret it, if they find there be any that think it their duty to waive awhile serving the temple of this or that party, as less considerable, to defend that one wherein all men have a common interest and concernment: since matters are brought to that exigency and hazard, that it seems less necessary to contend about this or that mode of religion, as whether there ought to be any at all.

"What was said of a former age, could never better agree to any than our own, 'that none was ever more fruitful of religions, and barren of religion or true piety.' It concerns us to consider, whether the fertility of those many doth not as well cause, as accompany, a barrenness in this one. And,—since the iniquity of the world hath made that too suitable, which were otherwise unseemly in itself, to speak of a temple as a fortified place, whose own sacredness ought ever to have been its sufficient fortification,—it is time to be aware, lest our forgetful heat and zeal in the defence of this or that outwork, do expose (not to say betray) the main fortress to assault and danger : whilst it hath long been, by this means, a neglected, forsaken thing, and is more decayed by vacancy and disuse than it could ever have been by the most forcible battery, so as even to promise the rude assailant an easy victory. Who fears to insult over an empty, dispirited, dead religion ? which, alive, and shining in its native glory (as that temple doth, which is compacted of ' lively stones' united to the 'living corner stone'), bears with it a magnificence and state that would check a profane look, and dazzle the presumptuous eye that durst venture to glance at it obliquely or with disrespect. The temple of the living God, manifestly animated by its vital presence, would not only dismay opposition, but command veneration also, and be its own both ornament and defence. Nor can it be destitute of that presence, if we ourselves render it not inhospitable, and make not its proper inhabitant become a stranger at home. If we preserve in ourselves a capacity of the Divine presence, and keep the temple of God in a posture fit to receive Him, He would then no more forsake it than the soul a sound and healthy body, not violated in any vital parts ; but if he forsakes it once, it then becomes an exposed and despised thing. And as the most impotent, inconsiderable enemy can securely trample on the dead body of the greatest hero, that alive carried awfulness and terror in his looks ; so is the weak-spirited atheist become as bold now, as he was willing before, to make rude attempts upon the temple of

God, when HE hath been provoked to leave it, who is its life, strength, and glory."

Parallel with this is another equally noble passage, and the counsel in which in many instances it should be our wisdom to follow, rather than be timorously and feverishly troubled and combative over every new assault of the "Higher Criticism" (so-called). I must also give it:—

"How highly shall *he* oblige them, that can furnish out a libel against religion; and help them, with more artificial spite, to blaspheme what they cannot disprove! And now shall the scurrilous pasquil and a few bottles work a more effectual confutation of religion, than all the reason and argument in the world shall be able to countervail! This proves too often the unhappy issue of misapplying what is most excellent, in its own kind and place, to improper and uncapable subjects.

"And who sees not this to be the case with the modern atheist, who hath been pursued with that strength and vigour of argument, even in our own days, that would have baffled persons of any other temper than their own, into shame and silence; and so as no other support hath been left to irreligion than a senseless stupidity, an obstinate resolvedness not to consider, a faculty to stifle an

---

* *Ibid.*, vol. iii., p. 18-20.

argument with a jest, to charm their reason by sensual softnesses into a dead sleep, with a strict and circumspect care that it may never awake into any exercise above the condition of dozed and half-witted persons; or, if it do, by the next debauch, presently to lay it fast again! So that the very principle fails in this sort of men, where in reasoning we should appeal and apply ourselves; and it were almost the same thing to offer arguments to the senseless images or forsaken carcases of men. It belongs to the grandeur of religion to neglect the impotent assaults of these men, as it is a piece of glory, and bespeaks a worthy person's right understanding and just value of himself, to disdain the combat with an incompetent or a foiled enemy. It is becoming and seemly that the grand, ancient, and received truth, which tends to and is the reason of the godly life, do sometimes keep state, and no more descend to perpetual janglings with every scurrilous and impertinent trifler, than a great and redoubted prince would think it fit to dispute the rights of his crown with a drunken, distracted fool or a madman.

"Men of atheistical persuasions, having abandoned their reason, need what will more powerfully strike their sense, —storms and whirlwinds, flames and thunderbolts, things not so apt immediately to work upon their understanding as their fear, and that will astonish that they may convince: that the great God make himself 'known by the judgments which He executes.' 'Stripes are for the backs of fools,' as they are justly styled that say in 'their hearts, There is no God.' But if it may be hoped any gentler method may prove effectual with any of them, we are rather to expect the good effect from the steady, uniform course of *their* actions and conversation, who profess reverence and devotedness to an Eternal Being, and the correspondence of their way to their avowed principle,—that acts on them agreeably to itself, and may also incur the sense of the beholder, and gradually invite and draw his observation,—than from the most severe and necessitating argumentation that exacts a sudden assent.

"At least in a matter of so clear and commanding evidence, reasoning many times looks like trifling; and out of a hearty concernedness and jealousy for the honour of religion, one would rather it should march on with an heroical neglect of bold and malapert cavillers, and only demonstrate and recommend itself by its own vigorous, comely, coherent course, than make itself cheap by discussing at every turn its principles: as that philosopher, who thought it the fittest way to confute the sophisms against motion only by walking.

"But we have nothing so considerably objected against practical religion, as well to deserve the name of a sophism (at least no sophism so perplexing in the case of religious as of natural motion); jeers and sarcasms are the most weighty convincing arguments. And let the deplorate crew mock on. There are those in the world that will think they have, however, reason enough to persist in the way of godliness; and that have already laid the foundation of that reverence which they bear to a Deity, more strongly than to be shaken and beaten off from it by a jest."

---

* *Ibid.*, vol. iii., pp. 21-23.

As the co-relative of his conception of God, John Howe had an exalted conception of man. This is A SEVENTH PRESENT-DAY TRUTH. His discussion of the Trinity and all his cognate discussions of the Being and Attributes and Providence of God, rest on a twofold solid basis of fact—viz., what he discerns in himself as he is a man, and what he finds himself as he is a Christian. He is fearless in arguing from what man *is* (being a Christian) to what God is : from how man (being a Christian) wills, chooses, does, to what God wills, chooses, does. He never forgets for a moment that by God's own Word this is among the certainties that man WAS made "in the image of God." I emphasize 'was:' for the problem is not 'Given man as he *is*—the old Greek, Roman, Persian, Egyptian, and the modern Englishman, Frenchman, Hindoo, Turk, etc.—required to find *what God is ;*' but 'Given man as he is as a Christian or restored to what he was, argue to what God is.' Man as he *is* is not = man as he *was*. That tremendous factor SIN—a fact of universal human nature, not of Christianity merely—has come into disastrous operation throughout the whole realm of man's being. Ere therefore we can legitimately argue up to God we must take into account the change that has been wrought in the creature's being. Man *as he is* is not the answer to the question, *What is* MAN? Man *as he is* is man fallen, disordered and defiled, not in his "natural state" but in a state utterly 'un-natural,' 'de-natural.' In man *as he is* we find untruth, unrighteousness, selfishness, fear, remorse, the deepest and most perplexing contradictions and antagonisms. Here is Howe's putting of mankind's "universal revolt and apostasy from God":—

"Every man's own reflection upon the vitiated powers of his own soul would soon, as to himself, put the matter out of doubt; whence each one's testimony concerning his own case would amount to a universal testimony. No man that takes a view of his own dark and blinded mind, his slow and dull apprehension, his uncertain, staggering judgment, roving conjectures, feeble and mistaken reasonings about matters that concern him most; ill inclinations, propension to what is unlawful to him and destructive, aversion to his truest interest and best good, irresolution, drowsy sloth, exorbitant and ravenous appetites and desires, impotent and self-vexing passions,—can think human nature, in *him,* is in its primitive integrity, and so pure as when it first issued from its high and most pure Original."*

Yet, rightly dealt with, this so strangely disordered being yields us knowledge concerning God. An organ tells about the man who devised it. Even though, having been injured by bad usage, it sends out most discordant sounds, and instead of playing out a consistent piece of music, gives forth only wild shrieks and screeches, along with tones that go to our soul—we can infer much about the contriver. And if we had knowledge that the instrument is not as it was when it came from the maker's hand, but has been spoiled, we would be able to tell more about the inventor still. So precisely with man *as*

---

* *Ibid.,* vol. iii., pp. 290-91.

he is. We do not take the 'is' of man and argue direct to the 'is' of God. We dare not treat man as if he were now "the image of the invisible God," but the image marred and in some cases scarcely recognisable. Yet is there a great deal more told of God through even fallen man than timorous theologians and preachers recognize. Two great sayings—one from the Old Testament and the other from the New Testament—occur to me: Psalm ciii. 13, "Like as a father pitieth his children, so the Lord pitieth them that fear Him." There human pity is the manner and argument of Divine pity. St. Matthew vii. 11: "If ye then, being evil, know how to give good gifts unto your children, how much more shall your Father who is in heaven give good things to them that ask Him." We have here the explicit recognition of man's "evil"; and yet evil though he be, he shews us something of God, only with a "How much more" that no mind can estimate. I fear that in their dread of un-orthodoxy, in their quivering alarm at any whisper of heresy, all the churches are faulty in refusing the help reached out by this so great fact that man *was* made "in the image of God," and its blessed counterpart that a Christian man is re-made in the same image—as Paul puts it (Eph. iv. 24), "which *after God* is created in righteousness and true holiness." Howe exults in this Divine and gracious restoration, and is never weary in working up and up from what man is by the "new birth" to what God is, and from what God is to what man is destined to be. Worthy to be written in letters of gold is this Paschal-like summary in "The Vanity of Man as Mortal":—"The truest notion we can yet have of the primitive nature and capacity of man, is by beholding it in its gradual restitution." More full, and yet condensed in its thinking, is his argumentative statement of the "image of God" in "The Blessedness of the Righteous," as thus:—

"There are some things to be found in the blessed God, not so incommunicable and appropriate, but that His creatures may be said to have some participation thereof with Him, and so far, to be truly like Him. This participation cannot be *univocal;* as the nature of a living creature in general is equal in men and brutes: so it is a self-evident principle, that nothing can be common to God and an inferior being. Nor is it only an *equivocal*, —a participation of the same name, when the natures signified thereby are altogether diverse; but *analogical*, inasmuch as the things spoken, under the same names, of God and the creature, have a real likeness and conveniency in nature with one another: and they are in God, primarily; in the creature, by dependence and derivation: in Him, essentially, as being His very essence; in them, but as accidents (many of them) adventitious to their beings; and so, while they cannot be said to be the same things in them as in Him, are fitly said to be His likeness.

"This likeness, as it is principally found in man among all the terrestrial creatures, so hath it in man for its seat and subject, his soul or spiritual part. The effects of Divine wisdom, power, goodness, are everywhere visible throughout the whole creation; and as there is no effect but hath something in it corresponding to its cause (wherein it was its cause), so every creature doth some way or other represent God: some in virtues, some in life, some in being only. The material world represents Him, as a house the Builder; but spiritual beings, as a child the Father. Other creatures (as one fitly expresses it) carry His footsteps; these, His image; and that, not as drawn with a pencil, which can only express figure and colour, but as represented in a glass, which imitates action and motion. To give the pre-eminence, therefore, in this point to the body of man, was a conceit so gross, that one would wonder how it should obtain, at least in the Christian world."*

Still more fully and forcibly and persuasively, after explaining and illustrating how "vital" and "intimate" the "image of God" is, through "restitution," he thus expatiates:—

"An image *connatural* to the spirit of man; not a thing alien and foreign to his nature, put into him purposely, as it were, to torment and vex him; but an ancient, well-known inhabitant, that had place in him from the beginning. Sin is the injurious intruder; which therefore puts the soul into a commotion, and permits it not to rest while it hath any being there. This image calms it, restores it, works a peaceful, orderly composure within; returns it to itself, to its pristine blessed state; being re-seated there as in its proper, primitive subject.

"For though this image, in respect of corrupted nature, be *supernatural*, in respect of institute and undefiled nature, it was, in a true sense, *natural*; as hath been demonstrated by divers of ours against the Papists, and, upon the matter, yielded by some of the more moderate among themselves. At least it was connate with human nature, consentaneous to it, and perfective of it. We are speaking, it must be remembered, of that part of the

---

* *Ibid.*, vol. i., pp. 65-66.

Divine image that consists in *moral* excellencies; there being another part of it, as hath been said, that is, even in the strictest sense, natural.

"There is nothing in the whole moral law of God—in conformity whereunto this image did *ab origine* consist—nothing of what he requires from man, that is at all destructive of his being, prejudicial to his comforts, repugnant to his most innate principles: nothing that clashes with his reason or is contrary to his interest; or that is not, most directly, conservative of his being and comforts, agreeable to his most rational principles, subservient to his best and truest interest. For what 'doth God the Lord require,' but fear and love, service and holy walking, from an entire and undivided soul? What, but what is good; not only in itself, but for us; and in respect whereof, His law is said to be holy, just, and good?

"And what He requireth, He impresseth. This 'law, written in the heart,' is this 'likeness.'

"How grateful then will it be, when after a long extermination and exile, it returns and repossesses the soul, is recognised by it, becomes to it 'a new nature,' yea, even a Divine; a vital living law, 'the law of the Spirit of life in Christ Jesus!' What grievance or burden is it to do the dictates of nature? actions that easily and freely flow from their own principles? and when blessedness itself is enfolded in those very acts and inclinations? How infinitely satisfying and delightful will it be, when the soul shall find itself connaturalised to everything in its duty, and shall have no other duty incumbent on it than to be happy! when it shall need no arguments and exhortations to love God, nor need be urged and pressed, as heretofore, to mind Him, to fear before Him ! when love, and reverence, and adoration, and praise, when delight and joy, shall be all natural acts. Can you separate this in your own thoughts from the highest satisfaction?"*

Again, and pregnantly, of Law as a gauge of man's departure from God, thus :—

"And how far he is swerved from what he was is easily conjecturable, by comparing him with the *measures* which show what he should be. For it cannot be conceived for what end laws were ever given him, if, at least, we allow them not the measures of his primitive capacity, or deny him ever to have been in a possibility to obey. Could they be intended for his government, if conformity to them were against or above his nature? Or were they only for his condemnation? or for *that*, if he was never capable of obeying them? How inconsistent were it with the goodness of the blessed God, that the condemnation of His creatures should be the first design of His giving them laws; and with His justice, to make His laws the rule of punishment to whom they never could be the rule of obedience and duty; or with His wisdom, to frame a system and body of laws that should never serve for either purpose, and so be upon the whole useful for nothing? The common reason of mankind teacheth us to estimate the wisdom and equity of lawgivers by the suitableness of their constitutions to the genius and temper of the

---

* *Ibid.*, vol. i., pp. 113-114.

people for whom they are made; and we commonly reckon nothing can more slur and expose government than the imposing of constitutions most probably impracticable, and which are never *likely* to obtain. How much more incongruous must it be esteemed, to enjoin such as never possibly could! Prudent legislators, and studious of the common good, would be shy to impose upon men under their power, against their genius and common usages (neither alterable easily), nor to any advantage. Much more absurd were it, with great solemnity and weighty sanctions, to enact statutes for brute creatures! And wherein were it more to purpose to prescribe unto men strict rules of piety and virtue than to beasts or trees, if the former had not been capable of observing them, as the latter were not?"*

I wish to follow in the footsteps of John Howe. In view of the sentimentalism and ritualism and making visible of things that are best left invisible; in recollection of our actual dealing in pulpit and platform and current literature, whereby appeal is made to feeling,

---

* *Ibid.*,vol. iii., pp. 298-9. Cf. Works, vol. i., pp. 14, 15 ("Blessedness of the Righteous"), for most eloquent and deeply-thought statement of man's "capacities" and the inconceivableness of God implanting longings and aspirations without corresponding objects. Our limits forbid further quotation.

sentiment, æsthetic nature, I re-assert as a present-day truth that Christianity recognizes and addresses our reason, our conscience, our moral nature. I would proclaim afresh that that is an anti-Biblical and anti-Christian teaching that so makes sin the master that nothing remains in man capable of response to his God. I affirm that, fallen though man be, he remains God's divinest work, God's nearest likeness, God's most homogeneous creature. I reverence man because he is man. I stand in awe of man's grandeur as I see the value God has put on him. I refuse to demean and deteriorate his nature. I grasp gratefully and adoringly the fact that it is I the man who become the Christian; that the restitution *is* of what I *was ;* and that the lowliest believer bears, nay, in a sense *is*, " the image of God."

It were unpardonable to omit in any Lecture on John Howe, his magnificent as pathetic, sublime as heart-shattering description of the ruined temple of man's soul, and the fitness of God's departure from it. As they will splendidly close our consideration of his HABITUAL REVERENCE, and related characteristics, I give them at this point.*

---

* My quotations thus far, and these, will speak to the exaggerated nonsense of HENRY ROGERS and others on Howe's style as unformed and obscure. I have no wish —quite the reverse—to undervalue the service rendered by Henry Rogers in his edition of Howe's Works for the Religious Tract Society (6 vols., 8vo., 1863). It was a great gift to all who value noble and devout thinking. But the good man pothered and pottered so long over the punctuation and involute sentences of Howe, that he came to imagine his own labours of transcendent magnitude and importance. It was, perhaps, well to revise the punctuation, and to remove the Scripture texts and quotations generally to foot of pages ; but after all Howe is "strong meat" for men, not milk-and-water for babes, and no one who has liking for Howe finds any difficulty worth naming in reading him just as he himself gave his books to the world. I protest against Rogers's preposterous hyperstatement of Howe's unformed style, punctuation, italics, etc. Need I add that, while enforced to say these things, I yield to none in gratitude for Henry Rogers's manifold gifts to our best literature ?

It seems expedient to vindicate Howe's style, as mere style, against such misdirected criticism, by a few examples taken *ad aperturam libri*, as thus :—

SATISFACTION AND DESIRE.—" For this satisfaction is the soul's rest in God ; its perfect enjoyment of the

He is pleading with men to yield to the persuasions of the Spirit of God, and reinstate

most perfect good; the expletion of the whole capacity of its will; the total filling up of that vast enlarged appetite; the perfecting of all its desires in delight and joy. Now delight or joy (for they differ not, save that the latter word is thought something more appropriate to reasonable nature) is fitly defined,—the rest of the desiring faculty in the thing desired. Desire and delight are but two acts of love, diversified only by the distance or presence of the same object; which, when it is distant, the soul, acted and prompted by love, desires, moves towards it, pursues it; when present and attained, delights in it, enjoys it, stays upon it, satisfies itself in it, according to the measure of goodness it finds there. Desire is, therefore, love in *motion;* delight is love in *rest:* and of this latter—delight or joy—Scripture evidently gives us this notion,—'He will rejoice over thee with joy' (unto which is presently added as exegetical), 'he will rest in His love:' which 'resting' can be but the same thing with 'being satisfied.'"

"BEING SATISFIED."—" And so doth this 'being satisfied' not only generally signify the soul to be at rest, but it specifies that rest; and gives us a distinct account of the nature of it: as, that it is not a forced violent rest; such as proceeds from a beguiled ignorance, a drowsy sloth, a languishing weakness, or a desire and hope of happiness, by often frustrations, baffled into despair,—to all which, the native import

God on the throne of their hearts. He grounds this on God's great offers to return. He then and propriety of that word 'satisfaction' doth strongly repugn. But it discovers it to be a *natural* rest; I mean, from an *internal* principle. The soul is not held in its present state of enjoyment by a strong and violent hand; but rests in it by a connaturalness thereunto: is attempered to it by its own inward constitution and frame. It rests not as a descending stone, intercepted by something by the way that holds and stops it, else it would fall further; but as a thing would rest in its own centre; with such a rest as the earth is supposed to have in its proper place; that, 'being hung upon nothing,' is yet unmoved,—*ponderibus librata suis,*—equally balanced by its own weight every way."

INCOMMENSURATE END.—"Now, who can think the satisfying of these lusts the commensurate end of man? Who would not, upon the supposition of no higher, say with the Psalmist, 'Wherefore hast thou made all men in vain?' To what purpose was it for him to live in the world a few years upon this account only, and so go down to the place of silence? What is there in the momentary satisfaction of this mortal flesh; in his pleasing view of a mass of treasure, which he never brought with him into the world, but only heaped together, and so leaves not the world richer or poorer than he found it; what is there in the applause and admiration of fools, as the greater part always are;

portrays the "desolate temple" of the human soul without God. A hush of awe may well

that we should think it worth the while for man to have lived for these things? If the question were put, 'Wherefore did God make man?' who would not be ashamed so to answer it: 'He made him to eat, and drink, and take his pleasure, to gather up wealth for he knows not whom; to use his inventions, that each one may become a talk and wonder to the rest; and then, when he hath fetched a few turns upon the theatre, and entertained the eyes of beholders with a short scene of impertinences, descend, and never be heard of more?' What! that he should come into the world furnished with such powers and endowments for this! It were a like case, as if one should be clad in scarlet to go to plough, or curiously instructed in arts and sciences to tend hogs."

REAL WORTH.—" Though it do not vaunt, will show itself; and while it doth not glare, yet cannot forbear to shine" (vol. i., p. 428).

CALM.—"*That we endeavour for a calm indifferency and dispassionate temper of mind towards the various objects and affairs that belong to this present life.* There are very narrow limits already set, by the nature of the things themselves, to all the real objective value that such things have in them; and it is the part of wisdom and justice to set the proportionable bounds to all the thoughts, cares, and passions, we will suffer to stir in our minds in reference to them. Nothing is a more come over our spirit as we read and re-read the portrayal:—

evident acknowledged character of a fool, than upon every slight occasion to be in a transport. To be much taken with empty things betokens an empty spirit. It is a part of manly fortitude to have a soul so fenced against foreign impressions, as little to be moved with things that have little in them; to keep our passions under a strict rein and steady command, that they be easily retractable and taught to obey; not to move till severe reason have audited the matter, and pronounced the occasion just and valuable: in which case the same manly temper will not refuse to admit a proportionable stamp and impress from the occurring object. For it is equally a prevarication from true manhood to be moved with everything and with nothing: the former would speak a man's spirit a feather, the latter a stone. A total apathy and insensibleness of external occurrents hath been the aim of some, but never the attainment of the highest pretenders; and if it had, yet ought it not to have been their boast, as upon sober thoughts it cannot be reckoned a perfection. But it should be endeavoured that the passions, which are not to be rooted up, because they are of nature's planting, be yet so discreetly checked and depressed that they grow not to that enormous tallness as to overtop a man's intellectual power, and cast a dark shadow over his soul."

RELUCTANT DYING.—"Who could ever by their love of this bodily life, procure it to be perpetuated? or by

"That He hath withdrawn Himself and left this His temple desolate, we have many sad and plain proofs before us. The stately ruins are visible to every eye, that bear in their front, yet extant, this doleful inscription : HERE GOD ONCE DWELT. Enough appears of the admirable frame and structure of the soul of man to show the Divine presence did sometime reside in it; more than enough of vicious deformity to proclaim He is now retired and gone. The lamps are extinct, the altar overturned; the light and love are now vanished, which did the one shine with so heavenly brightness, the other burn with so pious fervour. The golden candlestick is displaced and thrown away as a useless thing, to make their dread of mortality, make themselves immortal? Have not others, in all former ages, loved the body and this world as much? and what is become of them? Hath not death still swept the stage from generation to generation, and taken all away, willing or unwilling? To have all my good bound up in what I cannot keep, and to be in a continual dread of what I cannot avoid, —what can be more disconsolate? How grievous will it be to be torn out of the body! not to resign the soul, but have it drawn forth, *as a rusty sword out of the sheath;* a thing which our utmost unwillingness will make the more painful, but cannot deter!" (vol. vi., pp. 166-7).

The Reader will be richly rewarded by turning to the following :—i. 80, 437, 454 ; ii. 74-5, 97, 133, 193, 223, 237, 305, 377-8, 383, 389, 412-3, 421-2, 424, 427 ; iii. 22, 168-9, 274, 387-8.

room for the throne of the Prince of Darkness. The sacred incense, which sent rolling up in clouds its rich perfumes, is exchanged for a poisonous, hellish vapour; and here is, 'instead of a sweet savour, a stench.' The comely order of this house is turned all into confusion; the beauties of holiness into noisome impurities; the house of prayer to a den of thieves, and that of the worst and most horrid kind; for every lust is a thief, and every theft sacrilege: continual rapine and robbery is committed upon holy things. The noble powers which were designed and dedicated to Divine contemplation and delight, are alienated to the service of the most despicable idols, and employed unto vilest intuitions and embraces; to behold and admire 'lying vanities,' to indulge and cherish lust and wickedness. What have not the enemies 'done wickedly in the sanctuary'? How have they broken down the carved work thereof, and that too 'with axes and hammers;' the noise whereof was not to be heard in building, much less in the demolishing this sacred frame. Look upon the fragments of that curious sculpture which once adorned the palace of that great king: the relics of 'common notions,' the lively prints of some undefaced truth, the fair ideas of things, the yet legible precepts that relate to practice. Behold! with what accuracy the broken pieces show these to have been engraven by the finger of God, and how they now lie torn and scattered, one in this dark corner, another in that, buried in heaps of dirt and rubbish! There is not now a system, an entire table of coherent truths to be found, or a frame of holiness, but some shivered parcels; and if any, with great toil and labour, apply themselves to draw out here one piece and there another, and set them together, they serve rather to show how exquisite the Divine workmanship was in the original composition, than for present use to the excellent purposes for which the whole was first designed. Some pieces agree and own one another; but how soon are our inquiries and endeavours nonplused and superseded! How many attempts have been made, since that fearful fall and ruin of this fabric, to compose again the truths of so many several kinds into their distinct orders, and make up frames of science or useful knowledge; and after so many ages, nothing is finished in any one kind! Sometimes truths are misplaced, and what belongs to one kind is transferred to another, where it will not fitly match; sometimes falsehood inserted, which shatters or disturbs the whole frame. And what is, with much fruitless pains, done by one hand, is dashed in pieces by another; and it is the work of a following age to sweep away the fine-spun cobwebs of a former. And those truths which are of greatest use, though not most out of sight, are least regarded; their tendency and design are overlooked, or they are so loosened and torn off that they cannot be wrought in, so as to take hold of the soul; but hover as faint ineffectual notions that signify nothing. Its very fundamental powers are shaken and disjointed, and their order towards one another confounded and broken; so that what is judged considerable, is not considered; what is recommended as eligible and lovely, is not loved and chosen. Yea, the 'truth which is after godliness,' is not so much disbelieved as hated, 'held in unrighteousness,' and shines as too feeble a light in that malignant 'darkness which comprehends it not.' You come, amidst all this confusion, as into the ruined palace of some great prince, in which you see here the fragments of a noble pillar, there the shattered pieces of some curious imagery; and all lying neglected and useless amongst heaps of dirt. He that invites you to take a view of the soul of man, gives you but such another prospect, and doth but say to you, 'BEHOLD THE DESOLATION! all things rude and waste.' So that should there be any pretence to the Divine presence, it might be said, if God be here, why is it thus? The faded glory, the darkness, the disorder, the impurity, the decayed state in all respects of this temple, too plainly show the great Inhabitant is gone."

Of the fitness of the Divine departure he thus with solemn state and music speaks:—

" Now what could be expected to ensue upon all this, but that he should be forsaken of God? That the blessed presence be withdrawn, that had been so despitefully slighted, to return no more.

" No more; till at least a recompense should be made Him for the wrong done, and a capacity be recovered for His future converse ; namely, till both His honour should be repaired, and His temple ; till He might again honourably return and be fitly received.

" But who could have thought in what way these things should ever be brought to pass? That is, neither could

---

* *Ibid.*, vol. iii. pp. 306-9.

His departure but be expected, nor His return but be above all expectation.

"To depart was what became Him, a thing, as the case was, most Godlike or worthy of God, and what He owed to Himself. It was meet so great a MAJESTY, having been so condescendingly gracious, should not be also cheap, or appear unapprehensive of being neglected and set at naught.

"It became Him, as the self-sufficient Being, to let it be seen He designed not man His temple, for want of a house: that having of old 'inhabited His own eternity,' and having now the 'heavens for His throne, the earth His footstool,' He could dwell alone, or where He pleased else in all His great creation; and did not need, where He was not desired. That of the cynic was thought a brave saying, when his malcontented servant turned fugitive and left him: 'It were an unworthy thing Manes should think he can live without Diogenes, and that Diogenes cannot without Manes.' How much better would it suit with the real self-fulness of a Deity, where nothing of this kind can look like an empty hollow boast.

"It was becoming of His pure and glorious holiness not to dwell amidst impurities, or let it be thought He was a 'God that took pleasure in wickedness;' and most suitable to His equal justice to let them who said to Him, 'Depart from us,' feel that they spake that word against their own life and soul; and that what was their rash and wilful choice is their heaviest doom and punishment.

"It was only strange, that when He left His temple He did not consume it; and that not leaving it, without being basely expulsed, He hath thought of returning without being invited back again.

"Yea, and whatsoever was necessary thereto, is designed by His own so strange contrivance and done at His own so dear expense; His only begotten Son most freely consenting with Him, and in sundry capacities sustaining the weight and burden of this great undertaking."

Those of us who have to 'preach' the Gospel, or who have in any way to 'teach' out of THE WORD, will advantage ourselves by acting on the two-fold fact thus so invariably asserted by Howe—Man re-made in God's image: Man though fallen, capable of response to truth and grace. What bearing-down power, what urgency, what tenderness, what overwhelming wistfulness it gave to JOHN HOWE'S preaching, I would send the Reader to his Works to discover. There he is ever found dealing with Essentials.†

---

* "Works of John Howe," vol. iii., p. 311-312.

† "Essentials." He acted on his own aphoristic principles,—"We know that generally by how much anything is more disputable, the less it is necessary or conducible to the Christian life. God hath graciously provided that

I would close with one other characteristic that has for those to whom I mainly write a

what we are to live by should not cost us so dear. And, possibly, as there is less occasion of disputing about the more momentous things of religion, so there may be somewhat more of modesty and awe in reference to what is so confessedly venerable and sacred—though too many are over-bold even here also—than so foolishly to trifle with such things. Therefore more commonly, where that humour prevails, men divert from those plainer things with some slighter and superficial reverence to them, but more heartily esteeming them insipid and jejune because they have less in them to gratify that appetite, and betake themselves to such things about which they may more plausibly contend : and then, what pitiful trifles oftentimes take up their time and thoughts ; questions and problems of like weighty importance, very often, with those which, the above-named author * tells us, this disease among the Greeks prompted them to trouble themselves about ; as, what number of rowers Ulysses had ? which was written first, the Iliad or the Odyssey ? etc. So that, as he saith, they spent their lives very operosely doing nothing : their conceits being such that if they kept them to themselves they could yield them no fruit ; and if they published them to others, they should not seem thereby the more learned, but the more troublesome ; to this purpose he truly speaks. And is it not to be resented that men should sell away the solid

---

* Sen de Brev. Vit.

living message still, and is an EIGHTH PRESENT-DAY TRUTH. I have in my mind his PRACTICAL strength and vital joy, which a serious soul would find in substantial religion, for such toys ! Yea, and not only famish themselves, but trouble the world and embroil the Church with their impertinences ! If a man be drawn forth to defend an important truth against an injurious assault, it were treacherous self-love to purchase his own peace by declining it ; or if he did sometimes turn his thoughts to some of our petty questions, that with many are so hotly agitated, for recreation sake, or to try his wit and exercise his reason, without stirring his passions to the disturbance of others or himself ; it were an innocent divertisement, and the best purpose that things of that nature are capable of serving. But when contention becomes a man's element, and he cannot live out of that fire ; strains his wit and racks his invention to find matter of quarrel ; is resolved nothing said or done by others shall please him, only because he means to please himself in dissenting ; disputes only that he may dispute, and loves dissension for itself ;—this is the unnatural humour that hath so unspeakably troubled the Church and dispirited religion, and filled men's souls with wind and vanity,—yea, with fire and fury. This hath made Christians gladiators, and the Christian world a clamorous theatre, while men have equally affected to contend, and to make ostentation of their ability to do.

" And surely as it is highly pleasurable to retire one-self, so it is charitable to call aside others out of this noise and throng; to consider silently, and feed upon the known

APPLICATION OF ALL HE PREACHES AND TEACHES. Let one example out of abundant illustrate, from "The Redeemer's Tears Wept over Lost Souls":—

"That thou mayst, and not throw away thy soul and so great a hope, through mere sloth and loathness to be at some pains for thy life, let the text, which hath been thy *directory* about the things that belong to thy peace, be also thy *motive*, as it gives thee to behold the Son of God weeping over such as would not know those things. Shall not the Redeemer's tears move thee? O hard heart! consider what these tears import to this purpose :—

First, They signify the real depth and greatness of the misery into which thou art falling. They drop from an intellectual and most comprehensive eye, that sees far and pierces deep into things,—hath a wide and large prospect, takes the compass of that forlorn state into which unreconcilable sinners are hastening in all the horror of it. The Son of God did not weep vain and causeless tears or for a light matter; nor did He for Himself either spend His own or desire the profusion of others' tears : "Weep not for me, O daughters of Jerusalem," etc. He knows the value of souls : the weight of guilt,

---

and agreed things of our religion, which immediately lead to both the duties and delights of it."*

---

* "The Blessedness of the Righteous," To the Reader —vol. i., pp. 5-7. Cf. also vol. iii., p. 156.

and how low it will press and sink them ; the severity of God's justice and the power of His anger, and what the fearful effects of them will be when they finally fall. If thou understandest not these things thyself, believe Him that did,—at least believe His tears.

Secondly, They signify the sincerity of His love and pity, the truth and tenderness of His compassion. Canst thou think *His* deceitful tears? His, who never knew guile? Was this like the rest of His course? And remember that He who shed tears, did, from the same fountain of love and mercy, shed blood too ! Was that also done to deceive? Thou makest thyself some very considerable thing indeed, if thou thinkest the Son of God counted it worth His while to weep, and bleed, and die, to deceive thee into a false esteem of Him and His love. But if it be the greatest madness imaginable to entertain any such thought, but that His tears were sincere and inartificial, the natural, genuine expressions of undissembled benignity and pity, thou art then to consider what love and compassion thou art now sinning against, what bowels thou spurnest ; and that if thou perishest, it is under such guilt as the devils themselves are not liable to, who never had a Redeemer bleeding for them, nor, that we ever find, weeping over them.

"Thirdly, They show the remedilessness of thy case if thou persist in impenitency and unbelief till the things of thy peace be quite hid from thine eyes. These tears will then be the last issues of even defeated love,—of love that is frustrated of its kind design. Thou mayst perceive in these tears the steady, unalterable laws of heaven, the inflexibleness of the Divine justice, that holds thee in adamantine bonds, and hath sealed thee up, if thou prove incurably obstinate and impenitent, unto perdition; so that even the Redeemer Himself, He that is mighty to save, cannot at length save thee, but only weep over thee, drop tears into thy flame,—which assuage it not, but (though they have another design, even to express true compassion), do yet unavoidably heighten and increase the fervour of it, and will do so to all eternity. He even tells thee, sinner, 'Thou hast despised My blood: thou shalt yet have My tears. *That* would have saved thee,— *these* do only lament thee lost!'

"But the tears wept over others as lost and past hope, why should they not melt thee, while as yet there is hope in thy case? If thou be effectually melted in thy very soul, and looking to Him whom thou hast pierced, dost truly mourn over Him, thou mayst assure thyself the prospect His weeping eye had of lost souls did not include thee. His weeping over thee would argue thy case forlorn and hopeless; thy mourning over Him will make it safe and happy. That it may be so, consider further, that,—

"Fourthly, They signify how very intent He is to save souls, and how gladly He would save thine, if yet thou wilt accept of mercy while it may be had. For if He weep over them that will not be saved, from the same love that is the spring of these tears would saving mercies proceed to those that are become willing to receive them. And that love that wept over them that were lost, how will it glory in them that are saved! There His love is disappointed and vexed, crossed in its gracious intendment; but here, having compassed it, how will He 'joy over thee with singing, and rest in His love!' And thou also, instead of being involved in a like ruin with the unreconciled sinners of the old Jerusalem, shalt be enrolled among the glorious citizens of the new, and triumph together with them in eternal glory!"*

These appeals and 'applications' of previous reasoned-out truths, I am again old-fashioned enough to wish to see revived. I shall take occasion in bringing RICHARD BAXTER before my Readers, to enforce this. But in relation to the sermons of John Howe—as in kind to those of Jonathan Edwards—the heart of their power is to be found in their thick-coming, eager, intense driving-home on every hearer the doctrine that has been proved. I desiderate for to-day more of Howe's scholarly exegesis and INTELLECTUAL setting forth of the thought the inspired words clothe; and I emphatically covet for every preacher within all the Churches, more of direct, personal, present pressure on acceptance of whatever teaching is fetched

---

* "Howe's Works," vol. ii., p. 342-4.

from God's Word. To huddle up, as is so often done nowadays, an essay-like sermon or sermonette, or some pretty piece of sentence-making, with the merest pretence of 'application,' is a poor discharge of our august office, and a poor account of our God-given opportunity in being face-to-face with dying yet undying fellow-men.

I must leave the half untold of what might be told of Life and Works. It were not difficult to vindicate a potential influence alike in State and Church for John Howe, and pleasing to dwell on his 'inward' association with the foremost of his contemporaries, demonstrative of how great a space and place he filled in that great century. BAXTER reverenced him; OWEN loved and honoured him; ANDREW MARVELL held him to be of the greatest of the sons of men. Materials abound to illustrate his fidelity and yet considerateness of reproof in highest places. His books reveal modest but genuine scholarship and wide culture. His Letters remain to show with how touching sympathy he ministered to the mourning and despondent. His calm, dignified, conscience-ruled Nonconformity has been an inspiration to Nonconformists.* His end was 'peace,' and glory begun on earth. Looking to his Works, I may be blameworthy for not having given more prominence to his substantive contributions to the highest metaphysic. I regard his "Living Temple" and companion treatises—apart from their pricelessness as "Companions for the Devout Life"—and his Letters on the Trinity and its cognates, as furnishing special answers to present-day unbeliefs and disbeliefs. He anticipates these; for he breaks in their own hands and within their own standing-ground, the weapons of warfare lifted up against the existence of God and Revelation. The *possibility* of that existence he argues with unapproachable philosophic power, and not without jets of merited sarcasm and play of grave humour.

---

* Cf. vol. v., pp. 233-4.

I must perforce pass over these and other things.*

---

* I must here give one specimen of his lighter-touched yet most masterly thinking—the lightness only that of the foam on the surface of abyssmal depths—as thus, on " matter."

"A capacity of an *immortal state;* that is, that his nature is such that he may, if God so please, by the concurrent influence of His ordinary power and providence, without the help of a miracle, subsist in another state of life after this, even a state that shall not be liable to that impairment and decay that we find this subject to. More is not as yet contended for; and so much, methinks, none should make a difficulty to admit, from what is evidently found in him. For it may well be supposed that the admitting of this, at least, will seem much more easy to any free and unprejudiced reason, than to ascribe the operations before instanced in, to alterable or perishable matter, or indeed to any matter at all : it being justly presumed that none will ascribe to matter, as such, the powers of ratiocination or volition ; for then every particle of matter must needs be rational and intelligent,— a high advance to what one would never have thought at all active. And how inconceivable is it, that the minute particles of matter, in themselves each of them destitute of any such powers, should, by their mutual intercourse with one another, become furnished with them; that they should be able to understand, deliberate, resolve, and choose, being assembled and duly disposed in counsel

ROBERT HALL said to HENRY ROGERS "that as a *minister*, he had derived more benefit

together, but apart, rest all in a deep and sluggish silence! Besides, if the particles of matter, howsoever modified and moved to the utmost subtilty or tenuity, and to the highest vigour, shall then become intelligent and rational, how is it that we observe not, as any matter is more subtile and more swiftly and variously moved, it makes a discernibly nearer approach, proportionably, to the faculty and power of reasoning; and that nothing more of an aptitude or tendency towards intelligence and wisdom is to be perceived in an aspiring flame or a brisk wind than in a clod or a stone? If to understand, to define, to distinguish, to syllogize, be nothing else but the agitation and collision of the minute parts of rarified matter among one another, methinks some happy chemist or other, when he hath missed his designed mark, should have hit upon some such more noble product, and by one or other prosperous sublimation have caused some temporary resemblance, at least, of these operations. Or, if the paths of nature, in these affairs of the mind, be more abstruse, and quite out of the reach and road of artificial achievement, whence is it that nature herself,—that is vainly enough supposed by some to have been so happy as, by some casual strokes, to have fabricated the first of human creatures, that have since propagated themselves —is grown so effete and dull as never since to hit upon any like effect in the like way; and that no records of any time or age give us the notice of some such creature from John Howe, than from all other divines put together." I can well believe this. For he stands alone in his INTELLECTUAL SANCTITY; and it is magnetic. "As a minister," I feel in reading Howe that I breathe a more heavenly atmosphere than in any other divine in the

sprung out of some Epicurean womb of the earth, and elaborated by the only immediate hand of nature, so disposing the parts of matter in its constitution that it should be able to perform the operation belonging to the mind of man?

" But if we cannot, with any tolerable pretence or show of reason, attribute these operations to any mere matter, then there must be somewhat else in man to which they may agree, that is distinct from his corruptible part, and that is therefore capable, by the advantage of his own nature, of subsisting hereafter, while God shall continue to it an influence agreeable to its nature, as He doth to other creatures. And hence it seems a modest and sober deduction, that there is in the nature of man at least a *capacity* of an immortal state." *

---

* Works of John Howe," vol. i., p. 401-2. Cf. *ibid.*, pp. 56-7, of "apprehension" of God [= perception] as distinct from comprehension. See also iii., pp. 28, 36, 37-8, 139, 177; v. 85, 94-5. On *possibilities*, see iii., 144-5, 202; v. 88, 93.

whole range of our theological literature. His own purity and unearthliness are interfused with his words. His words connaturalize mind and heart with holiness. He so lifts up to serene heights, or rather from the very Alps of thought so elevates you that instinctively you are sent on your knees to adore, as before the apocalypse of stars in new-revealed skies. "As a minister," he awes me by the grandeur he imparts to my office, and by the blessed responsibilities he urges. For harmoniously-balanced and affluent variety of faculty, for disciplined and transfigured capacities, for grace-ruled serenity and sensitiveness of conscience, for potentiality throughout, I can think of no single man once to be named with JOHN HOWE. "As a minister," for stimulus, for aspiration, for fresh consecration, for deepening of belief in the power of the Gospel and in God's fulness of redeeming love in Jesus Christ so that every lost soul meets a self-elected doom, for quickening to urgency and pathos of entreaty—and all based on an intellect and a moral nature that might have served for ten ordinary men, and a scholarship and general culture that were noticeable even in his age—I know no works so absolutely supreme as those of John Howe.*

I agree with the Rev. S. W. CHRISTOPHERS in his "John Howe's Charge, Home and Church," that JOHN HOWE has self-described his own mature character in his "good man."

---

* It is pleasing to find Howe quoting with "pious" and "holy" before the name, George Herbert, at least three times. More noteworthy still, I have marked a finely-appreciative reference to Shakespeare, thus :—"At length he says, 'The butt-end of this hypothesis,' etc.,—I like not that phrase the worse for the author's sake of whom it seems borrowed, whose memory greater things will make live, when we are forgot" (A View of the late considerations addressed to H. H. about the Trinity: Works, vol. v., p. 173). The reference is to Richard III., ii. 2, "the butt-end of a mother's blessing." There is a Shakespeare touch of pride in "this England" in his Epistle-dedicatory of the "Living Temple" to Lord Paget:—" Hereby you have dignified England, in letting it be seen what it can signify in the world, when it is so happy to have its interests managed by a fit and able hand" (Works, iii., p. 3).

With this I conclude my inadequate but I trust inciting Lecture on this foremost of Nonconformists :—

"The life of a good man is under the sweet command of one Supreme Goodness, and Last End. This alone is that living form and soul which, running through all the powers of the mind and actions of life, collects all together into one fair and beautiful system, making all that variety conspire into perfect unity. . . . This is the best temper and composedness of the soul when, by a conjunction with our chief Good and Last End, it is drawn up into a unity and consent with itself; when all the faculties of the soul, with their several issues and motions, though never so many in themselves, like so many lines meet together in one and the same centre. . . . When religion enters into the soul it charms all its restless rage and violent appetite, by discovering to it the universal fountain-fulness of one Supreme Almighty Goodness ; and, leading it out of itself into a conjunction therewith, it lulls it into the most undisturbed rest and quietness on the lap of Divine enjoyment, where it rests with full contentment, and rests adequately satisfied in the fruition of the infinite, uniform, and essential Goodness and Loveliness." *

---

* "Homes of Old English Writers," 1 vol. (Haughton) —A very chatty and in some respects brilliant book. There are occasional churchy *bits*, but substantially it is finely catholic. In the paper on Howe one incidental

One word—in retrospect—from the Poet (Young) :—

> "How poor, how rich, how abject, how august,
> How complicate, how wonderful is man !
> How PASSING WONDER He who made him such !"

gibe is a childish and unworthy *anachronism*. He speaks of Cromwell's "devotional muscles . . . always under control" (p. 230).

RICHARD BAXTER:
Seraphic Fervour.

"I, who bow not to the priest
   Lean, or fed to sleekness,
Bend to one who holds of Christ
   Wisdom, love, and meekness.
When his intercession mild
   Hushed the critic's pæan;
He had caught a gentle tone
   From the Galilean."
        THE MASTER: *Passion Flowers* (1854).

"Take courage, Heart! For here below
What are such things but idle show;
Whose whole worth in thyself doth dwell
Created by thy magic-spell;
According as thou turn'st to good
Or evil use, Time's changeful mood:
So, like the wind the eagle's wings,
'Twill lift thy soul to higher things
Than those whereon the eye doth rest,
Or make thee level with the beast
Who lives but unto time and earth,
Whereof his food and joys have birth.
But thou that draw'st from such mean source
Only the body's brief-lived force,
Should'st not submit thy soul thereto
But to its service these subdue."
        HENRY ELLISON: *Mad Moments*, vol. i., pp. 295-6.

When Boswell asked Dr. Johnson what works of Richard Baxter he should read, he answered, "Read any of them, for they are all good."

"Baxter's face I think still more striking than Howe's. Where it used to hang in Dr. Williams' library, over the fireplace, I could have almost thought that it changed like a flame as I looked at it, and seemed to flicker with tenderness and with all kinds of delicacy of life."—DR. CHARLES STANFORD, *to the Lecturer*.

RICHARD BAXTER:

Seraphic Fervour.

Born at Eaton Constantyne, Shropshire, 12th November, 1615: *Died at London,* 8th December, 1691: *buried in Christ Church, London.*

THE epithets, 'Venerable' for BEDE, and 'Judicious' (by which I suppose 'judicial' is meant) for HOOKER, are not more irreversible down the ages, than is that of 'Holy' applied to RICHARD BAXTER. "The holy Baxter," says an able anonymous Essayist, "is just the verdict which a seraph, 'full of eyes within and without,' might be expected to pronounce after having deliberately reviewed the whole history and work of the sage of Kidderminster."* COLERIDGE—like WILLIAM ORME before him—

---

* Prefixed to "Practical Works," 4 vols., large 8vo. (Virtue), 1838.

was struck with the unearthliness and holiness of his character; and in relation to the great posthumous folio "Reliquiæ Baxterianæ," says "I would almost as soon doubt the Gospel's verity as Baxter's veracity." It were easy to adduce multiplied testimonies having the same burden,—from HOWE and CALAMY onward to Lord Macaulay and Principal Tulloch, and the present Archbishop of Dublin (Trench) in his noticeable lecture on the "Saint's Everlasting Rest:"* but I do not feel that it is needed. Such a man may well be taken as a REPRESENTATIVE NONCONFORMIST.†

The first thing that strikes me in studying the character and multitudinous Works of Baxter—and that I would note and illustrate—is, THE

---

* "Companions for the Devout Life."

† Baxter's prolonged and earnest efforts for 'Unity' among all who held the same fundamental truths and principles, tempt to a thorough discussion of them, more particularly their inherent elements of failure. But neither this, nor other prominent things in his Life, may I now notice. In the present Lecture, and in all, I fix on characteristics likely to be practically useful to-day.

VOLUME OF HIS BEING AND HIS PRODIGIOUS VITALITY. It was a penetrative criticism of GRAINGER'S Portraits, in apology for his brief notice, that "men of his size are not to be drawn in miniature." Intellect, moral nature, affections, force, power of work, actual achievement—all were on the largest scale. There are some one meets with, who have a restless and irritating vitality; and as a consequence they do everything loudly—know nothing of seclusion and silence—everything with fuss and edgedness, and *rasping* to one's patience. These are your small men who imagine themselves—big—giants of circumstance who sooner or later are shewn as what they are —pigmies. In Baxter the vitality that I name 'prodigious' informed a man of such a size, such height and depth and breadth as the word 'gigantic' alone can describe. So that his movements were intense yet deliberate, aggressive but reflective, eager nevertheless clear-eyed, and while splendidly daring, preceded by devoutest asking of higher help than his own. In his physical constitution naturally weak, and tainted from the outset with consumptive tendencies, and later, worn and valetudinarian, he so conquered the body, so made it serve not rule, that he did twenty ordinary men's work as an author alone; while outside of that was a ceaseless, tireless activity and ministry in Church and State, much more resembling the activity we think of in a seraph than an infirm mortal. He projected his own prodigious vitality into his century, and interpenetrated every movement for good in England. No one familiar with the Men and Books of Baxter's period can have failed to be arrested with his almost 'uncanny' omnipresence wherever in England men were aiming high for the nation's or the world's welfare. In the most unlikely and unexpected places and ways his personality turns up, and his directing brain and enkindling heart and inexhaustible energy. From the King to the House of Commons, from his Highness the Lord Protector to the Army, from the

Noble to the obscure village-Curate, from workers at home to workers " in the plantations," from the men of the Universities to the ignorant,—by spoken words, by preached sermon, by printed books, by 'catechizing' and fellowship meetings, by 'Commendatory Epistle,' by an ubiquitous correspondence, by journeyings hither and thither, by generous givings, by audiences with whoever might help forward a desired object or who seemed to hinder it, by days and nights of fasting and prayer — this one man touched, I believe, more of his fellow-countrymen and fellow-men than any other of his contemporaries who can be named in the same breath. I stand in admiration—in its old sense—I am awed by the quantity of being in him, and the prodigiousness of his vitality, as I come everywhere on proof upon proof that RICHARD BAXTER, in virtue of "the life of God" that was in him, wielded a controlling force throughout, comparable with gravitation in the physical world. It is no exaggeration to

8

affirm that this one man drew more hearts to the great Broken Heart than any single Englishman of any age.

Two simple facts may at this point be stated as illustrative of the BREADTH of this illustrious man. First—the Church of England is indebted to Richard Baxter for procuring the Charter of the Society for the Propagation of the Gospel. He was then 'ejected' by his mother-Church, in which he had refused a mitre; but none the less earnestly did he seek to obtain this charter for that Church.* His

---

* "At Acton, a personage of no mean importance watched over the ecclesiastical discipline of the parish. 'Dr. Ryves, rector of that church and of Hadley, dean of Windsor, and of Wolverhampton, and chaplain in ordinary to the King,' could not patiently endure the irregularities of his learned neighbour. The Dean, indeed, officiated by deputy, and his curate was a raw and ignorant youth, and Baxter (an occasional Conformist) was a regular attendant on all the sacred offices. But he refused the Oxford oath, and at his domestic worship there was sometimes found more than the statutable addition to the family circle ['five']. Such offence demanded expiation. He was committed to Clerkenwell

'field' was 'the world,' and his correspondence with JOHN ELIOT, the Apostle of the Indians, shows that, far ahead of modern Missions, he saw their possibility and urgent need. Second—Richard Baxter was among the first, if not the very first Englishman, to speak fearlessly out on the Slave-Trade. LORD BROUGHAM (it is believed) gratefully recalled this to our century in the *Edinburgh Review.* Here are our Worthy's presciently-sympathetic words, with their introduction :—

"The Slave Trade was very early—indeed almost from its first appearance—denounced in the strongest terms by many wise and good men in this country. The pious and fearless Richard Baxter was one of the first to express his disapprobation. 'They,' he said, writing in 1673, 'They

gaol, and when at length discharged from it was compelled to seek a new and more hospitable residence. He had his revenge. It was to obtain, through the influence of one of his most zealous disciples, the charter which incorporates the Church of England Society for the Propagation of the Gospel,—a return of good for evil for which his name might well displace those of some of the saints in the calendar."—SIR JAMES STEPHEN, Ed. Rev. lxxii., 199, 200.

who go as pirates and take away poor Africans to make them slaves and sell them, are the worst of robbers, and ought to be considered as the common enemies of mankind; and they who buy them, and make use of them as mere beasts of burden, are fitter to be called demons than Christians.'"*

That this vitality of Baxter was unspendable,—if I may coin a word,—let another simple matter-of-fact attest. It poured itself into well-nigh two hundred separate books, larger and lesser;† and nevertheless, alongside of all this writing—never once employing an amanuensis, and only for the pulpit, shorthand notes—as I have emphasized, he was doing day by day work for his Divine Master that drew on the same vitality measurelessly. For Richard Baxter, in a far other sense than ROBERT BURNS, gave a 'slice of his constitution' to all whose good he sought. His mental, moral,

---

* *Edinburgh Review*, vol. lxxix., p. 400, on Bandinel's "History of the Slave Trade," 1843. See also Reliq. Baxt. *s. v.*

† See my full Bibliographical List along with reprint of his long lost "What we must do to be saved."

and spiritual being was so seraphically fervent that he could not hold briefest interview, or write hastiest letter, or furnish a preface to some humble fellow-worker's book, without giving forth not merely light, but fire, and that seven times heated.

In the pulpit he was a JOHN KNOX, rather than a serene and august JOHN HOWE; and his books — more particularly those called 'practical'—were very much, in other form, what he had preached. As a corollary to this, be it recalled that through the full hundred and fifty years and upwards that have elapsed since his death, there never has been a day that some of his books have not been 'about our Father's business.' Such a thing as 'out of print' were a solecism applied to Richard Baxter. Even in his own lifetime the editions were almost countless, and I fear uncounted and un-accounted to him, by his publishers; while in Germany, and Holland, and France, his successive books were eagerly welcomed. The Fathers and Founders of New England sent over for them with loving messages. I found in Massachusetts and Scotland-like Connecticut, old copies of "The Saint's Everlasting Rest" and "Call to the Unconverted," and "Gildas Salvianus," and others, treasured as family heir-looms among the best in these States. So, too, away down in the South—in Virginia and the Carolinas and in the West Indies.

It is surely worth while our pondering this prodigious vitality of one slight and physically infirm man, of whom it has been said that his life was one long disease and suffering. I am reminded hereby of a jotting from some forgotten book: "Rabia, a devout Arabian woman, being asked in her last illness how she endured the extremity of her sufferings, made answer, 'They who look upon God's Face, do not feel His Hand.'"

I have named this prodigious vitality of Richard Baxter first, that I might, through it, SPEAK A MESSAGE TO MY READERS, ESPECIALLY TO MY FELLOW-MINISTERS, AND YOUNG MEN ENGAGED IN ANY WORK FOR

THEIR LORD. I do not forget many noble spirits housed in very frail tabernacles, who notwithstanding are doing marvellous service. These 'bruised reeds' who still give forth celestial music, or, unmetaphorically, consume themselves with toil, I profoundly revere. Far be it from me to hint of blame in their case. I recall abundant apostolic tender counsels to those who are strong. (Cf. 2 Cor. xiii. 9.) But it seems to me—looking beyond the really infirm—that there is sorrowfully too much *coddling* and sparing of ourselves, and giving way to the body's sluggishness and self-seeking. I do not think that there ought to be so very many ministerial 'sore throats,' or such frequent lying aside. Perhaps one secret of much of this is, that we spend a great deal of our vital force in doing a thousand-and-one little nothings, that yield no result. We may give out our electricity in great sparks—as lightning leaps from the thunder-cloud; but you may also lose it from a thousand pin-points and leave yourself helpless. I would caution against this restless activity in doing little nothings, and so misspending precious force that is demanded for higher and nobler and substantive work. My Worthy's vitality and unslackened service—spite of his body and *certes* not from his body (O ye materialists!)—seem to me to put many of us to burning shame; seem to me to appeal to us to get, at whatever cost, something of Richard Baxter's intensity, or, as I have designated it, seraphic fervour. I use the word 'seraphic' advisedly: for it is not to be disassociated from the fervour, neither the fervour from it. I regard the designation as peculiarly apt, seeing that seraph ministering is not mere active service, but active service in sacred work, in what concerns the public worship of God, 'liturgical spirit' being nearer to the original word. Baxter was pre-eminently a 'liturgical spirit,' as speaker, writer, worker. He did all as in presence of "Him Who is invisible." I like to vivify my conception of the angels or seraphs by musing on their lowly willinghood to do the meanest service as they 'hearken to His Word.' I glow with aspiration as I catch a vision of a mighty angel, Gabriel or Michael, before the Throne; but my heart is melted as I read of angels praising God for the Saviour born, or hushing the sorrows and terrors of the women at the sepulchre, or carrying the ransomed spirit of the beggar,—whose poor wasted corpse lay at the rich man's gate,—up and up on their lustrous wings. And so with RICHARD BAXTER,—I am stirred again and again into intellectual thoughtfulness by not a few of his metaphysical-theological treatises—over-subtle, even hair-splitting, yet rich with out-of-the-way lines of inquiry and speculation,—but tears come unbidden, and my heart leaps to my throat as I discover the tireless willinghood of this man to be helpful—with help drawn from God—wherever he possibly could be, with no standing on dignity, or well-won position, or patronizing airs, or plea of ill-health, or of pre-occupation. His fervour bore him through all, and fused all his activities. How pathetic in the light of this, is the sub-title of the 'Saint's Everlasting Rest,'—"written by the author for his own use in the time of his languishing, when God took him off from his public employment." One inevitably thinks of St. Paul, working so wonderfully, and for ever on his 'journeyings' for Christ, yet all the time having to bear about such a body—a body that "showed the dying of the Lord Jesus." Richard Baxter was the Paul of his century in manifold ways.

I venture to ask that we shall interrogate ourselves to-day whether there be not a miserable self-consciousness in the pulpits and Sunday-schools of all the Churches, whereby Preachers and Teachers seem afraid to let loose the vitality—Divine if it be "of grace"—that is in them. I must avouch that in my judgment, (so-called) refinement and culture and scholarliness are sorry substitutes for such heart-warm, passionate because compassionate, utterances as the multitudes heard from Richard Baxter, whether at loved Kidderminster or St. Margaret's. I can make allowances for dread of what is termed vulgarity, and enthusiasm, and fanaticism. I can, in a sort, sympathize with that fastidious reserve that dare not 'lift up the voice,' or startle the occupants of cushioned pews. I know it is a terrible thing to some—admittedly gentlemanly and scholarly and really men of God; for I do not for a moment question the equal genuineness of their Christianhood—to have their pulpit-bands awry, or their pulpit-gowns tossed—I limit myself, as a Presbyterian, to Presbyterian pulpit-gear— something shocking to find forehead or cheek or lip perspiring. But, as (mainly) addressing ministers of the Gospel, and students and young men, I feel constrained to pronounce all that a profound mistake. Essays are not sermons. Ethical or philosophical disquisitions are not messages. Symphonious elocution is not preaching, but saying. The secret of Richard Baxter's prodigious vitality was his seraphic fervour. We urgently need more of it; more and still more. Without fervour there is no vitality; without vitality, no power. Above all, without fervour there is no sympathy, no electric laying hold of the people, no sending home of "Thus saith the Lord." I do not see how a Preacher or Teacher can hope to fire his hearers if he be not himself fired. I do not believe that it is possible—humanly speaking—to make men realize the momentousness of the truths declared unless these truths rouse and agitate the speaker himself, ay though men should call it 'frenzy.' It is far from my wish to lessen the amount of pains taken to inform and cultivate and dignify candidates for the ministry and other service. But I am increasingly convinced that if God's 'Kingdom' is to 'come' by the preaching of the Word, the gospel of salvation, the Preachers must stand prepared not only to be in earnest, but to show it; not only to declare 'the *whole* counsel of God,' but by manner and bearing and tone, manifest that it is their own 'all in all,' and that they believe that everlasting issues, for weal or doom, are suspended on acceptance and rejection. I summon all of us to work not in frost but in fire, not only every sermon, but every phrase, shaped in the glow of a Divine heat. It was because Richard Baxter was the most earnest man in England of his century, that he wrought such work for God, and informed, with his own prodigious vitality, generations of men. I covet for to-day, I covet specially for my own beloved Church, his seraphic fervour. I want to stir all whom I can reach, to put HEART into their preaching and teaching, as well as brains.*

A second characteristic of the life-work of Richard Baxter is that he CONSECRATED HIS VARIED POWERS TO THE GOOD OF "THE COMMON PEOPLE." Whether in the pulpit or catechizing or holding prayer-meeting, or printing

---

* The old Scotch minister was warranted in his sarcastic rebuke of a young brother, who delivered an elegant polished essay, kid-gloved and emotionless, when he said, "I'd have given a few *thochts*" [thoughts] "the preference to all that tinkle-tinkle of sentence-making and studied elocution." Thoughts by all means, and thoughts aflame; "thoughts that breathe, and words that burn."

another and another book, his main thought was 'compassion on the ignorant, and on them out of the way.' It is historical that this was a 'new thing' in England. The Reformation was a proud memory. The names of the Reformers brought glory to the Anglican Church that paled the mythical saints of the Church of Rome; and they are their glory still, let degenerate sons malign them as they may. The great, the gentle-born, the learned, the rich and well-to-do, went to their parish churches. But it is a melancholy truth that it was only here and there that the National Church discharged the obligations for which it existed as a Church. SIR JAMES STEPHEN has pungently said, "A long interval had elapsed before the national temples and hierarchy were consecrated to the nobler end of enlightening the ignorant, and administering comfort to the poor."* Richard Baxter, whilst he had noblest eloquence and bravely direct speech for the

---

* *Edinburgh Review*, as before and onward.

noblest and learnedest in the land—and noblest and learnedest owned his spell—as a Preacher and as a Parish Clergyman spent himself in informing and, by God's grace, transforming the lowliest and poorest and most obdurate of his charge—pleading as nowhere men have been pleaded with, and warning and urging and entreating, 'lest a promise being left them of entering into that rest, they should seem to fall short of it.' And so he, like the Master, 'went out and in' among 'the people,' *his* people— and in season and out of season pressed home the glorious gospel of the blessed God. How immense and blessed was his success, what Kidderminster grew to under him witnesses, as adoringly told in the "Reliquianæ." Contrast him in this with even so saintly a man as GEORGE HERBERT. Very lovely was his ultimate character and life. Yet he was—after ordination—the veriest recluse—shrinking from contact with 'the people.' I am touched with his long ascetic fastings and prayers within his little church of Bemerton for his small flock.

But if he had prayed *with* them, gone among them, come closely near to them, how infinitely better! Richard Baxter was no recluse. He was a busy man, and it is your busy man who readiest makes time for duties, and the joy of 'serving.' He prayed and wept and thought and suffered *for* his people; but he did more. His sermons were *to* them; his prayers were *with* them; his whole energies *for* them. He was eminently contemplative, a meditative spirit; but he willingly tore himself away from his Study on any summons. It is not to be wondered at that the great Kidderminster Church was crowded, and the homes of whole streets vocal with praise and prayer every night. What might not the Church of England have done and been had a Richard Baxter been found in even a score of her parishes! For a man of his stamp is not merely like a street-lamp that shines and does its own useful service; but is a setter-on-fire of other souls.

Another side of this is—not polemical, but once more simply historical—that "rich beyond all Protestant rivalry in sacred literature, the Church of England, from the days of Parker to those of Laud, had scarcely produced any one considerable work of popular instruction. The 'Pastoral Care' which Burnet depicted, in the reign of William and Mary, was at that time a vision which, though since richly fulfilled, no past experience had realized. Till a much later time, the alphabet was among the mysteries which the English Church concealed from her catechumens." These are the judicial grave words of Sir James Stephen. As he was a devoted Churchman, I prefer to let him speak for me. If his language is startling, it is its sad realism that barbs it :—

"There is," he continues, "no parallel in the annals of any other Protestant State, of so wonderful a concentration, and so imperfect a diffusion of learning and genius, of piety and zeal. The reigns of Whitgift, Bancroft, and Laud WERE UNMOLESTED BY CARES SO RUDE AS THOSE OF EVANGELIZING THE ARTISANS AND PEASANTRY. Jewel and Bull, Hall and Donne, Hooker and Taylor, lived and wrote for their peers, and for future ages, but not FOR THE COMMONALTY OF THEIR OWN. Yet was not Christianity bereft in England of her distinctive and glorious privilege. It was still the religion of the poor. Amidst persecution, contempt, and penury, the Puritans had toiled and suffered, and had not rarely died in their service."*

I know not that a more damning charge could be brought against a Church than this of Sir James Stephen against the Church of England. I for one am saddened as I read the great sermons and other books of the great and good men named, in recollection of their utter forgetfulness of 'the people.' It is to exalt the ecclesiastical institute called the Church at the expense of Christ, not to mourn that a pseudo-apostolical succession vaunted by Whitgift and Bancroft and Laud was not rather exchanged for a succession of saintly Workers (large-brained and large-hearted too) in the line of the Puritans. *As it was*, that the 'Commonalty' of England, the vast body of 'the people,' were cared for at all, is mainly due to the genuinely apostolical labours

---

* *Edinburgh Review*, vol. lxx., pp. 183-4 : also in "Collective Essays."

of men of the stamp of Richard Baxter, as exemplified in Kidderminster. That the Bible was brought into their homes and made familiar as "household words" was also due to them. That FAMILY WORSHIP was set up in entire streets, was due to them. That there was Christian literature provided, cheap and easily read and understood and yearningly relished, is similarly due to them. For in the dark interregnum between the gracious books of the "preaching" and "lecturing" Puritans and the paganizing usurpation of Laud and onward, only such home-speaking cheap books as Richard Baxter's and later Puritans and Nonconformists kept the 'lamp alive' in the thick darkness. Except his historical-controversial treatises, which were addressed to those in "high places,"—for he feared to close with no antagonist,—the writings of our illustrious Worthy were 'practical,' and their supreme aim was usefulness in building up character and in nurturing the spiritual life and in guarding from the errors of contending factions and fractions.

I reckon it the glory of Richard Baxter that in the long roll of his Works so large a proportion were of the homeliest and most plain-spoken type, and brimming over with Bible texts and references. I look upon my complete collection of his Works—down to his single sheets and two and three sheets—as a treasure not to be outweighed by much more lauded literature. A light of life lies to my vision on such as these:—"The Right Method for Peace of Conscience and Spiritual Comfort" (1653): "Making Light of Christ" (1655): "Gildas Salvianus; or, The Reformed Pastor" (1656): "The Safe Religion; or, Three Disputations for the Reformed Religion against Popery" (1657): "A Treatise of Conversion" (1657): "A Call to the Unconverted" (1657):

The Crucifying of the World by the Cross of Christ" (1658): "Directions and Persuasions to a Sound Conversion" (1658): "A Treatise of Self-Denial" (1659): "The Vain Religion of the Formal Hypocrite" (1659): "The Fool's Prosperity" (1659): "The Last Walk of a

Believer" (1659): "The Mischief of Self-Ignorance and the Benefits of Self-Acquaintance" (1662): "A Saint or a Brute" (1662): "Now or Never" (1663): "Divine Life" (1664): "Two Sheets for Poor Families" (1665): "A Sheet for the Instruction of the Sick during the Plague" (1665): "Directions to the Converted for their Establishment, Growth and Perseverance" (1669): "The Life of Faith" (1670): "The Divine Appointment of the Lord's Day" (1671): "The Duty of Heavenly Meditation Revived" (1671): "How far Holiness is the Design of Christianity" (1671): "God's Goodness Vindicated" (1671): "More Reasons for the Christian Religion and no Reason against it" (1672): "Full and Easy Satisfaction which is the True and Safe Religion" (1674): "The Poor Man's Family Book" (1674): "Reasons for Ministerial Plainness and Fidelity" (1676): "A Sermon for the Cure of Melancholy" (1682): "Compassionate Counsel to Young Men" (1682): "How to do Good to Many" (1682): "Family Catechism" (1683):

Obedient Patience" (1683): "Farewell Sermon prepared to have been preached to his hearers at Kidderminster at his departure, but forbidden" (1683): "Dying Thoughts" (1683): "Unum Necessarium" (1685): "The Scripture Gospel Defended" (1690): "A Defence of Christ and Free Grace" (1690): "Monthly Preparations for the Holy Communion" (1696): "The Mother's Catechism" (1701): and "What we must do to be Saved" (1692-1868). Who may attempt to estimate the good, the undying good, such matterful and richly Scriptural books did wherever they went in their thousands and even tens of thousands?* Besides, he gave away enormous quantities of his own and kindred good books. Nor, as literature *per se* do the books of Richard Baxter need

---

* I ask that it be noted here that I include others along with Baxter as creators of our popular Christian literature. Earlier there was glorious old Latimer, and many cheap tracts and single sheets about in the world. Contemporary there was Flavel and Durant and others noticeable. Still, no one man did so much for popular Christian literature as Baxter.

to fear comparison with contemporaneous. I rejoice to be able to adduce hereon the testimony of a Master, the present Archbishop of Dublin—and what he thus says of the "Saint's Everlasting Rest" holds substantially of everything he wrote. "Let me mention here," observes his Grace, "before entering into deeper matters, one formal merit which it eminently possesses. I refer to that without which, I suppose, no book ever won a permanent place in the literature of a nation, and which I have no scruple in ascribing to it—I mean its style. A great admirer of Baxter has recently suggested a doubt whether he ever recast a sentence, or bestowed a thought on its rhythm, and the balance of its several parts; statements of his own make it tolerably certain that he did not. As a consequence he has none of those bravura passages which must have cost Jeremy Taylor, in his "Holy Living and Dying," and elsewhere, so much of thought and pains, for such do not come of themselves and unbidden, to the most accomplished masters of language. But for all this, there reigns in Baxter's writings, and not least in "The Saint's Rest," a robust and masculine eloquence; nor do these want from time to time rare and unsought felicity of language, which, once heard, can scarcely be forgotten. In regard indeed of the choice of words, the book might have been written yesterday. There is hardly one which has become obsolete; hardly one which has drifted away from the meaning which it has in his writings. This may not be a great matter; but it argues a rare insight, conscious or unconscious, into all which was truest, into all which was furthest removed from affectation and untruthfulness in the language, that after more than two hundred years so it should be; and one may recognise here an element, not to be overlooked, of the abiding popularity of the book."* Fine and finely put! Even more might be said. To-day his style

---

* Baxter and "The Saint's Rest" in "Companions for the Devout Life": 1877, p. 89.

seems to me a model of a spoken as distinguished from a merely written style. He wrote as Paul did; and even his letters are all *orations*.

I would concentrate attention on this double service rendered by Baxter (*a*) As a Preacher and 'Pastor' to 'the people,' (*b*) as the virtual creator of popular Christian literature. What Prelate or Dean or Canon or Preacher within the length and breadth of the National Church may for a single moment be put in comparison with this single man in either of these? This is not, I reiterate, matter polemical, but matter of fact. All honour and gratitude, therefore, to Richard Baxter for that seraphic fervour that enabled him to achieve so abundant and measurelessly blessed work in his long day and generation.

A third thing in Baxter that has—as I think—a living message for to-day, is his FAITH IN THE POWER OF CONSCIENCE IN OUR MORAL NATURE. No more than SAVONAROLA earlier, or GEORGE WHITEFIELD later, was he a man of exceptional intellect *qua* intellect. He had, beyond all debate, a sinewy, penetrative, almost morbidly acute brain. There are in his controversial writings multiplied evidences of special philosophical-metaphysical resources and aptitudes, and insight that has the look of intuition. I question if a shrewder, swifter, more indeceivable mind existed in England in his age. He looks within and without, above and beneath and all round, and in far perspective beyond his subject-matter. It must be conceded that—

"Other avenues stretching away to the right hand and to the left, he cannot always resist the temptation to explore ; and this though they may lead him far away from that which is his more immediate concern. Above all, let him only find himself in the neighbourhood of some perplexed question of the Schools, such a one as has tasked and divided the noblest intellects of Christendom for centuries, which has set Thomist against Scotist, Realist against Nominalist, and is likely to do the same to the end of time:—for these controversies are not dead, they have only a little shifted their ground;—and at once, like the war-horse of Job, he smells the battle afar off, 'the thunder of the captains and the shouting,' and nothing will content him till he finds himself in their midst."*

His many opponents discovered, to their cost, that they needed to be agile in weapon-use and wary in guard to escape his blows. He gave very much harder strokes than any he received. Some of the 'Dignitaries' are made to look extremely foolish under his irony and vehement exposures and unhesitating confutation. But it were to vindicate Richard Baxter's claims from a mistaken standpoint to magnify his intellect as compared with other contemporaries; *e.g.* it is John Howe's *intellectual* sanctity as distinguished from mere piety, the grandeur and richness and momentum of his thinking, that—as we have seen—is the inevitable impression left on every capable, modest and "considering" reader. You are not thus struck with Baxter's thinking, except here and there at long intervals—rather with its home-coming to men's businesses and bosoms. He was more of a Schoolman, less of a Philosopher than Howe. He himself

---

* *Ibid.,* p. 88.

writes:—"Next to practical divinity, no books so suited with my disposition as Aquinas, Scotus, Durandus, Ockham and their disciples" (Rel. Baxt.)*

Further: The facts of his Life—like those of John Bunyan, and perhaps of the supremest man of all literature, William Shakespeare—go to show that he had nothing like academic training. He had "little Latin and less Greek." His Latin folio swarms with evidences of defective scholarship. SIR JAMES STEPHEN thus summarizes his school-training : "The three remaining years of his pupilage .... were spent at the endowed school at Wroxeter, which he quitted at the age of nineteen, destitute of all mathematical and physical science—ignorant of Hebrew—a mere smatterer in Greek, and possessed of as much Latin as enabled him in after life to use it with reckless facility."† Correspondent with this is the absence of laden margins,

---

* See Abp. Trench's Lecture, as before, for excellent criticism on Baxter's 'School' affinities, etc.
† *Edinburgh Review*, as before, p. 182.

albeit you come on the most uncouth Latin names and authorities from whom he had spelled out their teaching. I accentuate the fact. His circumstances explain it. I do not—need I say?—infer from it that Baxter was without a certain culture. "A mind so prolific, and which yielded such early fruit, could not advance to manhood without much well-directed culture."* Neither do I infer from it that we ought now to pay less heed to the mastery of the "ancient learning." Contrariwise, I hold it is presumption in these days for any Church not to aim at a thoroughly educated and disciplined ministry and Sunday-school workers. Personally I regard that minister of the Gospel as underfurnished who cannot use his Hebrew Old Testament and Greek Septuagint and Greek New Testament with entire mastery. That would be my *minimum*; and the *maximum* can hardly be set too high, *cæteris paribus*. But Richard Baxter's life-work, based fundamentally on his English Bible, has surely a message for us to-day. Does it not put a re-

* *Ibid.*

proving finger on a weak spot of our modes of preaching? Does it not suggest reform in our presentation of 'the truth'? He had—I urge —no sovran intellect, he had little scholarship or culture proper; but he was the most successful preacher and winner of souls to Christ and nurturer of won souls, that England ever has had. What is the explanation? I answer that his temperament ennobled his intellect; his seraphic fervour did brain-work and heart-work in opulent amalgam. I answer again, that though he was no scholar and never was at a University (by no blame of his own), he was an omnivorous reader of books, and had a peculiar faculty of swiftly extracting their innermost marrow. So that, alike in his preaching and in his books, he is most apt with "apples of gold in basket-work of silver," from a wide range. For myself I have found quickening and instruction from his marginal words, and confirmations of his own arguments and pleadings.

But neither of these uncovers the whole secret of his power. I repeat and press,—

HE HAD FAITH IN THE HUMAN CONSCIENCE. Reasoning was all very well, imagination and fancy were all very well, spoils from good and learned books were all very well;—but the ultimate thing was that, in preaching or writing of the truth that he found in the Bible, he relied on the reality of conscience. He should have said 'amen' to Bishop Butler's classical words on conscience: "Had it strength as it had right, had it power as it had manifest authority, it would govern the world."* Consequently his works, broadly regarded, are appeals—not to intellect, not to imagination, not even to the affections, but emphatically to conscience. That was his real force. There he felt he had an ally for God and for the great facts and doctrines and messages of the Gospel. Therefore throughout this is his sustaining hope, viz., that the Spirit of God, taking "the things of Christ" proclaimed by

---

* Sermon i., on Conscience. The whole paragraph about conscience is vital.

him from the Word, does meet a response in every human conscience. It is impossible to over-state the fulness, the opulence, the variety or the wistfulness, the yearning, the intensity, the seraphic fervour of his addresses to the human conscience. If only he can get lodgement there for his present truth he has hope; if only he can obtain hearers through their moral nature, to the great words of God in Christ, he counts on success. He is convinced that in ninety-nine cases out of a hundred that issue in conversion, *i.e.*, that are won to believe the gospel and are led to Christ, the thing is done through Divine dealing with the conscience. Hence, though in his Episcopal as against Presbyterian, and in his Papal and Quaker and Independent controversies, he meets his antagonists in their own chosen regions, and proves their match; *e.g.*, almost playfully toppling down even such an one as Dr. John Owen;* yet as a Preacher and as

---

* With all his intellect and learning, Owen was singu-

a practical Writer, he presses home,—"Thus saith the Lord," "It is written." I would revive Richard Baxter's faith in conscience. For whatever be the relation of the Christian ministry to feeling, to the information and discipline of the intellect, and to all the parts of our complex nature, there can be no doubt but that—absolutely—it has to do with conscience. The Christian minister's chief function, as dealing with men for God, is to manifest the truth before their consciences; and in his pastoral work, as distinct from his evangelistic, he is to arouse, sustain, make mighty that 'rectorial' power in the human breast. Students of SIR WILLIAM HAMILTON of Edinburgh remember the golden-lettered motto of the famous classroom: "On earth there is nothing great but man: in man, nothing great but mind." I feel that I am safe in going farther and adding,

---

larly vulnerable to so agile an opponent as Baxter. His oppressive style was also terribly against him. None the less is John Owen foremost of the foremost rank in weight and worth.

'In mind, nothing is greater than conscience.' I would have us all grasp and realize this. If it be done it will save a man from that dreary childishness of Ritualism; it will save him from that rhetoric that passes itself off for eloquence; it will save him from sensationalism; it will save him from that cold-blooded logic that goes on splitting hairs and constructing syllogisms before men who are dead in trespasses and sins; it will save him from that offence to our deepest spiritual instincts, 'beautiful prayers,'—almost as sad as vulgar and bellowing prayers: (we do not want exhibitions of 'fine taste' in prayer, but something inspired of Christ: reverence will not be awanting in that case); it will save him from himself; it will give him a Divine courage. Who will make him afraid? The rich man? the proud man? the learned man? the political man? the infidel man? the sneering scientist? Nay! On the contrary, they shall one and all bow and quail as in the presence of the righteous judgment of God. In this matter

of dealing with conscience, let the preacher put forth all his knowledge, wisdom, learning, genius (if he have it), strength of manhood, fervour of nature,—fearless of all consequences, *e.g.*, of 'splitting up his party,' 'damaging his usefulness,' 'giving occasion to the adversary,' and so forth, and so forth. Do not let him zig-zag, with the character of being 'safe,' as one who knows how to preserve his popularity and his salary; do not let him 'cheep'— and I use the expressive Scotch word even if Englishmen do not understand it—when he ought to "lift up his voice like a trumpet."*
Even should he die by the roadside, let him earn an epitaph like this, " Here lies ———, who never feared the face of man."

All this, I must however observe, to be effective, must be combined with TENDERNESS AND SYMPATHY. Richard Baxter was in these pre-eminent. He 'melted' as he rebuked;

---

* 'Cheep' = chirp or chirrup—a thin scrannel voice and sanctimonious *tone* implied.

he quivered as he accused; he yearned as he warned; he pitied as he condemned; he urged and entreated as he showed the peril of delay. Consciences may be dealt with inhumanly. Your fire-and-brimstone men do that: indeed at times put them on a gridiron — over a painted fire : the inhumanness real enough if the fire be only painted. Logic may be very inhuman—sooth to say, Calvinistic logic, with its inferences and crotchets of interpretation exalted into 'inspired principles,' not unseldom is. Some of the comfort administered to mourners by men I know, and in books, strikes me as inhuman. With Baxter there is no merciless pushing of conclusions, or of facts of Scripture and human life. There is a consistent vein of HUMANITY all through. Let some brief *bits* from three of his finest books illustrate. In the " Saint's Everlasting Rest " he says :—

"But when in the other world, love meets love, it will not be like Joseph and his brethren, who lay upon one another's necks weeping : it will be loving and rejoicing, not loving and sorrowing."

It seems to me he touches us here with that "touch of nature which makes the whole world kin." Other two quotations relate to the death of his wife—that truest and noblest of 'elect' ladies. "Perhaps," he says, "love and grief may make me speak more than many will think fit." And then he goes on: "And I will not be judged by any that never felt the like." Again, speaking of his wife's monument in Christ Church, he says :—

"But Christ's Church on earth is liable to those changes of which the Jerusalem above is in no danger. In the doleful flames of London, 1666, the fall of the church broke the marble all to pieces ; so that it proved no lasting monument. I hope this paper monument, erected by one who is following even at the door, in some passion indeed of love and grief, but in sincerity of truth, will be more publicly useful and durable than that marble stone was."

Once more : his relentless and vulgarly libellous opponent, BAGSHAWE, died 'in prison,' and on the tidings reaching Baxter he closed their contention thus :—

"While we wrangle here in the dark, we are dying,

and passing to the world that will decide all our controversies, and the safest passage thither is by peaceable holiness."

Is there not a fine, tender, holy, sweet humanness in this? I could easily multiply proofs that 'stern' is just about the most absurd and false word possible to apply to Richard Baxter.* Equally decisive is the 'testimony' of DR. BATES in his noble funeral sermon, *e.g.* :—

"His prayers were an effusion of the most lively, melting expressions of his intimate, ardent affections to God: from the abundance of the heart, the lips spake. His soul took wing for heaven, and swept up the souls of others with him. Never did I see or hear a holy minister

---

* I must note however that in his reverence for conscience (other people's) and tenderness, he grew. In the outset, I think it is clear that he found it difficult to make allowance for persons who conscientiously differed from him on Church questions, and that he did not easily learn the rule, ' Put yourself in his place.' Barclay, in his *Religious Societies in the Commonwealth* (p. 333), speaks of how he grew in grace in this respect, and cites some of his gracious language owning a change of view about the Holy Spirit, so bringing him into more sympathy with his early opponents the Quakers.

address himself to God with more reverence and humility, with respect to His glorious greatness; never with more zeal and fervency, correspondent to the infinite moment of his requests, nor with more filial reliance on the Divine mercy.

"In his sermons there was a rare union of arguments and motives, to convince the mind and gain the heart; all the fountains of reason and persuasion were open to his discerning eye. There was no resisting the force of his discourses without denying reason and Divine revelation. He had a marvellous felicity and copiousness in speaking. There was a noble negligence in his style; for his great mind could not stoop to the affected eloquence of words. He despised flashy oratory; but his expressions were clear and powerful, so convincing the understanding, so entering into the soul, so engaging the affections, that those were as deaf as adders who were not charmed by so wise a charmer. He was animated with the Holy Spirit, and breathed celestial fire, to inspire heat and life into dead sinners, and to melt the obdurate in their frozen tombs."

I must not withhold part of the vivid summary of Orme:—

"Baxter's severity never partakes of the nature of misanthropy. He never seems to take pleasure in wounding. He employs the knife with an unsparing hand; but that hand always appears to be guided by a tender, sympathising heart. He denounces sin in language of tremendous energy, and exposes its hideous nature by the light of the flames of hell itself; but it is to urge the sinner to flee from the wrath to come, and to lay hold on the hope set before him. He never appears as the minister of Divine vengeance, come to execute wrath, and to make men miserable before the time; but as an angel of mercy brandishing a flaming sword to drive men to the tree of life. In his own words :—

> "' He preach'd, as never sure to preach again,
> And as a dying man to dying men.'" *

Beside BAXTER, JEREMY TAYLOR is a monk, and even JOSEPH ALLEINE, hard.

This allegiance to conscience, and faith in it, made the Bible to be, to him, without a shadow of doubt, God's Book. God had spoken, ay, speaks, in it. God's mind and heart and purpose are revealed there. God's House is a place of audience and communion with God. Prayer does reach Him. Faith does grasp Him. The "exceeding great and precious promises" are realities to be asked and counted on. Sanctification onward from conversion is no dream. God is no dumb or deaf or indifferent Governor of the universe, Who has

---

* Life, p. 486; Poet. Frag., p. 30.

wound it up like a watch and slipped it under
His pillow and gone to sleep till the Day of
Doom arrives. And so, as among everlasting
verities, Richard Baxter unladened himself of his
' burden,' as old Hebrew prophets did; stood up
to declare that so-and-so was God's eternal truth.
No more than does the Bible itself, did he stand
in the pulpit to prove, or to debate, or to reason-
out. Book on book he gave to the like of that,
and his confutations of error and unbelief are
simply priceless for their argumentative weight
and solid debating worth; but as a Preacher he
urged the 'Revelation' of God, the words of
God, the truth of God, the Gospel out of the
infinite heart of God. So doing, that seraphic
fervour of which we have already written, drove
home his sermons with more than mortal impetus.
Awed, rapt, believing, expectant, declarative,
dying-like himself, he took a *grip* of men's
thoughts and feelings and lives; made what
was still divine in them—their conscience—
answer, ay reverberate the facts and truths and
sanctions he pressed upon them.

A subsidiary element in Baxter's faith in conscience and his addresses to it deserves passing notice. I refer to the chastity of his presentations of 'the truth.' Nowhere else that I know will you find anatomy so trenchant of fallen human nature, and yet so modest. You have detection of disease, and 'lusts,' and sophistries, and miseries, and self-accusations, portrayed with terrifying exactitude; but there is no touch of the morbid, or of that suggestiveness of sinning that characterises Roman Catholic and modern 'High Church' literature. His manly, gentlemanly nature abhorred 'confessional' lines of thought and feeling. He is vivid but chaste, intense but consolatory, faithful but persuasive.

This DECLARATIVE preaching of Richard Baxter was doubtless sharpened by his realizing as few have done that a Christian church—humblest 'conventicle' as well as cathedral—is in very truth God's house. THERE he could not but have a kind of disdain of objectors and objections that ELSEWHERE, with his naturally combative temperament, he was always ready to meet with their own weapons. His books reveal that he had fought out his conclusions, wrestled on the sharp peaks of despair (the 'dark mountains') for his beliefs, struggled as for very life with spectres from the abyss of doubt, and enigmas, and perplexities, and mysteries of being, wept himself into tenderness over the hard facts of human existence and possibilities of destiny. It is all the more pathetic that in the pulpit he leaves doubt and fear and anguish and questioning behind him,—Abraham-like going up 'to worship.' It is to me infinitely affecting to mark the sharp line of division between no little of his controversies and his sermons. I read the grand seventy-third Psalm of Asaph more understandingly, as I find Richard Baxter so absolute, so joyous, so triumphant, so declarative and simply a 'voice' for God in the pulpit. The clear piercing light of the Word kindled all about him, and the still more piercing light of the Divine Face, and so he was lifted above all intercepting mists and all disturbing forces. Yet with all his declarativeness (called by some foolishly dogmatism), what fine and broad human Catholicity there was!

I am not more sure that we need Richard Baxter's seraphic fervour to-day than I am that we would do well to combine with our methods his faith in the human conscience and consequent declarative preaching. I have not a syllable to say against the most intellectual preaching that can be commanded. The loftiest intellect may well be dedicated to this grandest of human functions when a true man fills it. I regard any preaching that does not address and seek to convince our reason, as without the necessary basis of solid fact. I have little liking for either, on the one hand effusive sentimentalism, or on the other gushing exclamatoriness. I do not think the pulpit is a fitting place for that rhetorical elocution that cheats itself into a belief that it is oratory, or for that word-painting that weens it is imagination, or for gorgeous phrase-making that seeks to sensationalize the Gospel. I am disposed to think—though so far as I know my own heart, uncensoriously—that 'Christian

Evidence' literature has been sadly overdone. I must regard the seven-fold threshed-out controversies on inspiration and cognate topics, as mere dealing with the husk. I desiderate, in fine, DECLARATIVE preaching in the faith that the Bible vindicates its own inspiration. I long for a return to Richard Baxter's faith in human conscience. I would fain give impulse to our younger preachers and students, who are destined to take our vacated places, towards being fired with his seraphic fervour, and his fearless statement of all that "is written." I am anxious to see them with bearing-down power asserting, not arguing, the fundamental facts and doctrines of the Bible, or accrediting them equally with the facts and teachings of the outward world (on which God never breaks silence, or vindicates), and as realizing that they have witness in man's moral nature alike in its aspirations and unrest, in its yearnings and sorrows, in its hopes and terrors, in its strength and mutableness. I want less—oh, infinitely less—recognition of the awe-less and pragmatical objections and oppositions of "science falsely so-called," and a more resolute sounding out of what has been revealed and declared. I seek Richard Baxter's Biblical self-assertativeness, Biblical affirmation, Biblical glorious assumptions, if you will, Biblical silences, to be held fast and held faster, and so that in the very manner and bearing it shall be demonstrated that the Preacher tells of what he knows, testifies of what he has experienced—leaving ALL in the keeping of the human hearts and consciences within which they are placed, and in that of the ever-watching and magnanimously patient Holy Spirit, Who knows where every spoken or printed word falls, and nurtures every seed of the Word to its springing, blooming, and fruitage.

As the 'application' of all this—already hinted at in the lecture on JOHN HOWE—it is to me a sorrow and a bewilderment, that so vast a number of preachers and Sunday School teachers content themselves with informing. That is to say, I miss from our present-day sermons, to a deplorable extent, the "applications" all round, with which Baxter and his compeers invariably closed them. There may have been, perchance, disproportionate length and exaggerated divisions and sub-divisions. Yet withal there were point-blank shots, direct, personal, unmistakable speaking straight *to* (never the meanness and cowardice of *at*) the individual with a "Thou art the man" as of old. The trains of foregoing exposition and thinking, the riches of illustrative and anecdotical instruction, the illumined and engrandeured message, were all grasped in concluding appeals and warnings, and cogencies and urgencies, and importunities of declaration and enforcement. Now how all too often is the sermon huddled up without any attempt to individualize or to send arrowily home to each hearer what has been spoken. I am more and more satisfied that herein we are losers, and must return to the old-fashioned ways. With faith in the Word, and faith in human conscience, and faith in a present God, and Baxterian fervour, I should count on new life, new energy, new aggressiveness, new conquests. The old 'applications' demand revival, not neglect. It needeth that we return on ancient forms. It is the thing I urge. It is the poor stopping short at information, I lament.

I must give examples of Baxter's preaching confirmatory of what I have stated. In 1658 he published "The Crucifying of the World by the Cross of Christ." It was originally an Assize sermon; and the book is dedicated to Thomas Foley, Esq., High Sheriff of the county. Let us realize the assembled Court and the impression of these words as delivered with his "soft, flexible, melodious voice" and seraphic fervour:—

"Honourable, worshipful, and all well-beloved, it is a weighty employment that occasioneth your meeting here to-day. The estates and lives of men are in your hands. But it is another kind of judgment which you are all hastening towards: when judges and juries, the accusers and accused, must all appear upon equal terms, for the final decision of a far greater cause. The case that is then and there to be determined, is not whether you shall have lands or no lands, life or no life (in our natural sense); but whether you shall have heaven or hell, salvation, or damnation, an endless life of glory with God and the Redeemer, and the angels of heaven, or an endless life of torment with devils and ungodly men. As sure as you now sit on those seats, you shall shortly all appear before the Judge of all the world, and there receive an irreversible sentence, to an unchangeable state of happiness or misery. This is the great business that should presently call up your most serious thoughts, and set all the powers of your souls on work for the most effectual preparation; that if you are men, you may quit yourselves like men, for the preventing of that dreadful doom which unprepared souls must there expect. The greatest of your secular affairs are but dreams and toys to this. Were you at every assize to determine causes of no lower value than the crowns and kingdoms of the monarchs of the earth, it were but as children's games to this. If any man of you believe not this, he is worse than the devil that tempteth him to unbelief; and let him know that unbelief is no prevention, nor will put off the day, or hinder his appearance; but ascertain his condemnation at that appearance.

"He that knows the law and the fact, may know before your assize, what will become of every prisoner, if the proceedings be all just, as in our case they will certainly be. Christ will judge according to His laws; know therefore whom the law condemneth or justifieth, and you may know whom Christ will condemn or justify. And seeing all this is so, doth it not concern us all to make a speedy trial of ourselves in preparation to this final trial? I shall for your own sakes therefore, take the boldness, as the officer of Christ, to summon you to appear before yourselves, and keep an assize this day in your own souls, and answer at the bar of conscience, to what shall be charged upon you. Fear not the trial; for it is not conclusive, final, or a peremptory irreversible sentence that must now pass. Yet slight it not, for it is a necessary preparative to that which is final and irreversible. Consequentially, it may prove a justifying accusation, an absolving condemnation, and if you proceed to execution, a saving, quickening death, which I am now persuading you to undergo. The whole world is divided into two sorts of men: one that love God above all, and live for Him; and the other that love the flesh and world above all, and live to them. One that seek first the kingdom of God and His righteousness; another that seek first the things of this life. One that mind and savour the things of the flesh and of man; the other that mind and savour most the things of the Spirit and of God. One that account all things dung and dross that they may win Christ; another that make light of Christ in comparison of their business, and riches, and pleasures in the world. One, that live by sight and sense upon present things; another that live by faith upon things invisible. One, that have their conversation in heaven, and live as strangers upon earth; another that mind earthly things, and are strangers to heaven. One, that have in resolution forsaken all for Christ, and the hope of a treasure in heaven; another, that resolve to keep somewhat here though they venture and forsake the heavenly reward, and will go away sorrowful that they cannot have both. One, that being born of the flesh is but flesh; the other, that being born of the Spirit, is spirit. One, that live as without God in the world; the other, that live as without the seducing world in God, and in and by the subservient world to God. One, that have ordinance and means of grace as if they had none; the other, that have houses, lands, wives, as if they had none. One, that believe as if they believed not, and love God as if they loved Him not, and pray as if they prayed not,—as if the fruit of these were but a shadow; the other, that weep as if they wept not for worldly things, and rejoice as if they rejoiced not. One, that have Christ as not possessing Him, and use Him and His name as but abusing them; the other, that buy as if they possessed not, and use the world as not abusing it. One, that draw near to God with their lips when their hearts are far from Him; the other, that corporally converse with the world when their hearts are far from it. One, that serve God, who is a Spirit, with carnal service, and not in spirit and truth; the other, that use the world itself spiritually, and not in a carnal, worldly manner. In a word, one sort are children of this world; the other are the children of the world to come, and heirs of the heavenly kingdom. One sort have their portion in this life, and the other have God for their portion. One sort have their good things in this lifetime, and their reward here; the other have their evil things in this life, and live in hope of the everlasting reward.[*]

In another vein is his "Walking with God." It is full of beauty, and is instinct with his devotional force, as witness:—

---

[*] Works, by Orme, vol. ix., pp. 431-433.

"'To walk with God,' he says, 'is a word so high, that I should have feared the guilt of arrogance in using it, if I had not found it in the Holy Scriptures. It is a word that importeth so high and holy a frame of soul, and expresseth such high and holy actions, that the naming of it striketh my heart with reverence, as if I had heard the voice to Moses, "Put off thy shoes from off thy feet, for the place whereon thou standest is holy ground." Methinks he that shall say to me, Come see a man that walks with God, doth call me to see one that is next unto an angel or glorified soul. It is a far more reverend object in mine eye than ten thousand lords or princes, considered only in their fleshly glory. It is a wiser action for people to run and crowd together to see a man that walks with God, than to see the pompous train of princes, their entertainments, or their triumph. Oh happy man that walks with God, though neglected and contemned by all about him! What blessed sights doth he daily see! What ravishing tidings, what pleasant melody doth he daily hear, unless it be in his swoons or sickness! What delectable food doth he daily taste! He seeth, by faith, the God, the glory which the blessed Spirits see at hand by nearest intuition! He seeth that in a glass, and darkly, which they behold with open face! He seeth the glorious Majesty of his Creator, the eternal King, the Cause of causes, the Composer, Upholder, Preserver, and Governor of all worlds! He beholdeth the wonderful methods of His providence; and what he cannot reach to see, he admireth, and waiteth for the time when that also shall be open to his view! He seeth by faith the world of spirits, the hosts that attend the throne of God; their perfect righteousness, their full devotedness to God; their ardent love, their flaming zeal, their ready and cheerful obedience, their dignity and shining glory, in which the lowest of them exceed that which the disciples saw on Moses and Elias, when they appeared on the holy mount and talked with Christ! He hears by faith the heavenly concert, the high and harmonious songs of praise, the joyful triumphs of crowned saints, the sweet commemorations of the things that were done and suffered on earth, with the praises of Him that redeemed them by His blood, and made them kings and priests unto God. Herein he hath sometimes a sweet foretaste of the everlasting pleasures which, though it be but little, as Jonathan's honey on the end of his rod, or as the clusters of grapes which were brought from Canaan into the wilderness; yet they are more excellent than all the delights of sinners."*

Again: Here is another passage which reminded an able Essayist of the spirit in which those who stand by the sea of glass before the throne, cry down to man, whilst looking up to God :—

"'Who would not fear and glorify Thee, Thou King of saints; for Thou only art holy!' It is this :—'God is so

---

* Works, as before, vol. xiii., pp. 242, 243.

abundantly and wonderfully represented to us in all His works, as will leave us under the guilt of the most inexcusable contempt, if we overlook Him, or live as without Him in the world. The heavens declare the glory of God, and the firmament showeth His handiwork. Day unto day uttereth speech, and night unto night showeth knowledge. Cannot you see that, which all the world revealeth? nor hear that, which all the world proclaimeth? O sing ye forth the honour of His name; make His praise glorious. Can we pass Him by, that is everywhere present, and by every creature represented to us? Can we forget Him, when all the world are our remembrancers? Can we stop our ears against the voice of heaven and earth? Can we be ignorant of Him, when the whole creation is our teacher? Can we overlook that holy, glorious name, which is written so legibly upon all things our eyes ever beheld, that nothing but blindness, sleepiness, or distraction, could possibly keep us from discerning it?

"'I have many times wondered, that, as the eye is dazzled so with the beholding of the greatest light, that it can scarcely perceive the shining of a lesser, so the glorious, transcendent majesty of the Lord, doth not even overwhelm our understandings, and so transport and take us up, as that we scarce observe or remember anything else. For naturally the greatest objects of our sense are apt to make us insensible, at that time, to the smaller; and our exceeding great business is apt to make us utterly forget and neglect those (things) that are exceedingly small. And, oh, what nothings are the best and greatest of the creatures, in comparison with God! And what toys and trifles are all our other businesses in the world, in comparison of the business we have with Him!

"'But I have been stopped in these admirations by considering that the wise Creator hath fitted and ordered all His creatures according to the use He designeth them to. And therefore, as the eye must be receptive only of so much light as is proportioned to its use and pleasure; and must be so distant from the sun, that its light may rather guide than blind us, and its heat rather quicken than consume us; so God hath made our understanding capable of no other knowledge of Him here than what is suited to the work of holiness. Our souls, in this *lantern* of a body, must see Him through so thick a glass as not to distract us, or take us off the works which He enjoineth us: and God and our souls shall be at such a distance, as that the proportionable light of His countenance may conduct us, and not overwhelm us; and His love be so revealed as to quicken our desires, and draw us on to a better state, but not so as to make us utterly impatient of this world, and utterly weary of our lives. So that when I consider, that certainly all men would be distracted, if their apprehensions of God were any whit answerable to the greatness of His majesty and glory, (the brain being not able to bear such high operations of the soul, nor the passions which would necessarily follow,) it much reconcileth my wondering mind to the wise and gracious providence of God, in setting innocent nature itself at such a distance from His glory, though it reconcile me not to that doleful distance which is introduced by sin, and which is furthered by Satan, the world, and the flesh.

"'And it further reconcileth me to this disposure and will of the blessed God, when I consider that, if God, and heaven, and hell, were as near and open to our apprehensions, as the things are which we see and feel, this life would not be what God intended it to be, a life of trial and preparation for another. What trial would there be of any man's faith, or love, or obedience, or consistency, or self-denial, if we saw God stand by, or apprehended Him as if we saw Him? It would be no more praiseworthy or rewardable, to abhor all temptations to worldliness, ambition, gluttony, drunkenness, lust, cruelty, than it is for a man to be kept from sleeping that is pierced with thorns; or for a man to forbear to drink a cup of melted gold, which he knows will burn out his bowels.

"'But though in this life we may neither hope for, nor desire, such overwhelming sensible apprehensions of God, as the rest of our faculties cannot answer, nor our bodies bear; yet that our apprehensions of Him should be so base, and small, and dull, and inconstant, as to be borne down by the noise of worldly business, or by the presence of any creature, or by the tempting baits of sensuality, this is the more odious, by how much God is more great and glorious than the creature, and even because the use of the creature itself is but to reveal the glory of the Lord. It is no unjust dishonour or injury to the creature, to be accounted as nothing in comparison with God, that it may (thus) be able to do nothing against Him and His interests; but to make such a nothing of the most glorious God, by our contemptuous forgetfulness or neglect, as that our apprehensions of Him cannot prevail against the sordid pleasures of the flesh, and against the richest baits of sin, and all the wrath and allurements of man,—this is but to make a god of dust, and dung, and nothing. It is a wonder that man's understanding can become so sottish as thus to wink the sun itself into a constant darkness. O sinful man, into how great a depth of ignorance, stupidity, and misery, art thou fallen?'"*

I should scarcely be forgiven were I not to draw something from the "Saint's Everlasting Rest." I would preface my brief selection here with the finely catholic words of Archbishop Trench. He has quoted some choice *bits*, and remarks:—

"Certainly these are good; and it would be easy to multiply them a hundredfold; but there is more and better and higher behind. That pathos which I ascribed to Baxter just now does not manifest itself merely in those calls to the unconverted, full as those are of an inward bleeding compassion. There are passages not a few toward the end of the book, strains of the most passionate devotion, in which he seeks to initiate such as have yielded themselves to his guidance into the deeper mysteries of Divine meditation, to furnish them with some of the materials on which the soul may work, to lead them upward and onward, step by step, from

---

* See Baxter's "Practical Works," 4 vols. 8vo., vol. i., pp. xxix.-xxx. (Published by Virtue, 1838.)

strength to strength, from glory to glory, to the contemplation of the glory of God. Take, for example, this. He has spoken of some motives to love, and proceeds:—

"'But if yet thou feelest not thy love to work, lead thy heart further, and shew it yet more. Shew it the King of saints on the throne of His glory, who is the first and the last; who liveth and was dead. Draw near and behold Him. Dost thou not hear His voice? He that called Thomas to come near and to see the print of the nails, and to put his fingers into His wounds, He it is that calls to thee, Come near, and be not faithless but believing. Look well upon Him. Dost thou not know Him? Why, it is He that brought thee up from the pit of hell and purchased the advancement which thou must inherit for ever. And yet dost thou not know Him? Why, His hands were pierced, His head was pierced, His side was pierced, His heart was pierced with the sting of thy sins, that by these marks thou mightest always know Him. Hast thou forgotten since He wounded Himself to cure thy wounds; and let out His own blood to stop thy bleeding? If thou know Him not by the face, the voice, the hands, if thou know Him not by the tears and bloody sweat, yet look nearer—thou mayest know Him by the heart.

"'Hast thou forgotten the time when thou wast weeping, and He wiped the tears from thine eyes? when thou wast bleeding, and He wiped the blood from thy soul? when pricking cares and fears did grieve thee, and He did refresh thee and draw out the thorns? Hast thou forgotten when thy folly did wound thy soul, and the venomous guilt did seize upon thy heart; when He sucked forth the mortal poison from thy soul, though therewith He drew it into His own? Oh how often hath He found thee sitting weeping like Hagar, while thou gavest up thy state, thy friends, thy life, yea, thy soul for lost; and He opened to thee a well of consolation, and opened thine eyes also, that thou mightest see it. How oft hath He found thee in the posture of Elias, sitting down under the tree forlorn and solitary, and desiring rather to die than to live; and He hath spread thee a table of relief from heaven, and sent thee away refreshed, and encouraged to His work. How oft hath He found thee in such a passion as Jonas, in thy peevish frenzy aweary of thy life; and He hath not answered passion with passion, though He might indeed have done well to be angry, but hath mildly reasoned thee out of thy madness, and said, Dost thou well to be angry, and to repine against Me? How often hath He set thee on watching and praying and repenting and believing, and when He hath returned, hath found thee fast asleep; and yet He hath not taken thee at the worst, but instead of an angry aggravation of thy fault, He hath covered it over with the mantle of love, and prevented thy overmuch sorrow with a gentle excuse, The Spirit is willing but the flesh is weak? How oft hath He been traduced in His cause or name, and thou hast (like Peter) denied Him at least by thy silence, while He hath stood in sight; yet all the revenge He hath taken hath been a heart-melting look, and a silent remembering thee of thy fault by His countenance.'

"And hear him once and only once more; as he

rebukes with the same passionate earnestness those who, loving God, do not love Him better; who professing to seek, and in a sense seeking a heavenly country, are yet unwilling to reach it, and to find themselves (all life's tempest past) in the Fair Havens of the eternal rest :—

"'Ah foolish, wretched soul, doth every prisoner groan for freedom? and every slave desire his jubilee? and every sick man long for health? and every hungry man for food, and dost thou alone abhor deliverance? Doth the seaman long to see the land? Doth the husbandman desire the harvest? and the traveller long to be at home? and the soldier long to win the field? And art thou loth to see thy labours finished? and to receive the end of thy faith? and to obtain the things for which thou livest? Are all thy sufferings only seeming? have thy griefs and groans been only dreams? If they were, yet methinks we should not be afraid of waiting; fearful dreams are not delightful. Or is it not rather the world's delights that are all mere dreams and shadows? Is not all its glory as the light of a glow-worm, a wandering fire; yielding but small directing light and as little comforting heat in all our doubtful and sorrowful darkness. Or hath the world in these its latter days laid aside its ancient enmity? Is it become of late more kind? Who hath wrought this great change, and who hath made this reconciliation? Surely not the great Reconciler. He hath told us in the world we shall have trouble, and in Him only we shall have peace. We may reconcile ourselves to the world (at our peril), but it will never reconcile itself to us. Oh foolish unworthy soul, who hadst rather dwell in this land of darkness than be at rest with Christ; who hadst rather stay among the wolves, and daily suffer the scorpion's stings, than to praise the Lord with the Host of heaven! If thou didst well know what heaven is, and what earth is, it would not be so.'"*

I would only add that "Gildas Salvianus" is simply beyond price to the Minister of the Gospel and all Workers for Christ. Even Dean Goulburn's striking book of our own day is thin and formal beside it.

A fourth thing in the life-work of Richard Baxter that suggests itself to me as a message for to-day is THE USE HE MADE OF THE ENGLISH BIBLE ALONE.

I have already expressed my own judgment and conviction as to an increased rather than a lessened scholarliness and culture. Had I my own way I should greatly widen our ministers' and students' culture. I wish it were as discreditable to them not to know, for example, our transcendent Elizabethan-

---

* "Companions for the Devout Life," as before, p. 100, and pp. 100-3.

Jacobean literature as to be ignorant of the ancient classics. I have an idea also that in our colleges Arabic as a living language would be the best of all gateways by which to enter into Hebrew; and I would add other Semitic tongues. But while I stand up for a richly and variously educated ministry, I can scarcely find words contemptuous enough for surface-show 'tinkering'—whether in pulpit or Sunday-school—of our English Bible. To all intents and purposes it is *the* Bible of the English-speaking race, regarded broadly. It may safely be so. For the truest scholarship is the foremost to admit that whilst in process of time corrections and revisions are inevitable, yet substantially the outcome of the Jerusalem-Chamber long-continued labours will be a very *minimum* of change. The revision probably will show a difference in the translation of aorists and prepositions and consistency in rendering the same original words by the same English word. No doubt various passages will be found to have a different meaning from what hitherto has been attached to them. But I do not think of anything that will even touch fundamental fact or doctrine. The *textus* is another matter; but that is not in the province of the translator. But with reference even to it, we need have no fear. No doubt, *e.g.*, taking the Divinity of Christ, a revised text deprives us of some few proof-passages; but the grand truth shines out the same as ever.* It were pity if it were otherwise. It was a measurelessly grander gift than the Translators themselves ever dreamed of that they gave in the Authorized Version. All honour to Tyndale and Coverdale and other pioneers in making the Hebrew and Greek 'speak English;' far be it from us to abate from their high-hearted service. But in itself, as an English Book, there is nothing to be placed in competition or even comparison with our present English Bible. Nicely true—up to the available texts of

---

* This is simply saying that I have not less faith in the grand old Bible-truth because I use my Ginsburg and Tischendorff and Lachmann.

the period—to the originals, its English is the richest and finest and most musically idiomatic. How home-speaking and yet so far-brought! how coloured of the Orient and nevertheless so Western! how ancient and at the same time so youthful! how grand and also simple! how diverse in its congruousness, and how homogeneous in its diversity! How definite and yet how wide it is! how local and nevertheless cosmopolitan!

What a splendid history the English Bible has! It was accepted as the Bible of SHAKE-SPEARE and BACON and MILTON, and Sir THOMAS BROWNE and JOHN SELDEN. Its cloth-of-gold was worked by them into their supremest workmanship. Its words fitly uttered their noblest personal aspirations. When Oliver Cromwell in his war-tent read a Psalm ere he hurled his Ironsides against the Cavaliers, it was from his English Bible. It went across the wintry seas to "New England" with the Pilgrim Fathers, as before, in their exile to Holland. It was all the Bible the "immortal dreamer" ever knew. Scholars though they were, George Herbert and William Cowper clasp hands over the English Bible. The "Assembly of Divines" at Westminster—that added a book true in its deepest lines and most articulate teaching to the Bible, and that Presbyterians at least will not willingly let die—pondered over it—as later the 'Ejected' of 1660, when two thousand strong they resolved to leave their beloved National Church rather than violate conscience. In the lonely moors and bleak hill-sides of Scotland, the 'Covenanters' wrestled with God through its golden-worded promises. John Howe hewed hence the 'lively stones' of his "Living Temple." Richard Baxter found here his "Saint's Everlasting Rest." Charles Wesley drew from it his "Songs of Zion"; John Wesley his evangelical 'Gospel'; George Whitfield his burning appeals; our own Church's forefathers on both sides of the Tweed, their soul-satisfying "Marrow of the Gospel." SIBBES plucked his "Bruised Reed" from the side of its "living stream"; Leighton fetched from it his unction; Thomas Boston his "Fourfold State" and "Crook in the Lot." It was the English Bible Jonathan Edwards grasped when, as he discoursed of eternal realities, the great Church was transformed into a Bochim. It was it grand Dr. John Erskine called for when fronting the 'Moderates' in the General Assembly he cried out, '*Rax* [reach] me that Bible.' It was 'the one book' ("there is but one, Lockhart") that dying Sir Walter Scott asked his son-in-law to read to him. It was the English Bible whose strange revelation of himself to himself so moved Byron on receiving the memorable letter from John Sheppard.

It has inspired our noblest eloquence, it has barbed our most epoch-making speeches, it has burnished our divinest poetry, it has given a tongue to our grandest music, it has been the beating heart of our sweetest hymns, it has been the soul of our greatest sermons, it has given imperishable watch-words in the fight for freedom, civil and religious, it has sustained patience in the darkest days, piercing the thickest gloom with its light of immortal Hope. THOMAS CHALMERS and EDWARD IRVING, NEWMAN and FREDERICK MAURICE and ROBERTSON, CANDLISH and CAIRD and GUTHRIE, PUSEY and LIDDON and MOZLEY, LYNCH and MACLAREN and HULL and SPURGEON, BINNEY and ALLON and CHARLES STANFORD and ALEXANDER MCLEOD and JOHN KER,—to name only a representative few—'preached'—and so far as they being dead still speak, or being still with us still "preach"—their supremest sermons from the English Bible. It has gone into the prison and the hospital and the battlefield. It has been as a lamp in the valley of shadows. It has been the 'troth' [=betrothal] Bible of many lowly loving hearts—as of Robert Burns and his Highland Mary when that burning heart was at its best and purest. It has been the mother's gift-Bible to the sailor-lad going far away; and to myriad others on lifting up the anchors from home and setting out into the great world. It was "the big Ha' Bible" of "The Cotter's Saturday Night" as of the winsome lay of Robert Nicoll. It was the Bible whence our own Church's gentle Michael Bruce fetched his sweet paraphrases, and a leaf of which he folded down on the night he died. It was out of it "Robinson Crusoe" read for himself and "Friday," and brave-hearted "Jeannie" to her erring sister "Effie" Deans. It was over it Eva and "Uncle Tom" wept and prayed and hoped together. I name these because it rules in the sphere of imagination as in reality. It was by it the slave was made of a thing a man, and roused to flee from the rice-swamp to enfranchising Canada. It was to it DAVID LIVINGSTONE "in the shadows" turned as he lay dying "in the Dark Continent." It has been to untold millions the Marriage Bible, the Family Bible, hallowed by unforgetable memories and associations, and pathetic with old and faded entries of births and marriages and deaths. When we went to college or to city-life it was the Book of books that mothers' eyes and tears and broken words commended to us as she put it into our 'trunk.' It has made entombed miners die "in peace," leaving poorly-scrawled yet trusting words from it, on pieces of shale. It has interpreted to the sin-stung and penitent their own wildered anguish, and guided them back to their Father's House and Heart. It has brought back light of hope to eyes faded and worn and dry, in midnight mission and among the fallen, as out of it 'fair women and brave men' spoke of the redeeming love of Jesus Christ. Its promises are proverbs. Its proverbs are aphorisms. Its deepest sayings are crystalline-clear to the heart and look of faith. Its warnings come like motherly, sisterly voices. I love to think how in glory it shall be found that scarcely a text of the New Testament but has been a saving word to human souls. Weary, broken, humbled, backsliding, forsaken, desperate men and women have in the English Bible found at long-last their rest. Pure, inviolate, dedicated ones from dawn of thought and resolve have been won to Christ through it. What a cloud of witnesses glorify its every page! What joy and pathos, what gratitude and wonder, what hallelujahs and prayer, what incitement and restraint, what hope and anguish, what sunshine and shadow consecrate it all over the world!

If I have seemingly diverged from my subject in thus paying tribute to our English Bible, I am not reluctant to plead guilty. But after all it is only a seeming divergence. For I turn back on my observation that Richard Baxter preached as he preached, and achieved the life-work he did, from his English Bible. My earnest counsel therefore would be, that while by all means we continue to read in the original whatever we expound and enforce in the pulpit or elsewhere, and while I would have us all enrich ourselves with the fullest apparatus possible, we shall nevertheless keep in habitual recollection that to the mass of our auditories the English Bible is their only Bible, with—as we have heard—

deepnesses and tendernesses and heart-holdings of familiarity that furnish a capable Preacher with a means for profoundest influence second only to the conscience. I would have ministers and students grow more and more intimately acquainted with their English Bible.

A fifth and final thing that asserts itself in studying the character and life-work of RICHARD BAXTER—as of thousands more—is THE GUILT OF SCHISM THAT LIES ON OUR NATIONAL CHURCH OF ENGLAND THAT HAD NO ROOM FOR HIM WITHIN IT AND ROOM FOR THOSE WHO WERE WITHIN IT AND DISPLACED OTHERS. I do not, I confess, much care for the word schism. It has the hiss of the serpent in it. Neither have I polemical ends to serve in these Lectures. But with all calmness and gravity, I must assert that in my judgment, it was nothing short of schism for any Church to 'silence' and cruelly persecute and spoil such men as Richard Baxter. Equally is it schism to-day, of the most culpable type, to ignore, as so many Churchmen unhappily do, the insignia of Divine sanction accorded to the ministry and to 'the people' of Nonconformity. Richard Baxter was parish-clergyman of Kidderminster. Richard Baxter literally transformed his parish and beyond it, until it was a Goshen in the midst of Egyptian darkness. Richard Baxter was offered and pressed to accept a bishopric—of Hereford. His regard to conscience suffered him not to accept the insidious honour or to fall in with the godless 'Uniformity' sought, and the 'et cetera.'* His humble self-estimate made the lure no temptation. On the other hand, EDWARD REYNOLDS accepted the bishopric offered him at the same time, and died Bishop of Norwich. I do not sit in judgment on Reynolds. I name him simply to bring out the monstrousness and superstition and nonsense and schism of High-Church Episcopalianism. For who for one instant would compare poor Edward Reynolds in anything with Richard Baxter? And yet Richard

---

* As early as 1640 he had been troubled by this *et cetera* oath.

Baxter's mouth was shut and he was put in prison because he would meet with and exhort a few Christian friends in 'a private house'! For that and the like he was brow-beaten and insulted by the ermined ruffian Judge Jeffreys, doing the bidding of the Court and the Church. Who either would compare any two thousand of the 'clergy' in the mass within the National Church with the two thousand of 'The Ejected'? And yet again —as simple matter-of-fact—the former alone were held to have 'orders,' the latter none! Those 'within' were (and to-day are) God's clergy, those 'without' were (and to-day are) 'intruders.' And so down till to-day in High-Church theories —— and practice! "Good God!" as even calm JOHN HOWE was moved to exclaim—What are 'orders'? What constitutes a Divine 'commission'? What carries authority with it in this matter of preaching the Gospel and dispensing the ordinances of the New Testament? Surely, surely if God's grace finds and fashions such a man as RICHARD BAXTER and such men as were the two thousand of 1662, and gives them the 'character' He did, and the magnificent success they had in advancing His Kingdom on earth and peopling Heaven, there is witness and sanction unchallengeable! Here is the unanswered appeal of JOHN HOWE :—

"I do particularly believe,—as I doubt not but God is graciously present with those that in the sincerity of their hearts have chosen to serve Him in the way which the Lord prescribes,—so, that if Dr. Stillingfleet had known what proofs there are of that same gracious presence in these SO MUCH CENSURED MEETINGS, his thoughts would have been very different of them from that they are. I do not speak of proselyting men to a party, which I heartily despise as a mean and inconsiderable thing: but have known some and heard of many instances of very ignorant and profane persons that have been led, perhaps by their own curiosity or it may be by the persuasion of some neighbour or friend, to hear and see what was done in such meetings, that have (through God's blessing upon so despised means) become very much reformed men, and, for aught that could be judged, serious and sincere Christians. And whereas some, that have very prejudicial thoughts of all that frequent such meetings, may be apt to suspect all effects of that kind to be nothing else but illusions of fancy, or a disposition at least to enthusiasm, or an artificial and industrious hypocrisy; I am very confident that if the Doctor had had an opportunity frequently to observe and converse with such,—as we have had,—and heard the sobriety and consistency of their discourse, and seen the unaffected simplicity, humility, and heavenliness of their conversation, he could not have allowed himself the liberty of such hard censures, but would have judged of many such persons as you and I do." *

Bishop necessary for 'orders'! I could understand it if God were dead or dethroned, or if the Divine Head of the Church were not on His priestly Throne, or if God the Holy Spirit were not still on our earth. But with a living God to look to, and DEMONSTRATION of His sanction of the ministry and 'people' of Nonconformity,—as of Conformity in the measure of fidelity to preaching and believing and reproducing the Gospel,—it is the very senility of credulousness and also schism of a deadly sort, to so stand on 'Church' claims. Spiritual signs, Divine transformations, have all along gone with the work and labours

---

* "A Letter concerning Dr. Stillingfleet's Sermon:" Works, vol. v., as before, p. 252.

of Nonconformists equally with the like-minded of the Church of England and Church of Rome. There has been continuously, under Nonconformist ministries earlier, later and present, the turning of erewhile wanderers back to their Heavenly Father's Home; the purification of the erewhile fallen and shamed; the ennobling of the erewhile mean and debased; the liberating of erewhile enthralled and sordid natures. There have been consecrate and potential lives at home, and pre-eminently in the foremost Foreign Mission fields, outside of the National Church.* We are asked to disown the Divine 'witness' and the working of God's Spirit. We are asked to discredit these spiritual signs. We

---

* To-day, as from the first, Nonconformity admittedly is bearing "the heat and burden of the day" in FOREIGN MISSIONS, *e.g.*, in India, Carey, Marshman, and Ward earlier, and later, Wilson and Duff; in China, Morison and Medhurst, Legge and Burns; in the South Seas, Williams; in Africa, Moffat and Livingstone—were all Nonconformists. Yet I cordially admit that many of the Church of England missionaries have been co-equally noble men, and done co-equally noble service.

are urged to stand in doubt, even to brand our 'commission' thus ratified. We are supposed simple enough to shut up God in a temple made with hands, inscribed 'The Church of England,' or 'The Church of Rome.' It 'hurts our understanding' to hear such drivel of 'apostolical succession,' and violation of 'unity' dinned in our ears. It rouses a contempt we fain would not cherish, to be called to serve ourselves inferior to men of whom, man for man, we feel ourselves to be the equals. It moves to pity all round to find this exclusive and excluding 'clergy'—as we come in contact with them—largely by the thousand under-educated, and especially unfurnished theologically, and many habitually trafficking in sermons from January to January that are not their own. Arrogance anywhere is bad, but it is double-dyed bad when, by thousands, the men who claim to be 'priests' show no signs of Divine recognition that Nonconformists do not show.

The Church of England is a venerable and

illustrious section of the Church of Christ. Its roll of Worthies may compare with any other's. But really she is only a "little sister" in comparison with the vast aggregate of evangelical Nonconformity in England and her Colonies and Christendom. Emphatically the Church of England, I must solemnly reiterate, has been in the past, and is to-day, by a hundred proofs, guilty of schism in her attitude towards Nonconformity. The National Church sectarianizes and provincializes herself when she unchurches those whom God has churched, and holds aloof from those whom Christ has made part of His own Body. The serene assumption that she is '*The* Church,' and that refusal to believe in either her or Episcopacy is 'division,' etc., etc., etc., is not less unhistorical than it is ludicrous; is no less an impertinence than a wrong. It is a pain to me to say these things; but in the face of superciliousness and denial that Nonconformists are "ministers of religion" I dare not be silent. Methinks if we could get back Richard Baxter's seraphic fervour; if we could get his faith in the human conscience; if we could get his splendid declarativeness; if we could get his fulness of proclamation of "the old, old story"; if we could come to think more of Christ and less of the Church; if we could actualize to ourselves the need of every variety of gift and character and agency in meeting the forces in action against our common Christianity—I have little doubt that men's present ways of speech and bearing towards servants and believers of the same Divine Lord would be greatly altered. God speed the day!

WILLIAM ORME in his Life, and ARCHBISHOP TRENCH in his Lecture, close their estimate of Baxter with one of his poems, his "Valediction." In the latter's words,—

"Let me cite as *my* valediction a few verses from this, as showing that age had not dulled his longing desire for the Heavenly rest; being such also as may fitly quicken our own desire after the same":—

> "'What is the time that's gone,
> And what is that to come?
> Is it not now as none?
> The present stays not.

Time posteth, oh how fast,
Unwelcome death makes haste,
None can call back the past,
    Judgement delays not.
Though God brings in the light,
    Sinners awake not;
Because hell's out of sight,
    They sin forsake not.

"'Man walks in a vain shew;
They know, yet will not know,
Sit still, when they should go,
    But run for shadows;
While they might taste and know
The living streams that flow,
And crop the flowers that grow,
    In Christ's sweet meadows.
Life's better slept away
    Than as they use it;
In sin and drunken play
    Vain men abuse it.

" 'Is this the world men choose,
For which they heaven refuse,
And Christ and grace abuse,
    And not receive it?
Shall I not guilty be
Of this in some degree,
If hence God would me free,
    And I'd not leave it?
My soul, from Sodom fly,
    Lest wrath there find thee
Thy refuge rest is nigh,
    Look not behind thee.

" 'There's none of this ado;
None of the hellish crew,
God's promise is most true,
    Boldly believe it.

My friends are gone before,
And I am near the shore,
My soul stands at the door;
   O Lord, receive it.
It trusts Christ and His merits;
   The dead He raises.
Join it with blessed Spirits,
   Who sing Thy praises.'

SAMUEL RUTHERFORD:
Devout Affection.

"Visits of those friends who resided near were not unfrequent, such as the Gordons, Viscount Kenmure and his lady, and Marion M'Naught. But at times Anwoth manse [parsonage] was lighted up by the glad visit of unexpected guests. There is a tradition that Archbishop Ussher, passing through Galloway, turned aside on a Saturday to enjoy the congenial society of Rutherford. He came, however, in disguise, and being welcomed as a guest, took his place with the rest of the family when they were catechised, as was usual, that evening. The stranger was asked, ' How many commandments are there?' His reply was 'Eleven.' The pastor corrected him; but the stranger maintained his position, quoting our Lord's words, ' A NEW COMMANDMENT I give unto you, that ye love one another.' They retired to rest, all interested in the stranger. Sabbath morning dawned. Rutherford arose, and repaired, as was his custom, for meditation, to a walk that bordered on a thicket, but was startled by hearing the voice of prayer—prayer too for the host, and on behalf of the souls of the people that day to assemble. It was no other than the holy Archbishop Ussher; and soon they came to an explanation, for Rutherford had begun to suspect he had 'entertained angels unawares.' With great mutual love they conversed together; and at the request of Rutherford, the Archbishop went up to the pulpit, conducted the usual service of the Presbyterian pastor, and preached on 'The New Commandment.'"—Dr. Andrew A. Bonar's Sketch of Samuel Rutherford (Letters, vol. i., pp. 10, 11).

"He would send me as a spy into the wilderness of suffering, to see the Land, and to try the ford ; and I cannot make a lie of Christ's cross ; I can report nothing but good of Him and it" (Letter cxviii.)

SAMUEL RUTHERFORD:

DEVOUT AFFECTION.

Born at Nisbet, in Roxburghshire, Scotland, 'about 1600.' Died 20th March, 1661, at St. Andrew's: buried there, and it was Thomas Halyburton's dying request that he might be laid near his grave.

SAMUEL RUTHERFORD—of whom I have now to speak—is not a "household word" like the others of our quaternion. Only those who "turn aside" from the beaten highways of national history and literature to their by-ways, are at all likely to be familiar with it. None the less is it true in this case, as in that grander of old, that if we do "turn aside" we shall find if not (technically) a *"great* sight" yet a 'sight' not ill comparable with what Moses saw, "a bush burning yet not consumed." I fear that, except to a very few, now-a-days, the numerous writings of Rutherford are as if they had perished in the Great Fire of London. But when search is made, one relatively small book is discovered as *quick* to-day as at the first on its being sent forth in rudest and humblest form from the Dutch (Rotterdam) press; or to recur to our metaphor, one little 'bush' of his theological-literary growth—his "Joshua Redivivus; or Mr. Rutherford's Letters," 1664 *—retains all its original greenness and brightness and fragrance of bloom; nor is it at all likely that after surviving so long it ever will be forgotten.

It is through his LETTERS, and the DEVOUT AFFECTION shown in them, that SAMUEL RUTHERFORD is still—as in the past—a spiritual force. It is from what he was as the writer of these Letters, and for what he did

---

* With reference to the title "Joshua Redivivus," I imagine it was meant—the publication being posthumous—to designate Rutherford as a Joshua-like man, who though dead should now speak as if alive, by these Letters. Considering the 'leading' part that he had filled in the 'Kirk,' and at the Westminster Assembly, it was not a badly-chosen name.

by them and continues to do, that I seek to fetch a message from him for us to-day.

To make a clean breast of it at once, I must confess that exclusive of his Letters and "Trial and Triumph of Faith" (1645), and "Christ Dying and Drawing Sinners to Himself" (1647), and "Covenant of Life Opened" (1655), and "Influences of the Life of Grace" (1659), and some of his "Sacramental Sermons: taken by a Hearer" earlier and later—the Works of our worthy are in my judgment hard and ungracious reading. Even of these practical books it must be owned that there is little of penetrative thinking, or richness of spiritual experience, or memorable putting of things. There is a sweet incense of piety through all; but otherwise the books are thin and poor. Their method has all the vices of contemporaries, with only very occasional gleams of happy phrase. Their one merit is that they are full of the "exceeding great and precious promises" and truths of the Gospel, and that they hold forth with wistful and passionate entreaty, a crucified Saviour as the one centre for weary souls in their unrest, and the one hope for the world. He again and again bursts the barriers of his rigid creed under the spell of the all-sufficiency of the Lord Jesus. I have been touched with the pathos of his appeals to the impenitent and delaying. These are self-evidently the outcome of profoundest 'concern' for those to whom he 'preached.' The "wrath to come" was to him a very seer's "vision." The lightnings seemed to hurtle in the sky overhead. I do not marvel that his audiences were agitated even to outcries. It must be added that by temperament he had more reliance on love than terror. An English merchant said of him, even during controversies that sorely vexed and distracted his spirit, "I went to St. Andrew's, where I heard a sweet, majestic-looking man (Robert Blair), and he showed me the majesty of God. After him, I heard a little fair man (Samuel Rutherford), and he showed me *the loveliness of Christ.*"* It

---

* M'Crie's Sketches, *s.n.*

is also told that when he was expatiating on Jesus Christ, his manner grew so animated that it seemed as if he would have "flown out of the pulpit." *

I ask that all this be kept in grateful recollection. I ask that he may have all the benefit of accumulated testimony to his fidelity and gentle power and powerful gentleness as a "Preacher of the Gospel." For I must now state as a foil, that his controversial writings are of the most distressing type that I have ever come across, surpassed—if surpassed—only in those of the assailants of the great-brained and illustrious JOHN GOODWIN.† From his

---

* 'Rabbi' Duncan says of his "Christ Dying and Drawing Sinners to Himself"—"S. R. gives us in this book some unpretending but deep philosophy. He denies power in the will against the Arminian and asserts it against the Antinomian position. Any other doctrine of power uncreaturifies the creature. It either brutifies man or deifies him."—Brown's Memoir, p. 413. Dr. Bonar quotes a flowery passage from *De Providentiâ*. Cf. Knight's *Colloquia Peripatetica* (pp. 4, 6) on the same book by Dr. Duncan.

† John Goodwin : Would that for the (as a whole) arid

(so-called) "Peaceable and Temperate Plea for Paul's Presbytery in Scotland" (1642) to his "Lex Rex: the Law and the Prince" (1644), and from his "Divine Right of Presbyteries" (1644) to "The Divine Right of Church Government and Excommunication" and "A Dispute touching Scandal and Christian Duty" (1646), and from his "Survey of the Spiritual Anti-Christ" and "Modest Survey of the Secrets of Antinomianism" (1648) to his "Survey of Mr. [Thomas] Hooker's Church Discipline" (1658) —you have—speaking generally—such assumption of personal infallibility, such fierceness of contradiction, such unmeasured vituperation (*e.g.* "It is a lye! It is a lye!" exceeding often), such extreme narrowness of sectarian orthodoxy and such suspicion of all who differed from him, and would not pronounce his shibboleth (*e.g.*, "apostate Spottiswood," etc.), as is alike wonderful and sorrowful. Then there is his

and dreary works of Dr. Thomas Goodwin, we had a worthy collection of John Goodwin's. Dr. Jackson's Life of him is utterly unsatisfactory.

"Free Disputation against Pretended Liberty of Conscience" (1649), whose very title is an offence and an opprobrium, and which is a treatise simply confounding in its iron logic and (supposed) demonstrations. His "Lex Rex" is noticeable, and to be honoured for its brave speech for the liberty of the people, and its unflinching argumentative insistence that bad kings were "dethronable";*

---

* It is due to Rutherford to give in full, what I find nowhere, the title-page of "Lex Rex" :—

"Lex Rex: | The Law and the Prince. | A Dispute for the just | PREROGATIVE | of King and People. | Containing the *Reasons* and *Causes* of the | most necessary Defensive Wars of the Kingdom | of Scotland, and of their Expedition for the ayd | and help of their dear Brethren of England. | In which their Innocency is asserted, and a full | Answer is given to a Seditious Pamphlet, Intituled, | Sacro-Sancta Regum Majestas, or | The Sacred and Royall Prerogative of Christian Kings ; | Under the | Name of J. A. | But penned by *Jo: Maxwell* the Excommunicate P. Prelat. | With a Scriptural Confutation of the ruinous Grounds of | W. Barclay, H. Grotius, H. Arnisæus, Ant. de Domi. P. Bishop of Spalato, | and of other late Anti-Magistratical Royalists ; as the Author of | Ossorianum, D. Fern, E. Symmons, the Doctors of Aberdeen, &c. | In xliv. Questions. | Published but coming from these controversial writings of Rutherford, I am thankful that the small dust

by Authority. | 1 Sam. 12. 25. But if you shall still do wickedly, ye shall be | consumed, both ye and your king. | London : Printed for *Iohn Field*, and are to be sold at his house upon | Addle-hill, near *Baynard's* Castle, Octob. 7, 1644" 4to, 19 leaves and pp. 467. Here are some of the great questions debated : (xi.) Whether or no, he be more principally a king, who is a king by birth, or he who is a king by the free election of the people? Affir. posterius: (xvi.) "Whether or no a despoticall or masterly dominion agree to the king, because he is a king. *Negatur:*" (xix.) "Whether or no the king be in dignity and power above the people? *Neg.* Impugned by 10 argum:" (xxiii.) "Whether the king hath a prerogative royall above Laws? *Negatur.*" (xxv.) "Whether the supreme Law, the safetie of the people, be above the king? *Affirmed:*" (xxviii.) "Whether or no Wars raised by the Estates and Subjects for their owne just defence against the king's bloody Emissaries be lawfull? *Affirm.* :" (xxx.) "Whether or no passive obedience be a measure to which we are subjected in conscience by virtue of a Divine Commandment? *Neg.:*" (xxxvii.) "Whether the Estates of Scotland are to help their Brethren the Protestants in England against Cavaliers? *Affirmatur*, proved by 13 argum." While Rutherford held Monarchy to be the "best of Governments," there was no superstition or unreason in his loyalty. One wishes that Milton had come across " Lex Rex." See Appendix C for more.

of oblivion has fallen on them, not to be blown off. It is a mystery to me that BUCKLE did not disinter them that he might draw from them materials for his fulmination against Scotland in paradoxical association with Spain. It were to be patriotic at the cost of integrity, to be a Presbyterian first and a Christian second or third, not to condemn inexorably such kind of controversial writing, so utterly alien to the real spirit of Christianity and to intelligent Presbyterianism. I readily concede that throughout Samuel Rutherford was contending conscientiously for what he believed to be "the truth, the whole truth, and nothing but the truth." I am willing also to concede —as Sir William Hamilton of Edinburgh once said to myself with the "Divine Right of Church Government and Excommunication" in his hand—that in the most heated and bigoted of his books there is metaphysical ability, uncommon shrewdness, and an odd agility in putting an opponent in a dilemma. I do not forget either that in those troublous times men had to speak loud if they were to be heard at all, nor that the *mode* was to be violent as in crossing swords. Moreover, almost everybody then had the like spirit of combative intolerance. Even the Baptists and Quakers —near relatives though they were—could not be in the same jail together for the same cause, without passing the time in uttering sharp words—to say the least—of mutual undervaluation. But after every extenuating element is taken into account, we must not be sentimental in Apology for our favorites. All the more ought it to stir up the grace of indignation when we see such intolerance cleaving to a great saint. It remains sadly true that SAMUEL RUTHERFORD and contemporary Presbyterians, as advocates of the "Divine Right of Presbytery," wrote of and to the most venerable and saintly men, of Episcopacy and Independency, and Baptists and Quakers, as though they had been heretics of the deadliest sort. I cannot therefore here withhold John Milton's great scornful sonnet, albeit it must equally be kept in mind that his own invective is at times as fierce and intolerant as need be :—

ON THE NEW FORCERS OF CONSCIENCE UNDER THE LONG PARLIAMENT.

" BECAUSE you have thrown off your Prelate Lord,
    And with stiff vows renounced his Liturgy,
    To seize the widowed whore Plurality
    From them whose sin ye envied, not abhorred,
Dare ye for this adjure the civil sword
    To force our consciences, that Christ set free,
    And rule us with a Classic Hierarchy,
    Taught ye by mere A. S. and Rutherford?
Men whose life, learning, faith, and pure intent,
    Would have been held in high esteem with Paul,
    Must now be named and printed heretics
By shallow Edwards and Scotch What-d'ye-call !
    But we do hope to find out all your tricks,
    Your plots and packing, worse than those of
        Trent.
        That so the Parliament
May with their wholesome and preventive shears
    Clip your phylacteries, though baulk your ears,
        And succour our just fears,
When they shall read this clearly in your charge :
New *Presbyter* is but old *Priest* writ large." *

---

* " Milton's Poetical Works," 3 vols. 8vo., 1874 ; Vol. iii.,

When we recall that, in the words of PROFESSOR MASSON,—who is no enemy but a friend bold-spoken against the hasty traducers of Presbyterianism :—

"It was the uniform demand of the Presbyterian clergy that not only should Presbytery be established as the national system of worship and Church-government, but all deviations from it, all meetings for worship elsewhere than in the Presbyterian churches, and also all heresies and blasphemies, should be punished by the State; [and that] for some of the graver heresies, capable of being characterized as blasphemous, they demanded death,"*

it must be frankly and unreservedly admitted that much in Milton's Sonnet was warranted, though scarcely from him. There may still be (doubtless are) instances of the "New Pres-

---

p. 472. In the Cambridge MS. the reading is (line 12) 'hare-brained,' but erased for 'shallow,' as more stinging.

* *En passant*, it is pleasant to think that in the grand lines,

"Men whose life, learning, faith, and pure intent,
 Would have been held in high esteem with Paul,"

Milton, spite of his anti-prelatic feeling, paid tribute to Bishop Jeremy Taylor and Bishop Lancelot Andrewes.

byter, Old Priest," as there are instances in which the words of Milton are hurled fiercely at innocent heads; but it is matter of rejoicing that to-day in no quarter is Priestism less tolerated than in the 'free' Presbyterian Churches of England and Scotland.

I must further add, in favour of our Worthy, that his presence at the renowned Westminster Assembly for four years, and his observations in England, widened his opinions and conclusions; *e.g.*, in the preface to his "Survey of the Spiritual Antichrist," he writes:—

"I judge that in England the Lord hath many names, and a fair company, that shall stand at the side of Christ when He shall render up the Kingdom to the Father; and that in that renowned nation there be men of all ranks, wise, valorous, generous, noble, heroic, faithful, religious, gracious, learned."

It is questionable if Dickson, or Wodrow, or even Henderson or George Gillespie, would have said as much as this. But that Samuel Rutherford, if not so scurrilous as 'shallow' Thomas Edwards of the 'Gangræna'—who, however, was not so 'shallow' as he was 'hare-brained,'—was among the most strenuous asserters of the all-excluding "Divine Right" of Presbytery, it were uncandid as idle to deny; and thus the stigma of the Sonnet must go down to remotest posterity.

I do not think it would be difficult to prove that no single section of the Church of Christ, (as no political party in the State) given the power and opportunity to exalt itself, has not abused that power and opportunity. "Put a sceptre," says Lowell, "in any hand, the grip is instinctive." So that it is scarcely fitting that any should be forward to cast stones. Fitting rather, that all should antedate the song of the Church above, and acknowledge that only One is "Worthy to receive . . . . POWER, STRENGTH,"—the divinely-human, humanly-divine Head. Hallam's judicial words are unanswerable: "Persecution is the deadly sin of the Reformed Church, that which cools every honest man's zeal for their cause, in proportion as his reading becomes more extensive."* Let us rejoice in the ampler atmosphere that men breathe now, and in the clearer light in which men walk to-day, whereby it is being slowly but inevitably recognized that "Divine Right" can be affirmed of no one form of ecclesiastical government exclusively; that "Divine Right" may co-exist with many varieties of organization; that "The Word" of God has left large liberty as to everything merely ecclesiastical; and that not Church but Christ, not government and 'orders' but spiritual life, not lineage or circumstance but "the fruits of the Spirit," determine the claims of any Church to be Scriptural, or to have a "Divine Right" to exist. Personally I do not find it hard or recondite to affirm Bible-authority and "Divine Right" for our Presbyterian Church. I discern this increasingly, in its orderliness combined with freedom, congregational distinctness in union with corporate life, soundness in the faith with growth and expansion from generation to gene-

---

* History, *s. n.*

ration. I should not be a Presbyterian minister if I did not prefer my own Church to every other—and that on Bible grounds. But I should be ashamed of my Church and of myself, if I did not allow the same conviction to every other concerning their choice of Church-form. I read from the mouth of the Lord that there shall be not "one fold" but "one flock" under One Shepherd.* I reckon lightly of Church uniformity: I hold as priceless oneness *in* Christ Jesus now, and oneness *with* Him by-and-bye above.

Meantime be it ours to honour with our deepest gratitude, the 'elect few' to whom it was given in this England of ours, to assert the grand doctrine of FREEDOM OF CONSCIENCE. We come on individual utterances only; often by obscure individuals, in some long-persecuted 'Baptist' congregation or the like. They were somewhat inarticulate lispings of the true doctrine at the

---

* St. John x. 16: 'one fold,' like 'bishop' for 'presbyter,' was foisted in by order of King James, it is probable.

best, and changed circumstances I fear might have changed them. OLIVER CROMWELL under the temptation of power was true to the doctrine. Never has there been one truer. It was something in those days even to see the truth. He saw it, and with only a solitary exception, acted on it.

I need hardly say that among imperfect enunciations of the doctrine of freedom of conscience, I place the doctrine—if it be a doctrine—of Toleration. He who 'tolerates' me, usurps a place to which he has no right. He yields to me *ex gratia* what he is a traitor to God for invading.

Equally must I extend conscience-rights beyond a man's Church and religious opinions. It is to intrude into the very shekinah of human nature for anyone to maintain 'the truth' other than through its own persuasive power. I can enter into no truce with error,—as I regard it,— but I dare not fight it with other weapons than those of truth and righteousness.

I do not doubt that I should have been

branded as a Laodicean, if not worse, by SAMUEL RUTHERFORD for these sentiments. To him even 'Toleration' was a 'pretended liberty.' It may be that I shall be held for Latitudinarian to-day. So be it. I speak for myself alone. I have dwelt the more fully on the matter, because all the Signs of the Times go to show that in all the Churches these old problems are coming up for discussion and re-discussion. I have no alarms for the ultimate issue. As in the beginning, there is the grand " Nevertheless "— " Nevertheless the foundation of God standeth sure, having this seal, The Lord knoweth them that are His" (2 Timothy ii. 19). Be it ours to be forewarned by the fate of such-conducted controversies as those we have been characterizing. "*The Lord* knoweth them that are His." We do not. Therefore, do not let us pre-judge others. The second seal-word is—" Let every one that nameth the name of Christ depart from iniquity." Wherever we see that, wherever and under whatsoever Church-form we discern departure ' from iniquity,' and a meek, gentle, holy outcoming of the 'image' of Christ, let us accredit the reality of their Christian character as we accredit our own, and as we have self-respect. By all means let us stand ready, let us "hold fast" what we believe to be "the truth" against all comers; let us be well-informed and able to vindicate our own choice of Church-form, and even specialities of creed and ecclesiastical order. But in all controversy, let us be willing to allow to every other what we claim for ourselves. The golden words of "judicious Hooker"— equal to his more famous ones—may perchance give weight to my counsels:—"In the meanwhile it may be, that suspense of judgment and exercise of charity, were safer and seemlier for Christian men, than the hot pursuit of these controversies, wherein they that are most fervent to dispute be not always the most able to determine. But who are on His side, and who against Him, our Lord in His good time shall reveal."*

---

* Eccl. Polity, Book IV., ch. xiv. 6.

I right gladly turn from these ancient strifes to that in Samuel Rutherford which makes him one of the uncanonized saints of the Church Universal. I have characterized him as presenting to us an exemplification of such DEVOUT AFFECTION as I should like to have reproduced in our own day. I base this, with all confidence, on his Letters. These have long been a Christian classic in our own Scotland, and in Holland, and Germany, and in the United States of America and Canada, and our colonies. One still comes across the book, well-thumbed and not unseldom tear-blurred—the white tears of joy—in lowland cottages and shepherd-huts and farmsteads of the North. Not long since, a travelling friend met with two editions among the forsaken towns of the Zuyder-Zee. It went to my heart to meet with a copy under the shadow of Mount Hermon. In the backwoods of the Far West, the book lies side by side with the 'Pilgrim's Progress.' In Cumberland, Westmoreland, and Durham, and in the North of Ireland, it is in living demand. Originally published in lowliest guise, it has passed through, I suppose, really innumerable, or at least un-numbered, editions—many stereotyped. One—very beautiful and charming every way—is in two goodly octavos under the editorship of Dr. Andrew A. Bonar,—than whom none in all that was holy and tender and heavenly and sweet in Rutherford so abundantly inherits.* Such men as RICHARD BAXTER and DR. LOVE earlier, and SAMUEL WESLEY, and AUGUSTUS TOPLADY, and JAMES HERVEY and ROMAINE, and later RICHARD CECIL, and WILLIAM WILBERFORCE, and THOMAS CHALMERS, and THOMAS ERSKINE, of Linlathen, found in these Letters intellectual and spiritual nurture. All have written eloquently and gratefully of them. Richard Baxter, who was theologically opposed to much that Rutherford taught, said—"Hold off the Bible, and such a book the world never saw" as these Letters. RICHARD CECIL has said of Rutherford in these Letters: "He is one of my classics; he is a real original."

---

* 2 vols. 8vo., 1863.

Now turning to these Letters I must *in limine* put in a guarding word in relation to them. I would not for a moment utter one single syllable that would lower our estimate of the DEVOUT AFFECTION of Samuel Rutherford. But I should be false to a profound conviction if I were to be silent on a very subtle danger lurking in a not uncommon misuse of these Letters. I have seen in soft and passionate natures the growth of a sensuous, almost voluptuous religiousness, that meant the sapping of moral vigour. I have found such, turning for instance the Song of Solomon, into a seduction. The spiritualizing of the 'Song' does not in such cases neutralize its erotic imagery. Similarly I have met with those of both sexes who were—to speak straight out the simple truth—over-fond of texts from the Song of Solomon, equally over-fond of appropriating in speech and letter endearments from Rutherford that in certain moods and to certain constitutions are enfeebling (to say no more). You do not find the Apostles speaking of 'sweet Jesus,' 'dear Jesus,' or the like.

I feel bound to warn of the risk in reading the Letters of Rutherford of mistaking delicious feelings for delight in God. I would commend as an alterative JONATHAN EDWARDS on the "Affections"—a book which, though it favours introspective tendencies too much, distinguishes things that differ with great keenness, far beyond the casuistries of even Jeremy Taylor's "Ductor Dubitantium," or Richard Baxter's "Directory."

I should scarcely, perhaps, have indicated this peril of misuse of these Letters, were it not that I regard it as a present-day matter. "God forbid" that I should in the slightest speak evil of that great spring-tide wave of revival that swept over England and America in recent years, and that still keeps the spiritual life of individuals and communities high and strong. I can bear personal attestation to good done. But I dare not conceal that in after-meetings and inquiry-meetings, and other organized agencies, I have had reason to mourn that spiritual truths and experiences were explained and illustrated from the Song of Solomon, and the like, in a way that was liable—to say the least—to be turned to bad account in susceptible natures. I grant the ground I am treading is delicate. None the less is it duty to tread it and to speak unmistakably. I shall otherwise unreservedly recommend these Letters; but this risk I have felt bound to point out.*

The things by which the LETTERS of SAMUEL RUTHERFORD have a living message for to-day, I would now state and enforce. Each goes to exemplify his DEVOUT AFFECTION.

I. THE LORD JESUS AS A LIVING PERSON IS ALL IN ALL.—The 'burden'—to appropriate

---

* Words of endearment may have been genuine and loving when first used; but caught up by others, 'imitated,' they are apt to be untrue. Of course I do not forget that nice people have often the nastiest ideas; and that it is possible to go to an opposite extreme of reticence and restraint, *e.g.*, some miserable poetaster sought to tinker Charles Wesley's glorious hymn, "Jesus, lover of my soul," into "Jesus, refuge of my soul," and to transmogrify "Let me to Thy bosom fly" into "Let me to—I forget what—fly." Such prudery is simply abominable.

a suggestive Old Testament word—of all the Letters is to 'magnify' the Divine Saviour, and either to 'persuade' undecided and delaying to 'come' to Him, or to encourage and instruct those who have already come, to 'abide' in Him. To the still ever Living Person, Jesus Christ, not merely to THE BOOK about Him; or to THE BOOK only that it may 'direct' and draw to Him, these Letters from first to last seek to bring the various correspondents, whether gentle or simple. So that one is ready to apply to him Dr. Duncan's words about Chrysostom—"Though I disagree with his theology on some points, his views of the Person of Christ always kept him essentially right." The Biographer of McCheyne has excellently put this:—

"We have too often been satisfied with speculative truth and abstract doctrine. On the one hand, the orthodox have too often rested in the statements of our Catechisms and Confessions; and on the other the "election-doubters" (as Bunyan would have called them) have pressed their favourite dogma, that Christ died for all men, as if mere assent to a proposition could save the soul. Rutherford places the truth before us in a more accurate and also more savoury way, full of life and warmth. The Person of Him who gave Himself for His Church is held up in all its attractiveness. With him it is ever the Person as much as the work done; or rather, never the one apart from the other. Like Paul, he would fain know *Him*, as well as the power of His resurrection" (Phil. iii. 10).*

I agree with every word of Dr. Bonar here; and it is to me very delightful to mark the abounding evidences of Rutherford's own 'close walk' with his Lord and Saviour. You feel throughout that he is writing out of his own personal experience of the "Walk of Faith," and that grandest of personal realities, his own life 'hid' with Christ in God. Hence it is we recognise that he so wistfully and pathetically and joyously urges others to choose the same august and blessed friendship and fellowship. All this I regard as of deepest momentousness for to-day. I think that it is needed to-day that we instruct and warn against Bibliolatry or CHILLING-

---

* Letters, as before : Sketch, vol. i., pp. 29, 30.

WORTH'S watchword "The Bible the Religion of Protestants." Samuel Rutherford saw—and we must see—that not even the Bible is to be suffered to come between us and Christ. Wherever that is done, the old deadly Jewish error is repeated, which our Lord pronounced against, in words soft as light, yet giving the stroke of lightning:—"Ye search the Scriptures, for ye think ye have eternal life in THEM; and they are they which testify of ME; and ye will not come to ME that ye might have life" (St. John v. 39, 40). It is therefore a noticeable characteristic of these Letters, and a fine exemplification of their writer's DEVOUT AFFECTION, that to him the Lord Jesus IS—not historically '*was*'—a Living Person, and his own all in all. His ardent, loving, poetic diction, reminds us of Bernard de Morlaix and other old Catholic hymnists. His heart was ever ready to break into holy love-songs. 'I AM' was God to him, yet his very own most dear and intimate Friend; the 'I AM,' and not merely the "I WAS."

But I have a conviction that in relation to this living Personality of the Lord Jesus, there is room for a clearing up of Christian ideas respecting it. I would try to do so.

First of all I accentuate the fact of the immense predominance of the passages that represent 'faith' as coming to or trusting in a Living Person. We may say broadly that the New Testament is constructed after this fashion—'Come unto Me'—'Believe in the Lord Jesus Christ'—'Made accepted in the Beloved'—'I know Whom I have believed.' These suffice to demonstrate that it is not Christianity,—much less any one or two formulated doctrines,—that it is not THE BOOK as a revelation of that truth, but Jesus Christ Himself who 'Saves.'

Secondly, I am anxious to draw deep and distinct the march-lines (so to say) between the Person or the Living Personality of Christ and His 'body.' I find the two grievously confounded, and a brood of erroneous opinions and sentimentalism resulting. Thus, one asks me, 'Do you believe in the *personal reign* of Christ?' My answer is—'Of course I do.' But my questioner—as a rule—would be misled were I to say no more. He has marked out for himself a theory of the 'bodily' return of the ascended Saviour, and of His 'reign' on earth for 'a thousand years,' and other *fantastiques* of interpretation (*i.e.*, in my judgment, mis-interpretation). Specifically therefore, I would state that I believe in His 'personal reign' JUST NOW, and for these well-nigh 1900 years; for is not all power given Him *in heaven* and *on earth?* What 'is written'? When He was going away after His thirty and three years of awful exile and humiliation, He said, "Lo, I am with you alway, even unto the end of the world" (St. Matt. xxviii. 20). It is not—be it marked and re-marked—'I am on your side,' nor 'I will be with you figuratively,' but REALLY AND PERSONALLY; and that, too, just when they were about to see Him ascend up into heaven. But this personal presence of the

God-man is one thing, and 'bodily' manifestation something very different. If I wanted (or needed) a 'bodily image' of Christ that I could call up to the eye, I should turn to the Church of Rome. I am not very likely to do so. I believe too absolutely in His 'personal reign' as holding in His nail-pierced hands all the threads of Providence and grace, and working out His 'almighty purpose;' I remember too gratefully the grand words, 'Whom having not seen, YE LOVE' (1 Peter i. 8); I realize too deeply the grovelling superstition and the fanatical idolatry of 'bodily presence'; I too adoringly accept the magnanimously-patient 'ministry' of God the Holy Spirit—for an instant to acquiesce in ways of talking and writing that confound Person with 'body,' and 'personal reign' with 'bodily presence.' I find in the Letters of SAMUEL RUTHERFORD a habitual realization that the Lord Jesus was still 'alive' and governing, and blessedly accessible to the least and lowliest. I see that that clarified his faith and deepened his devout affection, and imparted an intense reality to his counsels to high and low, to 'live' in daily, hourly, momentary, continuous 'friendship' with Him. It were a benediction if we had more of this sense of the 'personal reign' of Christ NOW; if while grasping the historical 'bodily presence' we at the same time acted on the continuity of the promise of 'presence' to "the end of the world." It was this unbroken sovereignty and allegiance of myriad hearts to the 'dead Christ' (as men said) that so arrested Napoleon the Great; and I count it treason to Him to covet the poorer thing of 'bodily presence' for this magnificent, unseen, all-pervading government and 'personal reign.'

II. THE 'GLORIOUS APPEARING' OF THE LORD JESUS IS LONGED FOR.—The Letters are full of the most passionate 'breathings' and 'pantings' for the coming of the Lord. Those to MARION M'NAUGHT (Nos. 16, 48, and 49), and LADY KENMURE (Nos. 21 and 42), are unspeakably touching from their wistful heart-weariness and renewing of strength and ardour as he recalls " exceeding great and precious promises" of the Lord's coming. Every recurrence of the celebration of the Lord's Supper, whether at Anwoth or in exile in the North, burned in upon heart and memory the irreversible words, "Ye do show the Lord's death *till He come*" (1 Cor. xi. 6). Abounding sin and obstacles evidently led Rutherford, as it has similarly misled other good men, to think the 'end of the world' was close at hand, and the Advent of the Redeemer consequently near. But notwithstanding I do not discover in these Letters any expectation of the 'coming' of our Lord in the millenarian notion or interpretation. Dr. Bonar, I suspect, by "All who love that blessed hope, and the glorious appearing of the great God our Saviour,"* intends *his* and his co-equal brother's theory of the 'bodily presence' of the Lord for 'a thousand years' on our earth. If so—I cannot discover

---

* As before, p. 30.

it in the Letters, and as I cannot find it in the Bible I cannot believe it.

But though this millenarian-'appearing' of the Saviour, be neither in Rutherford's Letters nor the Bible, it would be an advantage to us to-day if we were more under the influence of the 'blessed hope and the glorious appearing of the great God and our Saviour Jesus Christ.' The more we love the Lord Jesus the more will we love His 'appearing,' and the more we *actualize* to ourselves that 'appearing' the holier we shall become. Let these aspirations of our Worthy put to shame our chill feeling as poor practice of the apostolic charge to 'look for and hasten unto the coming of the day of God." While in the 'far North' in 1637, he writes:—" O when will we meet! O how long is it to the dawning of the marriage day! O sweet Jesus, take wide steps! O my Lord, come over mountains at one stride! O my Beloved, flee as a roe or young hart upon the mountains of separation!" Again: "O fairest among the sons of men, why stayest Thou so long away? O heavens, move fast! O time, run, run, and hasten the marriage-day!" Once more: to Lady Kenmure his words are—" The Lord hath told you what you should be doing till He come. 'Wait and hasten,' saith Peter, 'for the coming of the Lord.' Sigh and long for the dawning of that morning, and the breaking of that day, of the coming of the Son of Man, when the shadows shall flee away. Wait with the wearied night-watch for the breaking of the eastern sky." These and kindred utterances, coloured with Scripture wording, seem to me born of personal longings to 'be with Christ, which is far better,' with an under-current of half-hope, half-expectation that the 'Second Coming' would take place in his day.

This being so, I would observe that though I differ fundamentally from millenarian interpretations of passages, I wish to protect myself from any suspicion of discrediting the "glorious appearing" as our "blessed hope," or saying anything that would interfere with an eager looking-forward to it. What I protest against is the vulgarization of the 'blessed hope,' the uncritical nonsense and fancies that ask our credence,—nay, our reverence. But these out-of-the-way, the 'Appearing' itself receives a prominence in the New Testament that we would do well to-day to note as Samuel Rutherford does in his Letters. Words of ineffable preciousness spring to one's memory on the instant—"This same Jesus shall so come"—"to all them that love His appearing"—"Ye turned to God from idols—to wait for His Son from heaven"—"Comfort yourselves with the words" of the Lord's 'descending' and 'judging.' Emphatically—to go back on the record—in the Lord's Supper we 'show His death TILL HE COME.' I do not quarrel with any for giving prominence to such texts. They had fallen too much out of sight, perhaps, when our modern millenarians recalled and vivified them; and therein they did noble service. The wretched thing has been the foolish fancies that have obtruded themselves as if part of Divine Revelation.

The self-evident expectation of the 'end of the world' in *his* time by Samuel Rutherford has been shared in every generation since, and is to-day held by many of the "excellent of the earth."* For myself I do not think that we have *data* that can enable us even to approximate the time of that 'end' and of the 'glorious appearing,' whether nearer or more remote. We have—so far as I know the New Testament— only the spiritual order or sequence of the event. It is 'written' as distinctly in the Second Epistle to the Thessalonians as anywhere. In the second chapter we find the 'mystery of lawlessness' working in St. Paul's day. It was then, however, held in check. The check is removed. Then comes the apostasy and the revelation of the man of sin, the son

---

* This was in the time of the Commonwealth. In the second edition of the *Westminster Confession* (1658) there is an address to the Christian Reader in the same strain. Dr. Thomas Manton, who signs it, says it was written by an eminent person, but does not tell his name. Could it have been Rutherford? or was it Baxter?

of perdition. The Lord puffs Him away (with the breath of His mouth) at His 'coming'— the 'coming' of the first chapter of 2nd Thessalonians and of the First Epistle. Such is the order—substantially—throughout the New Testament. But no one, I think, can get chronological *data* out of it. The death of the world is as certain as our individual death; but the time of it as uncertain to us as our individual death. Nevertheless it is 'certain' and 'appointed' to the Living Jesus upon the Throne. Therefore leaving the secret confidingly with Him, be it ours not to seek to be wise beyond what has been revealed. Be it ours to 'serve' as Samuel Rutherford served, and to long and aspire as he aspired. Let the second appearing of the Lord Jesus be an impulse and a motive to animate us to bring about the accomplishment of His great words of promise and prophecy—"The gospel of the kingdom shall be preached (= the herald-cry) in all the inhabited earth for a witness to all the nations; and *then shall the end come*" (St. Matt. xxiv. 14).

One other thing I cannot conscientiously overpass, on the same lines with preceding statements. At the close of his 'sketch' of Rutherford, Dr. Bonar writes:—" O for his insatiable desires Christward! O for ten such men in Scotland to stand in the gap!—men who all day long find nothing but Christ to rest in, whose very sleep is a pursuing after Christ in dreams, and who intensely desire to awake with His likeness." I run perhaps a risk of being misunderstood in what I am now going to say: I would not 'fault' one so reverenced and loved, of choice; but say it I must.

1. We have very many more than "ten such men" in Scotland in so far as Christian character and aspiration and genuine work are concerned.

2. Sleep is as divine a gift as Christ Himself. "He giveth His beloved sleep:" and to wish sleep to be visited by dreams, even such dreams, is mere sentimentalism.

3. To seek "ten such men" in Scotland, or anywhere, who "intensely desire to 'awake with His likeness,'" is virtually to ask the "ten such

men" to die, not live. Only through death and the resurrection do we 'awake with His likeness.'

III. THE WORK OF CHRIST IS PUT IN THE FOREGROUND.—It is not at all as an 'aside,' or by-the-bye, or in any way incidentally that these Letters set forth the redeeming love of God in Christ and the redeeming work of Christ in God. The writer's way to Jesus on the Throne is by the Cross. He is not 'ashamed' of it. The awful words 'Sin,' 'Guilt,' 'Condemnation,' 'Wrath,' and 'Wrath to come,' designate awful things. Hence to him the 'shed blood' is the most stupendous of realities, and 'received the atonement' the best of all 'good news.' He is not afraid to use deepest Pauline and Petrine sayings about Salvation being Redemption.

I like the Letters of Samuel Rutherford all the more for this. Here, by again quoting Dr. Bonar's words I am enabled to give my own estimate with more fulness and exactness. He says, then, as one of the elements of the Letters, that "all who delight in the Surety's imputed righteousness" will hold them as "precious"; and he thus enforces the observation:—" If thoroughly aware of the body of sin in ourselves, we cannot but feel that we need a *person* in our stead,—the person of the God-man in the room of our guilty person." " To us a Son is given;" not salvation only, but a Saviour. " He gave *Himself* for *us.*" These Letters are ever leading us to the Surety and His righteousness. The eye never gets time to rest long on anything apart from Him and His righteousness. We are shown the deluge-waters undried up, in order to lead us into the ark again : " I had fainted, had not want and penury chased me to the storehouse of all." *

I cannot help thinking that there is somewhat of confusion between Person and Thing here— as in much of our traditionary theological language about 'imputed righteousness;' and I regard it as a present-day duty, incumbent on us, to endeavour to clear away such con-

---

* As before, p. 27.

fusion. I used to hear, and I have not forgotten it, of Christ having "*made* propitiation." The Bible way of putting it is this—"Whom God hath set forth as a propitiation;" "He *is* the propitiation;" God "loved us and sent His Son *to be* the propitiation for our sins." So with Righteousness. Christ "doing and dying" *is* our Righteousness, the righteous reason of our acceptance, the ground of the justifying sentence. To see how this presentation of the case is given in the Bible itself, let us turn to passages like these:—Jeremiah xxiii. 6: "In His days Judah shall be saved and Israel shall dwell safely: and this is His name whereby He shall be called, THE LORD OUR RIGHTEOUSNESS"; Romans x. 4: "For Christ *is* the end of the Law for RIGHTEOUSNESS to every one that believeth"; 1 Corinthians i. 30: "Of Him are ye in Christ Jesus, Who of God is made unto us wisdom, and RIGHTEOUSNESS, and sanctification, and redemption."

Further: It must be borne in mind, that the phrase 'the righteousness of Christ,' 'unlike the righteousness of God,' is a purely theological-ecclesiastical one, and does not occur in the Bible. There is some appearance of ground for it in Romans v. 18: "by the righteousness of One;" but a glance into this passage, as distinct from a glance at it, reveals that the appearance is deceptive, and that the contrast is between "one offence" and "one [act of] righteousness." The word used is not δικαιοσύνη but δικαίωμα. When 'imputation' is connected with 'righteousness' in the Bible, it is 'Faith' that is imputed, reckoned, counted in—from Genesis xv. to Romans iv., the great 'imputation' chapter—that faith having no justifying merit in itself, but being the reception of Christ and all that is given in Him. I do not find Rutherford in his Letters getting into confusion here. I think it noticeable for to-day that (as a rule) his language was so Scriptural; and I should like us to abide by it. I confess that the way in which 'imputed righteousness' is at times preached of and written sounds sadly unreal and unrealizable to me; and I crave such preaching and writing as shall set forth that the 'Righteousness' which is the basis of the justifying sentence of God is, in Christ 'doing and dying,' no less a historical reality than sin.* Deeper still, I have a conviction that in their eagerness to bring the "good news" to men, and to give them 'peace,' the excellent men who so speak and sing, minimize the relation of the 'righteousness' to Law and to the God of the Law. The large statement, the rich unction of illustration, the vivid and memorable wording in these Letters wherever the work of Christ comes up, give to them, I conceive, price-

---

* For a very ingenious discussion on 'imputed righteousness,' I would refer to the second part of the Pilgrim's Progress," beginning where Great Heart takes charge of Christiana and the rest at the Interpreter's House : " But if He parts with His righteousness to us, what will He have for Himself?" and so onward, till we come to the paragraph beginning, "So then here is a righteousness that Christ, as *God*, hath no need of ; for He is God without it. Here is a righteousness that Christ, as *man*, hath no need of to make Him so ; for He is perfect man without it. Again, here is a righteousness that Christ, as *God-Man*, hath no need of," etc., etc.

less value. "*Let Him come down from the cross and we will* believe Him" was an old cry, and it reverberates to-day. But He came not down until the supreme work was achieved;—and though we rejoice that the Cross was exchanged for the Throne, none the less do we remember that no Cross and there had been no Throne as no 'free' all-gracious salvation. What I specially like in these Letters on the matter of the Work of Christ is the unreserve with which Rutherford proclaims and offers and urges that work on the acceptance of absolutely EVERY ONE. His stern logic and scholasticism, his ultra-Calvinistic readings (mis-readings) of texts, melt in the crucible of his devout affection; and no theory of Atonement or of Election or Predestination bars a universal and hopeful presentation of the Lord Jesus to all men and a demand of all men for Christ. The Letters contrast delightfully with his controversial books and their miserable limitations. I do not know that Samuel Rutherford would have dubbed me heretic had he read the title-page of my book:

"Jesus Mighty to Save: or Christ for All the World and All the World for Christ."

IV. PERSONAL HOLINESS IS STRENUOUSLY AIMED AT AND SPIRITUAL DECLENSION MOURNED.—These Letters never allow the Divine side of things to throw the human side into shadow. If the Christian has rights he has also duties; if he has privileges he has at the same time responsibilities. This is habitually recognized by Rutherford. Hence whilst he exults in his living friendship with his living Saviour, and breaks into singing as he expatiates on the Work wrought *for* him on the Cross, he never fails to test his 'faith' and 'hope' and 'peace' and 'joy' by what Christ is *in* him. Holiness is of value to him as he finds himself holy and holier. "Take Christ for sanctification as well as justification" is a frequent counsel in these Letters. Personally "we see in him a man who seems to have sought for *holiness* as unceasingly and as eagerly as other men seek for *pardon* and *peace*."* This sprang out of his close walk with

---

* Dr. Bonar, as before, p. 28.

his God. For as the old question puts it, "Can two walk together except they be agreed?" (Amos iii. 3). As he held high 'fellowship' with his ever-accessible Saviour, he yearned to grow 'like Him.' It was no mere text in the Bible, but a *bit* of his own actual experience, that we have "access by one Spirit to the Father through Him" (Ephesians ii. 18). It was his truest joy to be thus near his God and Father. Thus he writes: "I have been so near Him that I have said, 'I take instruments' [an old law-phrase and process] that 'this is the Lord.'" Nor was this mere enthusiasm, much less fanaticism. His 'aim' was to advance in holiness. "I dare avouch," he says, "the saints know not the length and largeness of the sweet earnest, and of the sweet green sheaves before the harvest, that might be had on this side of the water, *if we would take more pains.*" Remembering—as we are bound to do—how fierce and irascible and fluent of "bitter words" Rutherford was in controversy, I fear we must conclude that "Holiness to the Lord" was not inscribed on all the parts of his nature. It seems palpable that there remained a good deal of the 'old Adam' in him to the close: so that the Holiness he strove for must have been his ideal rather than attainment. I think I can recognize throbs of pain in his Letters as he urges others to a holiness that was not yet thoroughly his own possession. I wish that to-day all of us took more 'pains' to ante-date the holiness of heaven on earth, and to discharge our human part in forming our character.

These Letters equally abound in pathetic lamentations over his own spiritual declensions. With consummate shrewdness he wrote: "There is as much need to watch over grace as to watch over sin." He has piercing insight in laying bare the subtleties of sin,—its self-deceptions, its temptations, its sources, its drugging and dragging power. He shows like insight in warning against the peril of making a Saviour out of our own faith or peace or general grace, and so worshipping idols. Thus in his "Trial and Triumph of Faith" he remarks :—" As holy walking is a duty coming from us, it is no ground of true peace. Believers often seek in themselves what they should seek in Christ." Again, he writes:—"Your heart is not the compass that Christ saileth by." I should prize these Letters were it only for their lowliness, their self-abasement, the pathos of their confessions. I can strongly commend them to all who are desirous of help in self-examination. We, who are ministers of the Gospel, and others, need to realize that in having to preach and teach others so much we are in danger of neglecting ourselves. Self-scrutiny, if it be healthful and not morbid introspection, is a good thing.

As already indicated, Rutherford imagined the "end of the world" was near, because of the abounding wickedness around him. He is a very Jeremiah in 'weeping' over the corruption of public 'errors' (as he regarded them), and over the secret 'grey hairs' of spiritual decay. Thus he cries out, "There is universal deadness in all that fear God. O where are the sometime quickening breathings and influences from heaven that have refreshed His hidden ones?" And then he laments in the name of the saints: "We are half satisfied with our witheredness; nor have we as much of his shame who doth eight times breathe out that suit (Psalm cxix.), Quicken me!"—"We live far from the well, and complain but dryly of our dryness."

Dr. Bonar, in summing up his notice of this seeking of holiness by Rutherford, remarks:— "All this is from the pen of a man who was a metaphysician, a controversialist, a leader in the Church, and learned in ancient and scholastic lore. Why are there not such gracious, as well as great, men now?"[*] I must regard such unadvised words as these, as a mere repetition to-day of Elijah's despondent and utterly mistaken conception of his countrymen. I deny the premiss. I affirm that in respect of greatness of intellect, scholarship, leadership, grace,

---

[*] As before, p. 29.

there are fifty for one to-day true and living Christians in the front ranks of such capacity as is assigned—in part, mis-assigned—to Rutherford. It is well that we should have a keen apprehension of contemporary evils and shortcomings; but do not let us bear false witness to the grace of God, do not let 'brethren' turn 'accusers of the brethren,' or refuse to rejoice in the fact that never has there been a time when such myriad human hearts loved the Lord Jesus, and when all the signs of the times so magnificently betokened the ebb-tide of unbelief and the ever-advancing triumph—under the leadership of Jesus Christ—of truth and righteousness, and holiness and love. The self-conceited and bigoted scientists and dogmatists who would turn all into physiology, are a paltry minority. Hence, it is unhistorical, and uncritical, and ungrateful, to place either the piety and activities of individuals or churches in depreciatory contrast with the past. Two facts differentiate the present from the past immeasurably—the missionary spirit in action at home and abroad and the potential part now taken by the laity (so-called).

V. CONSOLATION TO THE AFFLICTED IS TENDER AND FULL.—No one who has been in sorrow of heart or spirit or conscience, will turn to these Letters in vain. It was as comforting him more especially that Richard Cecil said, " Rutherford's Letters is one of my classics." The secret of the comfort given is twofold: (1) That the writer fetches out of the treasury of the Bible " things new and old " with singular aptness. He had pre-eminently the " tongue " of the experimentally " learned, to speak a word in season to him that is weary." And " with what tender sympathy does he speak, leading the mourner so gently to the heart of Jesus!"* In his exile he was a man of one book ; and no consolation is equal to the tried words of the Bible. As an exile and " stranger " he knew the " heart of a stranger." " Let no man," he writes, " after me, slander Christ for His

---

* Dr. Bonar, as before, p. 29.

cross." Again, quaintly, "The lintel-stone and pillars of the New Jerusalem suffer more knocks of God's hammer and tools than the common side-wall stones." To Hugh McKail, uncle of the youthful martyr, he wrote: "Some have written me that I was possibly too joyful of the cross; but my joy overleapt the cross, it is bounded and terminated on Christ." This was the well of salvation out of which he drew 'living water' of consolation. (2) The writer dipped his pen—as Robert Nicoll, in our own day, said—in his own heart. He was a Son of Consolation because he was himself a Son of Affliction. Every Life and notice of him tells of the relentless persecution and privations that he endured. It is a blessing for a minister or any worker for Christ to know personally the sorrows of his people, so as not to speak or write from the outside.

One characteristic of the consolation of these Letters that deserves recognition and imitation is the healthiness of the comfort given. One meets with types of Christians who are always seeking—comfort; who for "Bread of Life" and "Water of Life" prefer 'honey, honey, honey.' This valetudinarian kind of Christianhood has tears right under the eyelash: a word, a touch, and they gush! Then they need—oh! ah!—they need 'comfort.' I have met with not a few of this sort. I could not conscientiously give in to them. I like rather to minister something drastic, to rouse them out of this spiritual coddling and self-indulgence. There are enough real, hard, lacerating sorrows in God's earth without artificial ones; and it is unmanly to acquiesce in such unrealities. Let us rather seek to put to shame, to energize, to summon forth to doing Christ-like work among sinners "for whom Christ died."

These Letters in so far as they bring comfort to the afflicted are genuine. Tempted, bereaved, backsliding, doubting, fearing men and women are written to while in the thick of the fight, or while bowed in wordless sorrow and lightless gloom.*

---

* As I read these proof sheets, a letter reaches me from

Looking now at the LETTERS more broadly, as really *the* life-work of SAMUEL RUTHERFORD, I think that the message they send across the two hundred years and upwards since they were first published is, that we shall do wisely TO REALIZE MORE THE GOOD THAT MAY BE DONE BY WELL-TIMED LETTER-WRITING. I have characterised and designated him by 'Devout

---

a 'brother beloved' in all the Churches. I cannot withhold one *bit*:—"I bear testimony to the preciousness of these Letters, from their tenderness of consolation. My copy is an old one, badly printed in Scotland, on what looks like fine grey flannel; but dim as it is, I hope that even in the valley of the shadow, I shall be able to read it. It has always been clearest and dearest to me when life has been lowest. A few Sundays ago I quoted Rutherford's saying, 'Lord, Thou seest a tired man coming up far behind Thee!' and although it was not my intention to apply it to myself, it really did express the very heart of me. Last Sunday, after my pulpit had been supplied for me in the morning, I was setting out to preach in the evening, when the doctor stopped me, saying that I should faint away if I made the attempt. Then Rutherford's words came home to me: 'Oh, what service can a silenced man do in Christ's house! I am a dry tree! Alas, I can neither plant nor water!' It is consoling to know how mistaken he was."

Affection.' I have done so because it was the 'burning heart' that he put into the Letters that is their glory. He thought no more about "picked and packed words" than a Quaker would have done. He only poured out his flowing heart as Richard Crashaw his poems. I know not anywhere to look for such cordial writing. Yet it is not mere heartiness that we feel, but the writing of one "whose heart beats toward the Lord." So I think, if, like David, he displeased God in some things belonging to his controversies, like him he was "a man after God's own heart." The elements of the Letters which I have named and illustrated, all go to demonstrate that with every abatement, he was a man who found his intensest and supremest delight in friendship with Christ. He was thus full of thoughts of Christ. He was equally full of 'blessings' from Christ. The Book sent him to Christ: Christ sent him to The Book. Its words were connected, like weft and woof, with his being. His spiritual gladness and sadness, his trials and raptures, his moans and aspirations, his failures and overcomings, his songs and his prayers, were of the substance of his life. His circumstances were an incentive to thoughts of others and feeling with others. In remote Anwoth he could only communicate occasionally with the "brethren." In exile at Aberdeen, he was cut off from all old associates and associations. It thus came about that letter-writing was laid to his hand. And thus we inevitably connect the message with the channel through which it comes, viz., that of Letters, written on the spur of occasion and opportunity.

One reads to-day the Letters of Pliny and Cicero, of Chesterfield and Chatham (to Lord Camelford), of William Cowper and Robert Southey and McCheyne and Thomas Erskine and McLeod Campbell, and recently-departed saintly Mrs. H. W. Taylor, with undying interest and gratitude. Deeper still, a third of the New Testament consists of Letters. It cannot be then that I shall be thought to exaggerate the message of Samuel Rutherford when I pronounce it a summons to us to-day to "go and do likewise."

In these days of post-cards and dainty note-paper and swift communication, the art of letter-writing seems in danger of lapsing. I have a growing conviction that that were a loss. I believe that if Ministers of the Gospel and their fellow-workers were to be more vigilant in outlook for opportunities, they would find themselves richly rewarded by embracing them. The sick-chamber and the death-chamber and the "house of mourning" admit of comparatively few words, and more particularly when the shadow lies broad and black over hearts and hearths, the best-intentioned words sound hollow and as platitudes. But if after recovery from illness, or after a death, or some family-incident that holds in it the future of the family (so-to-say) we write a well-thought-out letter, and Hezekiah-like "spread it before the Lord," *scripta manet;* and long years afterwards the yellowed page may excite renewed gratitude, and perchance stir to new activity. It often happens that we can put into a letter what we cannot *say*. In writing too you are better able to choose your words, and to employ those that will touch and persuade. Even should little good come from a letter at the time, it may come later. Need I state, that in writing such letter as I think of, a man should put himself—his very best self—into it? One's gorge rises at the imposition of a preachment or a string of cant phrases disguised as a letter. These Letters of Rutherford are delightful, vital reading to-day just because they were true from a true man.

I have uttermost faith in individualizing in congregation and Sunday-school; and as a co-relate, in addressing ourselves to the individual. "A word spoken in season, how good it is." More permanently good, more likely to be remembered, more likely to be fecund, is the WRITTEN WORD of DEVOUT AFFECTION.

It is manifest that Samuel Rutherford had an intense love for his people, a passionate yearning for their conversion and growth in grace. He self-evidently went out and in among them as a shepherd among his flock. Whether with gentle or simple, lord and lady or herd-lad or servant-girl, he had a quick eye and as quick an ear for the specialties of their needs spiritually and temporally; and so off went the letter that was to reveal thought and sympathy and interest, or give wise counsel, warning or incitement. How like a thunderbolt must this have fallen. "I would lay my dearest joys in the gap between you and eternal destruction." How wistful and persuasive this:—"My witness is in heaven, your heaven would be two heavens to me, and your salvation two salvations." The herd-boys were not beneath his special attention. He writes of them when at Aberdeen, and exclaims:—"Oh if I might but speak to thee, or your herd-boys, of my worthy Master." He had a heart for the young of all classes, so that he would say of two children of one of his friends, "I pray for them by name," and he could thus take time to notice one: 'Your daughter desires a Bible and a gown. I hope she shall use the Bible well, which, if she do, the gown is the better bestowed." He lamented over the few that cry " Hosannah "—felicitously sending them to their New Testament to read of the children's hosannas. He dealt—as I have noted—with individual parishioners so closely and so personally as to be able to appeal to them regarding his faithfulness in this matter. He addresses one of them, Jean McMillan: " I did what I could to put you within grips of Christ; I told you Christ's testament and latter-will plainly." He so carried them on his heart ("like the priest with the twelve jewels on his breast-plate," finely says Dr. Bonar) that he could declare to Gordon of Cardoness, "Thoughts of your soul depart not from me in my sleep "—" My soul was taken up when others were sleeping, how to have Christ betrothed with a bride in that part of the land," viz. Anwoth. He so prayed over them and for them, that he fears not to say, " There I wrestled with the angel and prevailed. Woods, trees, meadows and hills are my witnesses that I drew on a fair match between Christ and Anwoth." I greatly covet for us to-day something of this intensity of devout affection and swift readiness to write a letter when occasion is given or can be made. In the pulpit and Sunday-school desk we are far off from the people; I fear by the extent of our individual congregations, we are left in sad unacquaintance with the inner history of our flocks. I am satisfied that far beyond what is called visitation is the well-timed affectionate and faithful letter. For his Letters pre-eminently, Samuel Rutherford is to be held in grateful memory. I know not that the Latin lines prefixed to the early editions exaggerate when they say of them and him :—

"Quod Chebar et Patmos divinis vatibus olim;
Huic fuerant sancto claustra Abredæa viro."

Does anyone say I have no time for letter-writing? My answer and expostulation would be—'Make time, take time.' Rutherford, Baxter, and others, were busy men, but they could find time for letter-writing. Have faith in an over-watching living Head of the Church Who knows and values every spoken and written word for Him. Be swift and eager to 'write.' Be sympathetic and devout in writing!

I only add that as literature we cannot make a high claim for these Letters. There was no thought of authorship in any case. They are the heart-warm gushings of a fervid and intense nature. They are the Writer's affections rather than his thoughts made articulate. And yet there is an informing soul of poetic imagination in many of them, saintly raptures over the loveliness of Christ, and yearning pictures anticipative of heaven, that bear the stamp of genius. Side by side with George Gillespie, and Henderson, and Blair, and David Dickson, I place Samuel Rutherford in his own honoured niche in the Temple.

I would close my words on the Letters of Samuel Rutherford, and their loving message for to-day, with quaint and wise, wise and quaint words of T. H. WHITE in "A Pilgrim's Reliquary" on Letters, as thus :—

"I have heard and experienced much of the wonderful power of the Drama, of the Epic, of the Ballad, and of the Romance, in startling the passions and awakening the sympathies of human nature; but I know not the Tragedy, however powerful, or the Novel or the Poem, however pathetic, that possesses the spell of that little sheet, with its waxen lock, called a Letter.

"There is a noble passage in Shirley's 'Cardinal,' where the Duchess Rosaura is opening a letter in the presence of an attendant,—whose painful truth too many of us can testify.

> "'*Duchess.*—Wait at some more distance,
> My soul doth bathe itself in a cold dew;
> Imagine I am opening of a Tomb;   [*opens the letter*
> Thus I throw off the Marble, to discover
> What antic posture Death presents in this,
> Pale Monument to frighten me—Ha!   [*reads.*
> My heart, that call'd my blood and spirits to
> Defend it from the invasion of my Fears,
> Must keep a guard about it still, lest this
> Strange and too mighty joy crush it to nothing!'

"No gem is there, however precious, privy to such passions, such reverses, such mysteries as the Seal. Not the Cabalistic jewels of King Solomon boasted more dark sayings than the various sigillary impresses, that, with their mystic motto and device, form at once the clasp and frontispiece to this volume of a single sheet.

"What joys and loves—what upbraidings and endearments—do we find at once poured forth by the permission of this painted portcullis. The virgin's secret sigh—the anguish of the neglected wife—the child's affection, the mother's care—the dependent's just remonstrance—the patron's protracted evasions—the guilty flame of the seducer—the calculating greediness of the usurer—the glad summons to hospitality—the harsh menaces of a gaol. The advice of those we love, given but to be slighted—the anger of those we fear, inflicted to be defied—the betrayal of secrets—the detection of crimes —the warning, the disgust, and the final abandonment —the tidings of death, or (worse!) of sins that are the *sting of death*,—are among the million stirring topics of a letter! And the productions of the sublimest or most pathetic genius that ever wasted the midnight lamp in devising incidents of pity, of horror, or of marvel, are outdone by these unpremeditated effusions. While their prodigies task the toil of months or years, these spring forth, the spontaneous produce of every day, nay, every hour,—but, breathing ages of anguish in a sentence, and committing grief and ruin, the very thunderbolts of the soul, to the governance of that pretty, smooth, innocent-looking piece of Wax! Fair Bee! that singest in thy three-piled livery of black and tawny velvet, thou lover of the longest hour, thou artizan of the garden!— who does not rejoice that, in spite of dear Imogen's blessing upon thy toils, thou art not the manufacturer of a material which imprisons the earthquake, and lets loose the whirlwind! Who does not felicitate thy delicious labour—pursued in the straw hive under its yew hedge, with thyme and lavender and marigold beneath, by the calm cottage at the forest side—that it has never been made the warder of tidings that plunge the Palace in dismay, and fill the prison with unheard groans."*

---

* Pp. 217-19 : 1 vol., 1845 (Pickering).

Be it ours, then, to emulate the DEVOUT AFFECTION of Samuel Rutherford, as specifically manifested in his writing of LETTERS as opportunity offered or was made. Let us realize more and more the power of this instrumentality, and so " Strive, Wait and Pray:"—

> "STRIVE; yet I do not promise
>   The prize you dream of to-day
> Will not fade when you think to grasp it,
>   And melt in your hand away;
> But another and holier treasure,
>   You would now perchance disdain,
> Will come when your toil is over,
>   And pay you for all your pain.
>
> "WAIT; yet I do not tell you
>   The hour you long for now
> Will not come with its radiance vanished,
>   And a shadow upon its brow;
> Yet far through the misty future,
>   With a crown of starry light,
> An hour of joy you know not
>   Is winging her silent flight.
>
> "PRAY; though the gift you ask for
>   May never comfort your fears,
> May never repay your pleading,
>   Yet pray, and with hopeful tears;

An answer, not that you long for,
   But diviner, will come one day ;
Your eyes are too dim to see it,
   Yet strive, and wait, and pray." *

---

* The Poems of Adelaide A. Procter, pp. 72-3. Boston: 1864.

MATTHEW HENRY:
Sanctified Common-Sense

E'en as the bee has honey and a sting,
  So has each moment ; take thou then good heed
  To lay that up against thine hour of need,
And to avoid the other : if a thing
Tempt thee, first ask thyself if it will bring
  Pleasure but in the Present. Joy indeed
  When worthy of the name, doth ever breed
After its kind : the one, still ministering
  Unto the other; and the more they be
  Divine, the richer is their progeny ;
But earthly joys are barren, and they die
Homeless ; for if they at all could be
  Renewed, then Virtue were a mockery,
Whose essence is more pure, the more from these set free."

        HENRY ELLISON, *Mad Moments* (vol. i., pp. 65-6).

MATTHEW HENRY:

SANCTIFIED COMMON-SENSE.

Born October 18th, 1662: Died June 22nd, 1714.

THERE are few more beautiful and, towards the close, more pathetic stories, than the Life of Philip Henry,—as imperishably told by his son. Born in the palace of Whitehall—son of a page to James, Duke of York—he grew up a 'gentleman' of Nature's own fashioning. Well-educated, cultured, refined, quaint of speech, bookish, pronouncedly a Christian, he stands out a very distinct figure among the Worthies of England. When the Act of Uniformity and 'Black' Bartholomew-day of 1662 came, he was loyal to his conscience and his conscience's Lord. He was of the 'Two Thousand Ejected Ministers'—name of honour far beyond the cynical 'Socius Ejectus' that Thomas Baker wrote in his books (and that book-lovers so prize). Ripened and mellowed through suffering and anxiety, though lifted above the poverty that the 'Act' was timed inexorably to effect, he at last died in a good old age, leaving behind him a saintly memory, whose fragrance is not likely to expire, while the greatness of goodness is valued.

Philip Henry—who married 'Miss Mathews, a lady of fortune,' of Broad Oak, Flintshire—was father of Matthew Henry. Matthew was born at Broad Oak on October 18th, 1662; and thus his cradle was rocked in the shadow of the 'Ejection.' He was—in the fine old phrase —'a child of many prayers.' For father and mother alike were devout and 'believing.' One inevitably thinks of the paternal 'Ejection' from his church (of Worthenbury, Flintshire) in association with the 'flight' of mother and 'Holy Child' from Bethlehem. Persecution and opposition and silencing were stern realities under the 'Act of Uniformity;' and the infancy and childhood of little Matthew were baptized with tears and overshadowed by troubles. Half-consciously and half-unconsciously, the experiences of these years of sorrow and trial went into the very substance of the after-Commentator's life. He rejoiced indeed to avouch that his father's 'pithy sayings,' worked into his Commentary, were the best things in it. The times forbade a collegiate or academical training. But in Philip Henry, the youthful Matthew had a teacher who from Westminster to Christ Church, Oxford, was a scholar "ripe and good." If his discipline were perchance rigid, it was admirably formative. The home-school, I feel assured, gave a fuller and richer and more exact education than could elsewhere have been found. The atmosphere the lad breathed was as of heaven on earth. He had nothing but sunniest memories of all. Kindred with his paternal training was his further education under Thomas Doolittle, of Islington. He too was a 'man of God,' and in many ways far ahead of his age. Altogether, thoroughly grounded 'in the tongues' and other branches of a 'polite education,' Matthew Henry, though necessarily outside of the Universities, could have held his own with any within them. Latin, Greek, Hebrew, and living languages, were as familiar to him as his own. The observant reader of the 'Commentary' is at no loss to discover many modest insignia of this. In 1685, that is, in his twenty-fourth year, he entered Gray's Inn, as a student of Law. Circumstances were then unfavourable to his 'bent' to the ministry of the Gospel; and so Law was taken as a temporary refuge. Theology rather than Law, nevertheless, occupied his attention at Gray's Inn. So soon as 1686 he was back at Broad Oak with his parents; and invited to it by the excellent Mr. Illidge, of Nantwich, he began to preach in the neighbourhood. Report of his 'savoury' discourses went far and near. He was invited to preach at Chester in the private residence of a Mr. Henderson,—a sugar-baker,—to a small audience. This formed the nucleus of his subsequently great congregation in Chester. In 1687 James II. granted 'licence to Dissenters to preach,' as everybody knows, and knows why. Matthew Henry accepted a call to a 'dissenting congregation' (Presbyterian) in Chester. There he remained fully twenty-five years. His ministry in Chester was a remarkable one. For many-sidedness and fervour of activity and consecration of purpose, it might be compared with an Apostle's. His pulpit was as a throne. From thence he went through the entire Bible—Old and New Testament alternating each Sunday—more than once "in expository lectures." In 1712 he was transferred from Chester to Hackney, London. There he went along very much the same lines as in Chester. At the commencement of his ministry in London he re-began with the first chapter of Genesis in the forenoon, and the first chapter of St. Matthew in the afternoon. Thus gradually and steadily materials accumulated for his 'Commentary.'* He 'fed' his own flocks "out of the Scriptures"—as well as his own soul—he ministered to human actual interests, and with wistful fervour and prayerfulness 'watched' for results. Thus his 'Commentary' was the outcome not of mere learning or reading, or studious thought, but in combination therewith of living experience of the 'preached gospel' among the souls committed to his keeping under the Chief Shepherd.

It was his custom to pay an annual visit to Chester. In 1714 he set out on this journey May 31st. It was a delightful season. On his return he was taken ill at Nantwich, and the illness deepened into paralysis. His death-bed was tranquil as a little child's. Speaking to Mr. Illidge he said:—"You have been used to take notice of the sayings of dying men; this is mine: that a life spent in

---

* *Sic* in all the Memoirs; but as the first volume of the Commentary is dated Chester 1706, it is scarcely likely that he re-delivered its contents.

the service of God, and communion with Him, is the most pleasant life that any one can live in this world." His Diary shows that this was no death-bed saying. He died June 22nd, 1714, in his fifty-seventh year. He was buried in the graveyard of his former chapel at Chester. Within recent years Churchmen and Nonconformists equally—as with Baxter at Kidderminster and Bunyan at Bedford—united to do him honour, by the erection of a life-like statue, which to-day is one of the sights of Chester.

These main points in the Life of Matthew Henry—who is our fourth and last REPRESENTATIVE NONCONFORMIST in these Lectures —I have deemed it expedient to furnish, inasmuch as of none of the others is it so needful to know the facts of the LIFE in order rightly to estimate the LIFE-WORK.

The outstanding achievement of MATTHEW HENRY is HIS 'COMMENTARY' ON THE BIBLE. Whatever of message for us to-day that there is from him, must be sought for there. His minor writings are priceless, especially his Life of his Father and his "Walking with God" and his instructions on the "Lord's Supper." They are circulated still far and wide among all the English-speaking races. They are pre-eminently instructive and nurturing books. But on the 'Commentary' supremely, rests his unique and enviable fame.

Regarding the 'Commentary' broadly, there is one undoubted matter-of-fact that, in the outset, arrests attention. No single Commentary on the entire Bible has had a tithe of its circulation among all ranks and classes and orders of men. Rare JOHN TRAPP'S 'Commentary,' and co-equally rare though after another kind,—JOHN MAYER'S 'Commentary' on the Bible, spite of their wise wit and witty wisdom and fecundity of classical and patristic lore, never have had readers outside of scholars. The recent revival of TRAPP has enriched ministers of the Gospel and others selectly; but he remains and must remain *caviare* to the multitude. GILL has a very slender following—beyond his own denomination. Coming down to our own times, the 'Commentaries' of DR. CLARKE and DR. THOMAS SCOTT have found unquestionably many purchasers. But if I may venture to state my own opinion, a twofold sectarianism is at the bottom of the welcome to both. On the one hand the undigested and indigestible learning of Clarke is the boast and wonder of his own particular denomination; on the other the orthodoxy of Scott was welcome to the Evangelicals of the Established Church as releasing them from dependence on a Nonconformist like Henry for their 'evangelical' Commentary. Beyond these two sections, the circulation of Clarke and Scott has been extremely limited. I do not see that other than this was to be expected. Clarke is dreary reading; Scott is heavy, and dry as "remainder biscuit" of a long voyage. In contrast with either, the Commentary of Matthew Henry has passed into all Churches; and to-day is more extensively bought than any other. It never has been once 'out of print.' Its various editions

—since copyright expired—have been successive advances in beauty and value.*

I think this fact of A LIVING SALE THAT IS TO BE RECKONED BY TENS OF THOUSANDS in our country and colonies and the United States of America, is worth noting and pondering. For the incentive of personal attachment and reverence of his contemporaries; the heir-loom inheritance of the stately original folios; and the cleaving to the 'evangelical' teaching of the Commentary amid abounding 'falling away,' have long since ceased to be operative in winning readers. To-day on the testimony of publishers and booksellers of widest information, the Commentary of Matthew Henry is more largely sold than any other extant. That so large and comparatively costly a set of books should thus have held their own across the eighteenth century

---

* CASSELL'S in 3 large vols. 4to, and NISBET'S in 7 large vols. 8vo., are both excellent current editions. So too Bohn's in 6 large vols. In the United States and Canada, at least three stereotyped editions are being largely circulated; also in Australia.

and far forward into the nineteenth century, is to me most noticeable, and I will add most gladdening. It seems to me to be declarative of a fact that we are apt to let slip, viz., That our world after all has in it infinitely more of good men and women than some good (or goody) men and women are disposed to allow, else there should not be this commanding constituency of readers of a Commentary whose one absolute characteristic is its speaking to the spiritual life. I never have thought otherwise than that each successive generation is an advance upon the preceding. As I believe in a Living Head of the Church Universal, God in Christ "over all, blessed for evermore," and as I believe that in the Bible God has spoken and revealed Himself to man; or He never has spoken at all, and is dumb, deaf, blind, if not dead,—I equally believe that He is working out His everlasting purpose, coming into vitalizing contact with human souls, and continuously sending home the grand proclamation: "This is life eternal, that they might know Thee the only true God, and Jesus Christ Whom Thou hast sent" (St. John xvii. 3). I accept the immense sales of Matthew Henry's Commentary, as a testimony to a wide, deep, strong allegiance to the very truth of God.

This leads me to accentuate a second thing about the Commentary of Matthew Henry, that it is of the last moment to realize. This still-living circulation of the Commentary is RELIGIOUS, NOT LITERARY—IS FOR ACTUAL HUMAN NEED, NOT MERE BOOK-BUYING. Thus was it in the beginning. Thus has it continued. Thus is it to-day. As literature, the Commentary has its own high and special merits—of which more in the sequel; but it is as out-and-out a Commentary that magnifies the simple Gospel, that it has found and finds readers. Take its riches of spiritual insight and in-look and up-look away; empty it of its vivid and wistful personal appeals to come to the Lord Jesus Christ; leave out its searching and urgent summonses to penitence and confession over inadequate Christian living; evaporate its all-pervading aroma of devoutness, and yearning, and aspiration; eliminate its assertions of human indebtedness to the grace of God, and the God of grace for everything,—and you have indeed still pithy and quaint saying, apt and well-told anecdote, memorable aphorism and pleasant wit, but the beating heart of the grand old book is cloven. It has been a magnificent work, therefore, that this Commentary of Matthew Henry has been doing from generation to generation. It has been the very nurture and strength and delight of the "inner life" of myriads on myriads of the best in all the Churches. I speak from grateful personal recollection of what Matthew Henry was to myself as a child, and what it was to venerable and venerated ones who were all that mother and grandmother were to Timothy. I catch a vision to-day especially of a grandmother, whose life to a long and late and beautiful old age was as of a saint already out of this 'body of sin and death'; and it goes to my heart to recall how with alternate praise and prayer the chapter in the Old Testament and the chapter in the New Testament were daily read. The wise, 'sappy,' heart-touching words went down and in, and were as oil to the flame of daily devotion and daily growth in the 'divine life.' My experience and observation as a minister for fully seven years in a typical country parish of Scotland, gave me ratification and glad demonstration of the unspent force of Matthew Henry. I know I am within the mark rather than without, when I name one hundred copies of the Commentary as possessed by the godly in the small county of Kinross. In lowly homes, in back-lanes, in hard-driven households, and up among the Galilee-like "hill country" in scattered farmsteads, and shepherd's hut, and solitary cottage along sweet Lochleven, it was my joy to come on copies of Matthew Henry that were the daily helpers of their owners. I remember—and since he is dead, and gone (I believe) to glory for years, I may mention it—one godly farm-servant. He was a humble peasant. His work was toil. His wages low. The 'mouths to feed' many. And yet I never once met that man or his true 'help-meet' wife, that there was not a beaming look, and absolute contentment and hopefulness. His knowledge of Scripture was simply wonderful. It was a spiritual treat to mark how Bible words and ways of putting things were natural—indeed, inevitable with him. His spiritual penetrativeness, whereby the obscurest text was illumined, I was often humbled by. Talking with him one day, I discovered that Matthew Henry—inherited from a grandfather—was the feeder of his soul in association with 'The Word' itself. No day ever passed that he did not read in the Commentary. "I would not give one chapter of comment of Matthew for all the new books put together," was his fervid saying as he finished, if I err not, his tenth reading through and through of the Bible and the Commentary. I could similarly tell of many others; and I suppose—indeed I know—that my brethren could give the same testimony. Multiply all this by the aggregate of readers since the Commentary was first published—vol. i., preface,

Chester, October 2nd, 1706—and on to 1712—and by the aggregate of copies now in living use, and you have a spiritual force whose influence human arithmetic cannot estimate. Looking back in the eighteenth century, I hesitate not to avouch that the great Revival under the WESLEYS and GEORGE WHITEFIELD had been prepared for by the hidden "spiritual life" that had been nourished on Matthew Henry's Commentary. Looking back on the relapse of our own ancestral churches in England, I am of opinion that the lamp was kept alive very much from the copies of Matthew Henry's Commentary that were held by Presbyterian families, and which were carried with them into the evangelical Independent and Baptist and Wesleyan congregations of their choice when the mildew of Socinianism fell on their own Church. The Day only will declare how much the Commentary of Matthew Henry contributed to preserve faith in the old Gospel; how many hearts it drew to the foot of the Cross; how many lives it went to transfigure from bare morality into celestial grace. I speak from knowledge when I affirm that within and without the National Church, the Commentary of Henry was *the* Commentary whence the clergy and old preachers who walked in the "old paths" fetched at once their sermons and their own spiritual strength. Practically there was no other to be named beside it for a moment. But the force is to be emphasized especially in relation to the vast mass of the commonalty. This Commentary went to the roots of the people's every-day life. This Commentary was the interpreter to them of the Bible. This Commentary was the opener of eyes to see and of hearts to receive and of consciences to obey "the truth." This Commentary was thus a factor inestimable in its informing, transforming, upbuilding power in sustaining evangelical doctrine. I cannot conceive anyone gainsaying this. Nor can I suppose that I shall be thought guilty of exaggeration when I pronounce the Commentary of Matthew Henry as the most outstanding conservative spiritual force of the eighteenth century. It touched the spiritual life of England at innumerable points. It went like nurturing dew and rain into "waste places." It was as the "springs among the hills." It drew those who loved the Lord together. It brought down—I do not doubt—abundant answers to prayer and multiplied blessing.

Another element that is noticeable in this blessed heaven-like working of Matthew Henry's Commentary onward until now, demands statement. This Commentary is FINELY CATHOLIC. The word—like Charity and others—has deteriorated and been usurped by that Church which is flagrantly uncatholic; but it is the one word that I can think of whereby to designate the unsectarianism of the Commentary from beginning to close. You have no arid sect-exalting controversies. You have no wild-fires of bigotry. You have no narrownesses of church-order or church-creed. You have no taking of a man by the throat because he cannot pronounce your shibboleth. By heritage and training and deliberate choice Matthew Henry was a

Presbyterian. As such the "Westminster Confession of Faith," and the "Larger and Shorter Catechisms," were venerated symbol-books of his own faith. But Episcopalian and Baptist and Independent could and did and do turn to the Commentary with no risk of offence by gibes or jeers at their peculiarities or specialities of belief and practice. With all this there is no false liberality, no dealing in compromises, no discipleship to Mr. Facing-both-ways. I must regard this Catholicity and (in a good sense) breadth, as of no common notableness and of no common value. The Commentary is expository of the Bible as from chapter to chapter, and from verse to verse it is 'commented.' What "is written" is set forth and applied and urged. The result is that it is found that in ninety-nine cases out of a hundred, the things about which fellow-Christians differ are as nothing to the fundamentals, wherein they agree. More than this—it is found that the one out of a hundred in which they do differ is all too often HUMAN INFERENCE FROM BIBLICAL STATE-

MENT RATHER THAN BIBLICAL STATEMENT. It was a beatitude to our country, therefore, that the Commentary of Matthew Henry obtained such a welcome in all the Churches, and that it continues to hold its first place. It was a grand thing that such spiritual richly evangelical teaching, was going like a living current through all the Churches, and about the roots of so many lives. It was pre-eminently well-ordered that the Commentary that was thus potential and that to-day is so potential, was so lifted above the sectarianism of any one part of the Church, so untouched of rancour, so large and true and Christ-like in its charity. DR. DUNCAN thus speaks of our Worthy:—" Matthew Henry is not deep, but broad. He had not a deep insight, but his was an exceeding broad religion, because he cast himself with equal reverence *on the whole of the Bible*, and had no favourite texts."

A sentence before I pass on to details. I am very well aware that some will put me down as old-fashioned, as of the 'old school,' because

I thus claim so determinate a place and power for the Commentary of Matthew Henry. I do not reckon very much the supercilious sneer of scholars and preachers and students of a certain *grade*, who think it the right thing to hold cheap any expounder of the Bible who does not make a *parade* of learning. I have not one word to utter against learning. As already stated and re-stated, I am proud that our Church—in Scotland and England alike—has held a high standard of scholarship and culture for her ministers and students. I would increase rather than decrease the culture now exacted. But I dare not forget that the Bible is a book not for scholars but for universal man. Consequently I am satisfied that to-day that minister of the Gospel and student will best equip himself for "feeding the flock of God" who seeks to place alongside human lives the spiritual truths and facts of Bible experiences. Toward this he is a fool—it may be like a certain king, "a learned fool"—who imagines that he can afford to despise such practical humanities of teaching as Henry's Commentary so unfailingly furnishes. This brings me to that central controlling characteristic of Matthew Henry after which we have designated him—SANCTIFIED COMMON-SENSE.

The most uncommon thing I meet with is just this that we vaingloriously call 'common-sense.' The scarcest article I find in pulpit and pew is this 'common-sense.' The want of the times is more of it. What with sensationalism and picturesque sentimentalism and quasi-philosophical speculation on the unrevealed and the indeterminable on this hither side, and supra-subtle judgment on what is and what is not authentic and authoritative in the text of Holy Scripture, I am forced to think of many as living in balloons. I long for descent to mother-earth and nearness to the actualities of human interests and human needs. I estimate superlatively GOOD PLAIN COMMON-SENSE CLEAR OF THE ACCRETIONS ALIKE OF TRADITIONARY AND SECTARIAN OPPOSITIONS.

This I regard as a supreme characteristic of

Matthew Henry's Commentary. By the make and order of his intellect, by the entire discipline of his training, by temperament and specific sagacities, Matthew Henry was impatient of the merely speculative, had no sympathy with so-called spiritual allegorizing, swept aside beclouding mists of super-imposed learning, and went straight to the heart of the words before him. Spiritually he is hundred-eyed. He is piercing and he is perspective. He sees the innermost truth, and he sees all round to its widest circumference. John Foster, in one of his Essays, has pregnantly said of him :—

"Although Matthew Henry furnishes much less to afford gratification in a literary point of view, than do the works of many who are justly designated 'fine writers,' he possesses a vigour which, without the least endeavour to attract, awakens and sustains the attention in an uncommon degree. In a single sentence he often pours upon Scripture a flood of light; and the palpableness he gives to the wonders contained in God's law occasions excitement not unlike that which is produced by looking through a microscope. The feelings, too, which his subject had called forth in himself, he communicates admirably to others. In his whole manner—the same at nine years old as at fifty—there is a freshness and vivacity which instantly put the spirits into free and agile motion—an effect somewhat similar to that play of intellectual forgetfulness which some minds (obviously the greatest only) have the indescribable faculty of creating. But the crowning excellency remains; nothing is introduced in the shape of counteraction. There are no speeches which make his sincerity questionable; no absurdities to force suspicion as to accuracy in theological knowledge, or inattention to the analogy of faith; no staggering and untoward and unmanageable inconsistencies; nothing by which 'the most sacred cause can be injured,' or the highest interests of men placed in jeopardy; or which can render it imperative, exactly in proportion as the understanding is influenced, to repress or extinguish the sentiments, in order to listen with complacency to the Lord Jesus and His apostles."

All this results from his fine sanity and all-pervading common-sense. I dare to affirm that an ounce of it will go further than all acquired aids, in practically dealing with the Bible and men's souls. But it must be '*sanctified*' common-sense. There lies a profound distinction. 'Common-sense' *per se* is not enough, nor is 'sanctity' *per se* enough. The two must be combined. The two were combined in Matthew

Henry. By his 'common-sense' he fell in with the tendency of things in the eighteenth century, while in its being 'sanctified' common-sense, he retained the virtue of Puritanism in the seventeenth for the eighteenth century.*

Thus far I have been speaking of Matthew Henry. It will now be well to let him speak

---

* As stated in the beginning, Matthew Henry was a child of many prayers. The influence of his father was lifelong. I can well understand that Philip Henry's own Baptismal Covenant,—signed October 20th, 1686, when Matthew was in his twenty-fourth year,—was adopted by his son. It is a model for succinctness and comprehensiveness. It may well find a place here :—

"I take God the Father to be my chiefest good, and highest end.

" I take God the Son to be my Prince and Saviour.

" I take God the Holy Ghost to be my Sanctifier, Teacher, Guide, and Comforter.

" I take the word of God to be my rule in all my actions.

" And the people of God to be my people in all conditions.

" I do likewise devote and dedicate unto the LORD my whole self ; all I am, all I have, and all I can do.

" And this I do deliberately, sincerely, freely, and for ever."

for himself. At first he seems like a homely old father talking over the Bible at family prayer, and your spirit is very quiet with the home-feeling. Presently you fancy a twinkle of kind, sly humour, or you are charmed with some quaint, lively grace of expression, or struck with tense, tight words, and startled as he puts a sudden sharp light into a practical text, making a lamp of it to show the road. Dr. Doddridge says to students, " Perhaps Matthew Henry is the only commentator so large who deserves to be entirely and attentively read through." I say 'yes' to this. Still, remarkable things should be marked. And this is my purpose in the sequel, albeit Matthew Henry is no aimer at saying brilliant things, and no mere proverbialist. As Dr. Duncan observed—as we saw—he loved and revered the whole Bible in all its breadth as well as depth. Sometimes he is poetic, or at any rate dramatic—as on the story of the Prodigal Son. Sometimes there is a gleam and sparkle of grave wit. Sometimes you have a saying Baconian in its concinnity.

Well! turning to such characteristics as I have selected, I would first of all give proof of that SANCTIFIED COMMON-SENSE that he brought to his reading of the Bible, and so has put into his immortal Commentary. I must necessarily limit myself in illustrating this and other characteristics. I cherish a hope that the very imperfectness of representative quotations will send the reader to the complete Commentary for himself. If in any single case I decide a brother-minister or fellow-student to return on it may be his long-neglected Matthew Henry, I shall be rewarded. I may state that a goodly number of my brethren who had thus allowed Matthew Henry to be overlaid by more recent commentaries, have thanked and re-thanked me for stirring their first love for him.

I go at once to Genesis ii. 15, and I read with reference to our First Parents' appointment to "dress and to keep" the garden of Eden this:—" Secular employments will very well consist with a state of innocency, and a life of communion with God. The sons and heirs of heaven, while they are here in this world, have something to do about this earth which must have its share of their time and thoughts; and if they do it with an eye to God, they are as truly serving Him in it as when they are upon their knees." So in Genesis xxx. 25-36:—"Faith and charity, though they are excellent things, must not take us off from making necessary provisions for our own support and the support of our families. We must, like Jacob, 'trust in the Lord, and do good;' and yet we must, like him, 'provide for our own homes' also: he that doth not so is 'worse than an infidel'" (1 Timothy v. 8).

Further: on Exodus iv. 18-23:—"Note—The honour of being admitted into communion with God and employed for Him, doth not discharge us from the duties of our relations and callings in this world. Moses said nothing to his father-in-law (for aught appears) of the glorious appearance of God to him: such favours we are to be thankful for to God, but not to boast of before men." Be it noted how the robust common-sense of the Commentator writes folly on that sentimentalism which inculcates such living above mundane concerns as is destructive of all carrying on of the business of every-day life. Equally does it smite that weak-kneed Christianhood that sequesters and retires itself from fellow-men and ordinary affairs; and effectively too, all hasty proclamation and publication of spiritual experiences.

Of kin with this is his teaching on temptation (Genesis iii. 1-5):—" It is a dangerous thing to treat with a temptation, which ought at first to be rejected with disdain and abhorrence. The garrison that sounds a parley is not far from being surrendered. Those that would be kept from harm must keep out of harm's way. See Prov. xiv. 7-19, 27." You have there no casuistries or hair-splitting, such as we meet with even in the "Ductor Dubitantium" of Jeremy Taylor and the "Directory" of Richard Baxter. Common-sense dictates and enforces the decisive-given counsel.

Unspeakably consolatory and wise is the

'Note' on Abraham's sorrowful lament that he had no child (Genesis xv. 2-6) :—" Though we must never complain *of* God, yet we have leave to complain *to* Him, and to be large and particular in the remonstrance of our grievances ; and it is some ease to a burdened spirit to open its case to a faithful and compassionate friend : such a friend God is, whose ear is always open." I once tranquillized a greatly troubled good woman, as she lamented bitterly that her mouth was filled with 'complaints' rather than 'praise,' by taking down my Matthew Henry and reading these choice words. Many a year afterwards this excellent Christian assured me that that distinction between complaining *of* God and complaining *to* God, had been as a cup of living water to her in seasons of despondency.

Practical and useful is this on Abraham's intercourse with his covenant-God (Genesis xviii. 23-33) :—"Communion with God is kept up by the Word and prayer. In the Word God speaks to us; in prayer we speak to Him. God had spoken to Abraham His purposes concerning Sodom; now from thence Abraham takes occasion to speak to God on Sodom's behalf. Note—God's Word doth us good when it furnishes us with matter for prayer and excites us to it."

Very admirable seems to me the lessons drawn from Isaac's repetition of his father Abraham's sin concerning his wife (Genesis xxvi. 6-11):—"We see—1. That very good men have sometimes been guilty of very great faults and follies. Let those therefore that stand take heed lest they fall, and those that are fallen, not despair of being helped up again. And—2. That there is an aptness in us to imitate even the weaknesses and infirmities of those we have a value for: we have need therefore to keep our foot, lest while we aim to tread in the steps of good men, we sometimes tread in their by-steps."

Here are effective rebukes to your intermeddlers with "curious questions" (1) on Genesis xxxii. 24-32:—"Spiritual blessings, which secure our felicity, are better and much more desirable than fine notions that satisfy our curiosity. An interest in the angel's blessing is better than an acquaintance with his name. The tree of life is better than the tree of knowledge. Thus Jacob carried his point. A blessing he wrestled for, and a blessing he had; nor did ever any of his praying seed seek in vain." (2) Exodus xxv. 1-9 :—" The Scripture is designed to direct us in our duty, not to fill our heads with speculations, or please our fancies."

How like an outstretched hand to one "fainting and failing" is this on Exodus vi. 10-13 :—" Though our infirmities ought to humble us, yet they ought not to discourage us from doing our best in any service we have to do for God. His strength is made perfect in our weakness."

How 'composing'—the old word—on differences, this on Genesis xxxiii. 1-4 :—" Jacob bowed to Esau. Note—1. The way to recover peace where it has been broken, is, to do our duty, and pay our respects upon all occasions, as if it had never been broken. It is the remembering and repeating of matters, that separates friends and perpetuates the separation.

2. An humble and submissive carriage goes a great way towards the turning away of wrath. The bullet flies over him that stoops."

Over-rigid parents would do well to act on this weighty counsel on Genesis xxxiii. 5-15:—"This prudence and tenderness of Jacob ought to be imitated by those that have the charge of young people, in the things of God. They must not be over-driven at first, by heavy tasks in religious services; but led as they can bear, making that work as easy to them as possible."

How superior native sagacity and common sense are to the subtleties of the schools, let this on Genesis xliii. 11-14 prove:—"Jacob had said (ch. xlii. 38), My son shall not go down;" but now he is over-persuaded [= persuaded-over] to consent. Note—It is no fault, but our wisdom and duty, to alter our purposes and resolutions, when there is a good reason for our so doing. Constancy is a virtue, but obstinacy is not." So on 1 Samuel xxv. 32-35: "Oaths cannot bind us to that which is sinful. David had solemnly vowed the death of Nabal: he did ill to make such a vow, but he had done worse if he had performed it."

One meets sometimes with your all-important self-important Christian (in pulpit and pew alike), who monopolizes work as though he (or she) were responsible for all the ten talents, while actually perhaps one or one-and-a-half were better measure. This, ministers and Sunday School Superintendents find the most troublesome type of worker—so exalted is his (or her) own idea of capacity and fitness. Let such pause over this on Exodus xviii. 13-26 :— "There may be over-doing even in well-doing; and therefore our zeal must always be governed by discretion, that our good may not be evil spoken of. Wisdom is profitable to direct, that we may neither content ourselves with less than our duty, nor over-task ourselves with that which is beyond our strength." Equally home-spoken is this on Exodus xx. 12-17 :—"As religion towards God is an essential branch of universal righteousness, so righteousness towards men is an essential branch of true religion. Godliness and honesty must go together." Alas for the divorce in this present day! Let this still further speak, on Deuteronomy xii. 5-32:—" It is not only our wisdom, but our duty, to live according to our estates, and not to spend above what we have. As it is unjust on the one hand to hoard what should be laid out, so it is much more unjust to lay out more than we have; for what is not our own, must needs be another's, who is thereby robbed and defrauded."

With what admirable sobriety is the purpose of Holy Scripture limited here, on Exodus xxv. 1-9:—

"We must own that we have our all from God's bounty, and therefore ought to use all for His glory. Since we live *upon* Him, we must live *to* Him. He that gave us no account of the lines and circles of the globe, the diameter of the earth, or the height and magnitude of the stars, has told us particularly the measure of every board and curtain of the tabernacle; for God's Church and instituted religion is more precious to Him and more considerable than all the rest of the world. And the Scriptures were written not to describe to us the works of nature, a general view of which is sufficient to lead us to the knowledge and service of the Creator; but to acquaint us with the methods of grace, and those things which are purely matters of Divine revelation."

Much logomachy would be spared if controversialists would only keep within these bounds. On the same lines is this; and it ought to carry weighty dissuasion to those who feel called on to spiritualize every jot and tittle of the Word: on Exodus xxxvii. 10-24 :—

"God's manifestations of Himself in this world are but candle-light compared with the daylight of the future state. The Bible is a golden candlestick: it is of pure gold (Psalm xix. 10). From it light is diffused to every part of God's tabernacle, that by it His spiritual priests may see to minister unto the Lord and to do the service of His sanctuary. This candlestick has not only its bowls for necessary use, but its knops and flowers for ornaments. Many things which God saw fit to beautify His Word with, we can no more give a reason for, than for those knops and flowers; and yet must be sure they were added for good purpose."

I like this reminder on the robes that as Ministers of the Gospel we wear: on Exodus xxxix. 1-31 :—

"The priest's garments are here called 'clothes of

service.' Note—Those that wear robes of honour must look upon them as clothes of service; for those upon whom honour is put, from them service is expected. It is said of those that are arrayed in white robes, that they are 'before the Throne of God, and serve Him day and night in His temple' (Rev. vii. 13-15). Holy garments were not made for man to sleep in, or strut in; but to do service in: and then they are indeed for glory and beauty."

Here again are inestimably sober-minded words on the Church (Lev. iv. 13-21) :—

"This is the law for expiating the guilt of a national sin, by a sin-offering. If the leaders of the people through mistake concerning the law, caused them to err, when the mistake was discovered, an offering must be brought, that wrath might not come upon the whole congregation. Observe: It is possible that the Church may err, and that her guides may mislead her. It is here supposed that the whole congregation may sin, and sin through ignorance. God will always have a Church on earth, but He never said it should be infallible, or perfectly pure from corruption on this side heaven."

In the same spirit is this on Lev. xxiv. 1-9 :—

" The priests were to attend the lamps; they must snuff them, clean the candlesticks, supply them with oil morning and evening. Thus it is the work of the ministers of the Gospel to 'hold forth that word of life,' not to set up new light, but by expounding and preaching the Word, to make the light of it more clear and extensive. This was the ordinary way of keeping the lamps burning ; but when the Church was poor, and in distress, we find its lamps fed constantly with 'oil from the good olives,' immediately, without the ministry of priests or people (Zech. iv. 2, 3), for though God has tied us to means, He has not tied Himself to them ; but will take effectual care that His lamps never go out in the world for want of oil."

Thomas Brooks names one of his Funeral Sermons "A String of Pearls." I place these 'Notes' together as just such an im-pearled string.

1. Deuteronomy xiv. 22-29 :—" The way to obtain that blessing [of God] is to be diligent and charitable. The blessing descends upon the working hand. Expect not that God should bless thee in thy idleness, and love of ease, but in all the work of thy hand."

2. *Ibid.* xvii. 14-20 :—" Let not those that call themselves men of business think that will excuse them from making religion their business ; nor let great men think it any disparagement to them to write for themselves those 'great things of God's Law which He hath written to them ' (Hosea viii. 12)."

3. *Ibid.* xxx. 10-29 :—" All our knowledge must be in order to practice, for this is the end of all Divine revelation; not to furnish us with curious subjects of speculation and discourse, with which to entertain

ourselves and our friends, but that 'we may do all the words of this Law,' and be blessed in our deed."

4. 1 Samuel i. 19-28 :—" Those that are detained from public ordinances by the nursing and tending of little children, may take comfort from this instance of Hannah's not going up to the yearly sacrifice until Samuel was weaned, and believe that if they act with an eye to God, He will graciously accept them therein ; and though they tarry at home they shall divide the spoil."

5. 1 Kings xix. 9-18 :—" There are more good people in the world than some wise and holy men think there are. Their jealousy of themselves and for God, makes them think the corruption is universal ; but God sees not as they do. When we come to heaven, as we shall miss a great many whom we thought to have met there, so we shall meet a great many whom we little thought to have met there. God's love often proves larger than man's charity, and more extensive." *

6. 2 Kings viii. 7-15 :—" Those that are little and low in the world cannot imagine how strong the temptations of power and prosperity are, which, if ever they arrive to, they will find how deceitful their hearts were, and how much worse than they suspected."

---

* This is the source of similar sayings varyingly ascribed to (I think) John Newton, Richard Cecil, and others—with the addition, " The greatest surprise of all will be to find myself there."

7. 1 Chronicles xx. 1-3 :—"We have had a more full account of what is here recorded in 2 Samuel xi. and xii., and cannot but remember by this sad token, that while Joab was besieging Rabbah, David fell into that great sin in the matter of Uriah. But it is observable that though the rest of the story be repeated, that is not; but only a hint given of it in those words which lie in a parenthesis, 'But David tarried at Jerusalem.' If he had been abroad with his army he had been out of the way of that temptation; but indulging his ease he fell into uncleanness. Now as the relating of that sin David fell into is an instance of the impartiality and fidelity of the sacred writers; so the avoiding of the repetition of it here, when there was a fair occasion given to speak of it again, is designed to teach us that though there may be just occasion to speak of the faults and miscarriages of others, yet we should not take delight in the repetition of them; but should always be looked upon as an unpleasing subject, which though sometimes we cannot help falling upon, yet we would not choose to dwell upon, nor love to rake in a dunghill. Those persons or actions we can say no good of, we had best say nothing of."

8. 2 Chronicles xxxiii. 11-20 :—" It becomes penitents to take shame to themselves, to give thanks to their reprovers, and warning to others. Penitents may recover their comfort sooner than their credit."

9. Esther ix. 20-31 :—" The history of the transactions here recorded was written by Mordecai, and copies of it dispersed among all the Jews in all the provinces of the Empire, 'both nigh and far.' And if this book of Esther be the same that he wrote— as many think it is—I cannot but observe what a difference there is between Mordecai's style and Nehemiah's. Nehemiah at every turn takes notice of the Divine Providence and 'the good hand of his God' upon him, which is very proper to stir up devout affections in the minds of his readers; but Mordecai never so much as mentions the name of God in the whole story. Nehemiah wrote his book at Jerusalem, where religion was in fashion, and an air of it appeared in men's common conversation; Mordecai wrote his at Shushan the Palace, where policy reigned more than piety; and he wrote according to the genius of the place. Even those that have the root of the matter in them, are apt to lose the savour of religion, and let their leaf wither, when they converse wholly with those that have little religion. Commend me to Nehemiah's way of writing; that I would imitate, and yet learn from Mordecai's, that men may be truly devout though they do not abound in the expressions of devotion : and therefore we must not judge or despise our brethren."

10. Job xi. 7-12 :—" God's nature infinitely exceeds the capacities of our understandings. We may by searching find God (Acts xvii. 27) ; but we cannot find Him out in anything He is pleased to conceal.

We may *apprehend* Him but cannot *comprehend* Him; may know *that* He is, but cannot know *what* He is. The eye can see the ocean, but cannot see over it. We may, by a humble, diligent, and believing search find out something of God, but cannot find Him out to perfection; may know, but cannot know fully what God is, nor find out His word 'from the beginning to the end' (Eccles. iii. 11)."

11. *Ibid.* xvii. 10-16 :—" Those do not go wisely about the work of comforting the afflicted, who fetch their comforts from the possibility of their recovery and enlargement in this world : though that is not to be despaired of, at the best it is uncertain, and if it should fail, as perhaps it may, the comfort built upon it will fail too. It is therefore our wisdom to comfort ourselves and others in distress with that which will not fail, the promise of God, His love and grace, and a well-grounded hope of eternal life."

12. *Ibid.* xix. 23-29 :—" Serious godliness is the one thing needful. We are to believe that many have the root of the matter in them who are not in everything of our mind, who have their follies and weaknesses and mistakes : and it is at our peril if we persecute such."

13. Psalm xxx. 6-12 :—" As David's plunge into trouble from the height of prosperity, and then when he least expected it, teacheth us to rejoice as though we rejoice not, because we know not how near trouble may be; so his sudden return to a prosperous condition teacheth us to weep as though we

wept not, because we know not how soon the storm may become a calm and the formidable blast may become a favourable gale."

14. Psalm lxxxvi. 1-7 :—" It is our duty to pray always without ceasing, and to continue instant in prayer; and then we may hope to have our prayers heard which we make in time of trouble, if we have made conscience of the duty at other times, at all times. It is comfortable if an affliction find the wheels of prayer a-going, and that they are not then to be set a-going. Then we may hope that God will meet us with His mercies, when we in prayer send forth our souls as it were to meet Him."

15. Proverbs vi. 12-19 :—" It is an evidence of the good-will God bears to mankind, that those sins are in a special manner provoking to Him which are prejudicial to the comfort of human life and society. Those things which God hates, it is no thanks to us to hate in others, but we must hate them in ourselves."

16. Isaiah iii. 10-22 :—" It is possible that sin may be both loathed and left, and yet not truly repented of; loathed, because surfeited on; left, because no opportunity of committing it; yet not repented of out of any love to God, but only from a slavish fear of His wrath."

17. Jeremiah xv. 10-14 :—" Note—Even those who are most quiet and peaceable, yet if they serve God faithfully, are often made 'men of strife.' We can but 'follow peace;' have the making only of one side of the bargain, and therefore can but 'as much as in us lies' live peaceably."

18. *Ibid.* xxxvii. 1-10:—"Note—It is common for those to desire to be prayed for, that yet will not be advised; but herein they put a cheat upon themselves; for how can we expect that God will hear others speaking to Him for us, if we will not hear them speaking to us from Him and for Him? Many that despise prayer when they are in prosperity, will be glad of it when they are in adversity: now 'give us of your oil.' When Zedekiah sent to the prophet to pray *for* him, he had better have sent to the prophet to pray *with* him; but he thought that below him: and how can they expect the comforts of religion that will not stoop to the services of it?"

Another String of Pearls—equally precious—and of the same number with the other, must complete our exemplification of the practical sanctified common-sense of Matthew Henry:—

1. Jeremiah xxviii. 10-17:—"If what we have spoken be the truth of God, we must not unsay it because men gainsay it: for 'great is the truth, and will prevail.' It will stand, therefore let us stand to it, and not fear that men's unbelief or blasphemy will make it of no effect."
2. Ezekiel xxxviii. 1-14:—"God's grace can save souls without our preaching; but our preaching cannot save them without God's grace, and that grace must be sought by prayer. Ministers must faith-

fully and diligently use the means of grace, even with those that there seems little probability of gaining upon. To 'prophesy upon dry bones' seems as great a penance as to 'water a dry stick;' and yet whether they will bear or forbear, we must discharge our trust, must prophesy 'as we are commanded,' in the name of Him 'who raiseth the dead' and is the fountain of life."

3. Daniel iii. 8-18 :—" Those that would avoid sin must not parley with temptation. When that which we are allured or affrighted to, is manifestly evil, the motion is rather to be rejected with indignation and abhorrence than reasoned with. Stand not to pause about it, but say as Christ has taught us, 'Get thee behind me, Satan.'"

4. *Ibid.* :—" Here were they who formerly resolved not to defile themselves with the king's meat, and now they as bravely resolved not to defile themselves with his gods. Note—A stedfast self-denying adherence to God and duty in lesser instances, will qualify and prepare us for the like in greater."

5. Hosea ii. 6-13 :—" Crosses and obstacles in an evil course are great blessings, and are so to be accounted. They are God's hedges, to keep us from transgression; to restrain us from wandering out of the green pastures; to 'withdraw man from his purpose' (Job xxxiii. 17); to make the way of sin difficult, that we may not go on in it, and to keep us from it whether we will or not. We have reason to bless God both for restraining *grace* and for restraining *providences.*"

6. *Ibid.* iv. 12-19 :—" It is a sad and sore judgment for any man to be 'let alone' in sin ; for God to say concerning a sinner, he is joined to idols, the world and the flesh, he is incurably proud, covetous or profane, an incurable drunkard or adulterer. Conscience, let him alone ; minister, let him alone ; providences, let him alone. Let nothing awaken him till the flames of hell do it. Those that are not disturbed in their sin, will be destroyed for their sin."

7. St. Matthew vi. 25-34 :—" If we were by faith as unconcerned about the morrow, as the fowls of the air are, we should sing as cheerfully as they do ; for it is worldly care that mars our mirth and damps our joy and silenceth our praise as much as anything. 'Take therefore no thought for the morrow.' This doth not forbid a prudent foresight and preparation accordingly ; but a perplexing solicitude and a prepossession of difficulties and calamities, which perhaps never may come ; or if they do may be easily borne, and the evil of them guarded against. The meaning is, let us mind present duty, and then leave events to God ; do the work of the day in the day, and then let tomorrow bring its work along with it."

8. *Ibid.* xiii. 1-23 :—" There are many who are very glad to hear a good sermon that yet do not profit by it ; may be pleased with the word, and yet not changed and ruled by it : the heart may melt under the word, and yet not be melted down by the word, much less into it as into a mould."

9. *Ibid.* xiv. 22-3 :—" Looking at difficulties with an eye of sense, more than at precepts and promises with an eye of faith, is at the bottom of all our inordinate fears, both as to public and personal concerns. Christ rebuked Peter for the weakness of his faith."
10. *Ibid.* xviii. 1-6 :—" Besides the first conversion of a soul from a state of nature to a state of grace, there are after-conversions from particular paths of backsliding, which are equally necessary to salvation. Every step out of the way by sin, must be a step into it again, by repentance. When Peter repented of his denying his Master, he was 'converted.'"
11. *Ibid.* 15-20 :—" It is a good rule, which should ordinarily be observed among Christians, not to speak of our brethren's faults to others, till we have first spoken of them to themselves. This would make less reproaching and more reproving ; that is, less sin committed and more duty done. It will be likely to work upon an offender, when he sees his reprover concerned not only for his salvation, in telling him his fault, but for his reputation in telling him it privately."
12. St. John ix. 13-34 :—" This man doth not here give a nice account of the method of the cure, nor pretend to describe it philosophically, but in short says, ' Whereas I was blind, now I see.' This is the work of grace in the soul, though we cannot tell when and how, by what instruments and by what steps and advances the blessed change was wrought, yet we may take the comfort of it, if we

can say, through grace, 'Whereas I was blind, now I see.'"

13. *Ibid.* xii. 42-3 :—" Perhaps these chief rulers were true believers, though very weak, and their faith like smoking flax. Note—It may be there are more good people than we think there are. Elijah thought he was left alone, when God had seven thousand faithful worshippers in Israel."

14. *Ibid.* xiv. 15-17 :—[Jesus] "premiseth to this a memorandum of duty. 'If ye love me keep my commandments.' Observe—When Christ is comforting them, He bids them 'keep His commandments ;' for we must not expect comfort but in the way of duty."

15. *Ibid.* xx. 1-10 :—" The grave-clothes in which Christ had been buried, were found in very good order, which serves for an evidence that His body was not 'stolen away while men slept.' Robbers of tombs have been known to take away 'the clothes' and leave the body ; but none ever took away 'the body' and left the clothes, especially when they were 'fine linen' and new (St. Matt. xv. 46). Any one would rather choose to carry a dead body in its clothes, than naked. Or, if they that were supposed to have stolen it, would have left the grave-clothes behind, yet it cannot be supposed they should find leisure to 'fold up the linen.'"

16. Romans i. 19-32 :—"The being of a God may be apprehended but cannot be comprehended. We cannot by searching find Him out (Job xi. 7-9). Finite understandings cannot perfectly know an infinite

Being; but blessed be God, there is in that which may be known, enough to lead us to our chief end, the glorifying and enjoying of Him; and these things revealed belong to us and to our children, while secret things are not to be peered into" (Deut. xxix. 29).

17. Romans xi. 1-32 :—"Things are oftentimes much better with the Church of God than wise and good men think they are. They are ready to conclude hardly, and to give up all for gone, when it is not so."

18. *Ibid.* xvi. 1-16 :—" Paul sends greeting, not only to Aquila and Priscilla, but likewise 'to the church in their house.' It seems then a church in a house is no such absurd thing as some make it to be. Perhaps there was a congregation of Christians that used to meet at the house at stated times ; and then, no doubt, it was like the house of Obed-Edom, blessed for the ark's sake."

Other characteristics of the Commentary of Matthew Henry, and which bear a message to us to-day, are these, his—Brevity and Wisdom—Pungency and Ingenuity—Savouriness and Quaint-felicities of wording. These I shall now illustrate successively.

I. BREVITY AND WISDOM.—There is a proverbial saying that "Brevity is the soul of wit."

This must be taken *cum grano salis*. For as a preacher of a fashionable ten-minutes' sermon once learned from Canning, it is not at all impossible to be brief and—tedious. I should prefer putting it, that 'wit is the soul of brevity.' *Per se* brevity may arise from mere ellipsis, or meagreness of thought, or poverty of words, or ineptitude of style. But when wit—in the old sense of wisdom—is put forth in brief form, it is an informing soul to the words. Then you have of the imperishable things that go down into the memory, and even the heart of Humanity. This Brevity of Wisdom and Wisdom in Brevity, belongs peculiarly to Matthew Henry. You have many Commentaries as 'brief'; few so witful. You have others—as John Trapp's—as witful; few so brief. It is the combination of wit with brevity and brevity with wit, that makes his Commentary such racy and delightful reading, and so memorable. You recognize that the man says something because he has got something to say. You have no 'padding,'—as for instance of cob-webbed lore in the present Bishop of Lincoln's arid Commentaries, that for bread give grit.

I would now bring together, without note or comment, a number of such brief pregnant unforgetable things as offer themselves inexhaustibly to the student of Matthew Henry. I do not give the references to the places of their occurrence; but as before I begin with Genesis, and so go onward. My headings of each may be helpful:—

EVE.—" That wife that is of God's making by special grace, and of God's bringing by special providence, is likely to prove a help-meet to her husband."

FORBIDDEN FRUIT.—" When there is thought to be no more harm in forbidden fruit than in other fruit, sin lies at the door, and Satan soon carries the day."

CHURCH-FREQUENTERS.—" The Pharisee and the Publican went to the temple to pray " (St. Luke xviii. 10).

NON-HEREDITARY GRACE.—" A sinner begets a sinner, but a saint doth not beget a saint."

COMFORT NOT SPLENDOUR.—" Observe, God doth not bid Noah *paint* the ark, but *pitch* it."

FAME.—" These Babel builders put themselves to a great deal of foolish expense to make them a name ; but they could not gain even this point ; for we do not find in any history the name of so much as one of them."

INCREASE.—"God reveals Himself and His favour to His people by degrees. Before He had promised to *show* Abraham this land, now to *give* it him. As grace is growing, so is comfort." Again: "God had told Abraham long before, that he should have a son, but never till now that he should have a son by Sarah."

FEARS.—"Note—where is great faith yet there may be many fears" (2 Corinthians vii. 5).

GOD PUNCTUAL.—"God is always punctual to His time. Though His promised messages come not at the time we set, they will certainly come at the time that He sets, and that is the best time."

FORGETFUL.—"We are apt to forget former promises when present providences seem to contradict them."

OBEDIENCE.—"God's commands must not be disputed but obeyed. We must not consult with 'flesh and blood' about them (Gal. i. 15, 16), but with a gracious obstinacy persist in our obedience."

MAKING OUR WILL.—"Isaac lived above forty years after this: let none therefore think that they shall die the sooner for making their wills, and getting ready for death" (on Genesis xxvii. 1-5).

CONTRASTS.—"Saying and doing are not two things with God, whatever they are with us."

JOSEPH.—"It is better to lose a good coat than lose a good conscience."

ANGER.—"To be angry at nothing but sin, is the way not to sin in anger."

Duty.—" God's bounty leaves room for man's duty. It did so even when manna was rained : they must not eat till they have gathered."

Confession.—" Usually, the more particular we are in the confession of sin, the more comfort we have in the sense of pardon."

Sense of Affliction.—" There may be a deep sense of affliction even where there is a sincere resignation to the will of God in it."

Forbidden Meats.—" Most of the meats forbidden as unclean were also unwholesome."

Work and Help.—" Those whom God finds work for, He will find help for."

Balaam's Ass.—" It is good for us often to consider how useful the inferior creatures are, and have been to us, that we may be thankful to God, and tender of them."*

Death.—" We are not better than our fathers or brethren ; if they are gone, we are going."

Endings.—" If men did consider, as they ought, what would be the end of sin, they would be afraid of the beginnings of it."

Desires.—" We should never allow any desires in our hearts which we cannot in faith offer up to God by prayer ; and what desires are innocent, let them be presented to God."

Passion.—" A just cause needs not anger to defend it, and a bad one is never made better by it."

---

* This contains really all Samuel Cox tells us in a long and elaborate paper in his " Expositor."

CROSSES.—"It is sometimes hard, but never impossible, to reconcile cross providences with the presence of God and His favour."

REPENTANCE.—"True repentance is not only *from* sin, but *for* sin."

THE WHOLE HEART.—"If God have not all the heart, He will soon have none of it."

MINISTRY.—"The ministry is the best calling, but the worst trade in the world."

RUTH.—"High spirits can easier starve than stoop. Ruth was one of those. She does not tell her mother she was never brought up to live upon crumbs. Though she was never brought *up* to it she is brought *down* to it, and is not uneasy at it."

IMPATIENCE.—"Saul lost his kingdom for want of two or three hours' patience."

SHADOW AND SUBSTANCE.—"It is common for those that have lost the substance of religion, to be most fond of the shadow of it, as here is a deserted prince courting a deserted priest" (1 Samuel xiv. 1-15).

VEXATION.—"That will break a proud man's heart, that will not break an humble man's sleep" (2 Sam. xvii. 22-29).

PIOUS CHILDREN.—"The Divine image in miniature, has a peculiar beauty and lustre in it."

GODLY FEAR.—"Those that most *fear* God's wrath, are least likely to *feel* it."

SILENCE.—"Scripture silence sometimes speaks."

SCANDAL.—"Next to the sinfulness of sin, we should dread the scandalousness of it."

LEADERS.—"The pilot needs not haul a rope; it is enough for him to steer."

Joy and Sorrow.—" Holy joy must not indispose us for godly sorrow, no more than godly sorrow for holy joy."

Thanksgiving.—" Giving thanks for former mercies, is a decent way of begging further mercies."

A Jest.—" To forbid sackcloth to enter, unless they could have forbidden sickness and trouble and death to enter, was a jest."

Money.—" Money is like muck, good for nothing if it be not spread."

Possessions.—" What we have in the world, may be either used with comfort, or lost with comfort, if it was honestly gotten."

Influence.—" It is good lodging with an old disciple" (Acts xxi. 16; Titus ii. 4).

God's Care.—" God will not only deliver His people out of their troubles, in due time, but He will sustain them and bear them up under their troubles in the meantime."

Reward.—" There is a reward not only after keeping but in keeping God's commandments; a present reward of obedience in obedience."

Desires.—" A gracious soul though still desiring more of God, never desires more than God."

Prayer.—" You may as soon find a living man without breath, as a living Christian without prayer."

Meetening.—" Those that are made meet *for* heaven shall be brought safe *to* heaven."

Trust.—" Those that will deal with God, must deal upon trust."

God's Goodness.—" God's goodness appears in two things, giving and forgiving."

REPROOF.—"It is a great instance of wisdom to take a reproof well, and to give it well."

ARGUMENTS.—"Hard arguments do best with soft words."

FOOLISH.—"Rather than lose a jest some will lose a friend, and make an enemy."

HARD WORDS.—"Hard words indeed break no bones, but many a heart has been broken by them."

COMMUNION.—"We must seek for communion with Christ in communion with saints." Again: "A gracious soul can reconcile itself to the poorest accommodations, if it may have communion with God in them."

GOD'S FORGIVENESS.—"When God forgives, He forgets.'

PRINCES.—"Rich princes shall do what poor prophets have foretold."

TEARS.—"First or last, sinners must be weepers."

GOD.—"There is an admirable decency and congruity in the worshipping of God only. It is fit that He that is 'God alone' should alone be served; that He that is Lord 'of all' should be served by all; that He that is 'great' should be 'greatly feared' and 'greatly praised.'"

CHARACTERS.—"To render good for good, is human; evil for evil, is brutish; good for evil, is Christian; but evil for good is devilish."

GOD'S JUSTICE.—"There is no fleeing from God's justice but by fleeing to His mercy."

SECURE.—"Those are least safe that are most secure" (Jeremiah xxi. 8-14).

SYMPATHY.—"Those that are in distress should not only

be relieved but relieved with compassion and marks of respect."

TRIFLES.—" See what a good use even old rotten rags may be put to ; which therefore should not be made waste of, no more than broken meat' (Jeremiah xxxviii. 1-13).

TALK.—" Great talkers are little doers."

FALSE TRUSTS.—" The reed will break that is leaned on."

LEADERS.—" The sins of leaders are leading sins."

VANITY.—" Affecting an acquaintance and correspondence with 'great people' has often been a snare to 'good people.'"

WARNINGS.—" Those that will not be *warned* by the judgments of God, may expect to be *wounded* by them."

OCCASIONS.—" Those that would be kept from sin . . . must not come upon the devil's ground."

WISE MEN.—" Whatever sort of wise men they were before, now they begin to be 'wise men' indeed, when they set themselves to inquire after Christ."

GODLY FEAR.—" Those that truly fear God, need not fear man ; and those that are afraid of least sin, need not be afraid of the greatest trouble."

FAITH.—" Because of all graces faith honours Christ most, therefore of all graces Christ honours faith most."

MADNESS.—"Anger is a short madness, malice is a long one."

REPENTANCE.—" Though it is certain that true repentance is never too late, it is certain that late repentance is seldom true."

TRUE CHRISTIAN.—"I reckon him a Christian indeed, who is neither ashamed of the Gospel, nor a shame to it."

CHEERFULNESS.—"God is a Master who likes His servants to sing at their work."

PRAYER.—"Some of our enemies are best fought upon our knees."

THE BIBLE.—"God's word will destroy either the *sin* or the *sinner*."

OBEDIENCE.—"To obey is better than sacrifice. Angels obey, but angels do not sacrifice."

DIVINE CORRECTION.—"God's corrections are rods and whips, not swords and axes."

PROSPERITY.—"The wicked after all flourish only 'as a green *bay* tree,' which is all leaf and no fruit. The righteous are like the green *olive* tree, which is fat as well as flourishing."

THE LIFE.—"Thanks*giving* is good; thanks*living* is better."

RESPONSIBILITY.—"It is better to *be a* beast than to be a man who is *as a* beast. Beasts are at least indemnified as to the next world."

EXPECTATION.—"We cannot expect too little from men, nor too much from God."

CHIDING.—"'He will not always chide.' How unlike are they to God who are always chiding and never cease!"

WAR.—"War is a tragedy which destroys the stage upon which it is acted."

BOTTLE AND BOOK.—"God has a book and a bottle for the tears of His saints. He notes whether they are for sorrows or for sins."

ETERNITY.—" Between a minute and a million of years there is a proportion; between time and eternity none."

I must hold that it were well if to-day our sermons and addresses could be thus shotted (so-to-say) with brief, pointed, cleanly-cut, memorable things. I confess that it is a weariness to read very much of popular religious literature—so thin and beat-out and unroughened by thought, is it.

II. PUNGENCY AND INGENUITY.—The illustrations given thus far of the sanctified common-sense and the pregnant brevity and wisdom of Matthew Henry, have equally revealed his pungency and ingenuity of explication and application of Bible facts and truths and sayings. But I think it right to exemplify these by themselves. For—as I take it— one need of to-day all round, is speaking and writing that has this union of pungency and of arrestive ingenuity, whereby attention is awakened and sustained. "Smooth things," a flow and flow of "words, words, words," do no earthly and no celestial good. I have now to place in order such examples of pungency and ingenuity as have struck me in gladly re-reading the entire Commentary for this Lecture.

MAN'S CREATION.—" Observe that man was made last of all creatures, that it might not be suspected that he had been any way a helper to God in the creation of the world. That question must be for ever humbling and mortifying to him. 'Where wast thou, or any of thy kind, when I laid the foundations of the earth?' (Job xxxviii. 4). Yet it was both an honour and a favour to him that he was made last: an honour, for the method of the creation was to advance from that which was less perfect to that which was more so; and a favour, for it was not fit he should be lodged in the palace designed for him, till it was completely fitted up and furnished for his reception."

WOMAN.—" The man was but dust refined, but the woman was dust double-refined; one remove further from the earth. The woman was made 'of a rib out of the side of' Adam: not made out of his head to top him, nor out of his feet to be trampled upon by him; but out of his side to be equal with him; under his arm to be protected, and near his heart to be beloved."

POWER.—" Those that have so much power over others as to be able to oppress them, have seldom so much power over themselves as not to oppress."

WICKEDNESS.—" Things are bad when ill men are not

only honoured notwithstanding their wickedness, but honoured *for* their wickedness and the vilest men exalted. Wickedness is then great when great men are wicked."

DIVINE REPENTANCE.—"God repented that He had made man, but we never find Him repenting that He redeemed man, though that was a work of much greater expense."

TRUE NOBILITY.—"A family of saints is more truly honourable than a family of nobles ; Shem's holy seed than Ham's royal seed ; Jacob's twelve patriarchs than Ishmael's twelve princes (Gen. xvii. 20). Goodness is true greatness."

OUR RELIGION.—"Abram did not leave his religion behind him in Egypt, as many do in their travels."

ENJOYMENTS.—" It is just with God to deprive us of those enjoyments by which we have suffered ourselves to be deprived of our enjoyment of Him."

RETRIBUTION.—"We justly suffer by those whom we have sinfully indulged ; and it is a righteous thing with God to make those instruments of our trouble, whom we have made instruments of our sin."

GIVING.—" It is better to feed five drones, or wasps, than starve one bee."

CHOOSING.—" Of two evils we must choose the less ; but of two sins we must choose neither, nor ever do evil that good may come of it."

LOT.—" Lot that a while ago could not find room enough for himself and his stock in the whole land, but must jostle with Abraham and get as far from him as he could, is now confined to a hole in a hill, where he has scarce room to turn him, and there is solitary and trembling. Note—It is just with God to reduce those to poverty and restraint who have abused their liberty and plenty."

ISAAC.—"Abraham made this feast, not on the day that Isaac was born : that would have been too great a disturbance to Sarah; nor the day he was circumcised : that would have been too great a diversion from the ordinance ; but the day he was weaned, because God's blessing upon the nursing of children and the preservation of them through the perils of the infant age, is a signal instance of the care and tenderness of the Divine Providence, which ought to be acknowledged to His praise. See Psalm xxii. 9, 10; Hosea xi. 1, 2."

A MOTHER'S DEATH.—" What an affectionate son Isaac was to his mother. It was about three years since her death, and yet he was not till now comforted concerning it (Genesis xxiv. 67). The wound which that affliction gave to his tender spirit bled so long, and was never healed till God brought him into this new relation."

MEMORIALS.—"Jacob set up a pillar in remembrance of his joys (Genesis xxxv. 14), and here (vers. 16-20) he set up one in remembrance of his sorrows ; for, as it may be of use to ourselves to keep both in mind, so it may be of use to others to transmit the memorials of both."

JOSEPH.—"Observe Joseph dreamed of his preferment, but he did not dream of his imprisonment. Thus may young people, when they are setting out in the world, think of nothing but prosperity and pleasure, and never dream of trouble."

MODEST REQUEST.—"What a modest request Joseph makes to the chief butler; only 'think on me.' Pray do me a kindness if it lie in your way. And his particular petition is, 'Bring me out of this house.' He doth not say, Bring me into Pharaoh's house, get me a place at court. No; he begs for enlargement, not preferment."

WRONG.—"Whenever we think we have wrong done us, we ought to remember the wrong we have done others" (Eccl. vii. 21, 22). Again: "We should be more careful not to do wrong than not to suffer wrong, because to suffer wrong is only an affliction, but to do wrong is a sin; and sin is always worse than affliction."

JUDAH.—"How fitly doth the apostle, when he is discoursing of the mediation of Christ, observe, that 'our Lord sprang out of Judah' (Heb. vii. 14); for like his [fore] father Judah, he not only made intercession for the transgressors, but he became a surety for them, and it follows there (v. 22) testifying therein a very tender concern both for his father and for his brethren."

DEATH.—"Death will not always come just when we call for it, whether in a passion of sorrow, or in a passion of joy. Our times are in God's hand, and not in our own. We must die just when God pleases, and not either just when we are surfeit with the pleasures of life, or just when we are overwhelmed with grief."

JACOB AND JOSEPH.—"Seventeen years Jacob had nourished Joseph; for so old he was when he was sold from him (Genesis xxxvii. 2), and now by way of requital, seventeen years Joseph nourished him" (*ibid.* xlvii. 1-12).

REPROOF.—"We ought always, in the expressions of our zeal, carefully to distinguish between the sinner and the sin; so as not to love or bless the sin for the sake of the person, nor to hate or curse the person for the sake of the sin."

CONVICTIONS.—"A mighty struggle here was between Pharaoh's convictions and his corruptions. His convictions said, let the children of Israel go; his corruptions said, yet not very far away; but he sided with his corruptions against his convictions, and it was his ruin."

COUNTERFEITS.—"Counterfeit repentance commonly cheats men with general promises, and is loth to covenant against particular sins."

SPIRITUAL SERVICE.—"Thus far Moses was tried, 'his hands were heavy.' We do not find that Joshua's hands were heavy in fighting, but Moses' hands were heavy in praying. The more spiritual any service is, the more apt we are to fail and flag in it."

REDEMPTION-MONEY.—"The tribute to be paid for the ransom of the soul was half a shekel, about fifteenpence of our money. The rich were not to give more nor the poor less; to intimate that the souls of the rich and poor were alike precious" (Exodus xxx. 11-16).

OBEDIENCE.—"When the tabernacle and the furniture of it were prepared, they did not put off the rearing of it till they came to Canaan, though they now hoped to be there very shortly; but in obedience to the will of God, they set it up in the midst of their camp, while they were in the wilderness. Those that are unsettled in this world, must not think that will excuse them in their continued irreligion; as if it were time enough to begin to serve God when they begin to get settled in the world."

THE BIBLE. —"As before the tabernacle was set up, the Israelites had the cloud for their guide, which appeared sometimes in one place, and sometimes in another, but from henceforward rested on the tabernacle and was to be found there only; so the Church had divine revelation for its guide from the first, before the Scriptures were written; but since the making up of that canon, it rests in that as its tabernacle, and there only is it to be found."

IGNORANCE.—" Perhaps there was some allusion to the law concerning sacrifices for sins of ignorance in that prayer of Christ's, just when He was offering up Himself a sacrifice, 'Father, forgive them, for they know not what they do.'"

MAY DO.—"We should not only ask what *must* we do, but what *may* we do, for the glory and honour of God."

COMPLAINTS.—" When we complain without cause, it is just with God to give us cause to complain."

SIN.—" That affair can never end well that begins with sin."

END.—" Many . . . would be saints in heaven, but not saints on earth."

REFUGE.—"Even the suburbs or borders of the city [of refuge] were a sufficient security to the offender. So there is virtue even in the hem of Christ's garment for the healing and saving of poor sinners. If we cannot reach to a full assurance, we may comfort ourselves on 'a good hope through grace.'"

CHRIST IN OLD TESTAMENT.—" We have reason to think that the man who appeared to Jonah was the Son of God, the Eternal Word, who before He assumed the human nature, frequently appeared in a human shape. Joshua gave Him divine honours, and He received them, which a created angel would not have done; and He is called Jehovah (Joshua vi. 2). He had appeared as a soldier, with 'His sword drawn in His hand.' To Abraham in his tent, He appeared as a traveller; to Joshua in the field, as a man of war. Christ will be to His people what their faith expects and desires."

TROUBLE.—"Those that are troublesome shall be troubled."

NONCONFORMITY.—"Those that are bound for heaven, must be willing to swim against the stream, and must not do as the most do, but as the less do."

FORCED ABSENCE.—"Forced absence from God's ordinances and forced presence with wicked people, is a great affliction; but when the force ceaseth and it is continued of choice, then it becomes a great sin."

CHURCH IN THE HOUSE.—"It is no new thing for God's ark to be thrust into a private house. Christ and His apostles preached from house to house, when they could not have public places at command."

LOST ONES.—" If it were the business of the men of God to direct for the recovery of lost ones, they would be consulted much more than they are now [when] it is their business to direct for the recovery of lost souls."

SAUL.—" Saul among the prophets is a wonder to a proverb. Let not the worst be despaired of; yet let not an external show of devotion and a sudden change for the present, be too much relied on; for Saul among the prophets, was Saul still."

MAN'S RUIN.—"It is not sinning that ruins men, but sinning and not repenting."

FRIENDS.—" God's persecuted people have often found better usage from Philistines than from Israelites, in the Gentile theatres than in the Jewish synagogues. The king of Judah imprisoned Jeremiah, and the king of Babylon set him at liberty."

FLATTERERS.—" Great men ought always to be jealous of flatterers, and remember that Nature has given them two ears, that they may hear both sides."

UZZIAH.—" He invaded the office of the priests in contempt of them, and God struck him with a disease which in a particular manner made him subject to the inspection and sentence of the priests; for to them pertained the judgment on leprosy (Deut. xxiv. 8)."

MELANCHOLY.—" In melancholy times we must see and observe what makes for us as well as what makes against us."

POOR.—" God will be deaf to their prayers that are deaf to the poor's cries, which if they be not heard *by* us will be heard *against* us (Exod. xxvi. 23)."

THE ACCEPTED.—"It is only the penitent soul that God will accept; the heart that is broken, not the head that is bowed down like a bulrush only for a day; David's repentance, not Ahab's."

SPECIOUS RESPECT.—"A secret disaffection to God is often disguised with the specious colours of respect to Him; and those that are resolved they will not trust God, yet take on them to say they will not tempt Him."

SIN.—"The pleasures of sin will soon surfeit but never satisfy. A man may quickly tire himself in the pursuit of them, but can never repose himself in the enjoyment of them." Again: "Prosperity in sin is a great bar to conversion from sin. Those that live at ease in their sinful pleasure and raise estates by their sinful projects, are tempted to think God favours them, and therefore they have nothing to repent of." Further: "What buds in sin, will blossom in some judgment or other."

PEN AND SWORD.—"The honours of the pen exceed those of the sword. They were angels that bore the sword, but He was the Lord of angels that made use of the writer's ink-horn" (Ezek. ix. 1-4).

EZEKIEL AND JEREMIAH.—"Ezekiel is now among the captives in Babylon; but as Jeremiah at Jerusalem wrote for the use of the captives, though they had Ezekiel upon the spot with them (chap. xxix.), so Ezekiel wrote for the use of Jerusalem, though Jeremiah himself was resident there; and yet they were far from looking upon it as an affront to one another, or an interfering with one another's business;

for ministers have need of one another's help, both by preaching and writing. Jeremiah wrote to the captives for their consolation, which was the thing they needed. Ezekiel is here directed to write to the inhabitants of Jerusalem, for their conviction and humiliation, which was the thing they needed."

AFFLICTION.—" When an affliction has done its work, it shall be removed in mercy, as the locusts of Canaan were from a penitent people; not as the locusts of Egypt were removed in wrath, for an impenitent prince, only to make room for another plague."

JONAH.—" What a strange sort of a man was Jonah to dread the success of his ministry! Many have been tempted to withdraw from their work because they have despaired of doing good by it; but Jonah declined preaching because he was afraid of doing good by it; and still he persists in the same corrupt notion; for it seems the whale's belly itself could not cure him of it." .... " See how mildly the great God speaks to this foolish man; to teach us to 'restore' those that are fallen, with a spirit of meekness and with soft answers to 'turn away wrath.' "

US, NOT I.—" The two blind men did not each of them say for himself, 'Have mercy on me,' but both for one another, 'Have mercy on us.'"

SUPERFLUITIES.—" The piece of money which Peter took out of the mouth of the fish was just enough to pay the tax for Christ and himself. Christ could as easily have commanded a bag of money as a piece of money; but He would teach us not to covet superfluities, but having enough for our present occasions therewith to be content, and not to distrust God though we live from hand to mouth."

SINGING.—" Singing of Psalms is a gospel ordinance. Christ's removing the hymn from the close of the Passover to the close of the Lord's Supper, plainly speaks, that He intended that ordinance should continue in His Church; that as it had not its birth with the ceremonial law, so it should not die with it."

PRAYER.—"The waterman in the boat, who with his hook takes hold of the shore, doth not thereby pull the shore to the boat but the boat to the shore. So in prayer we do not draw the mercy to ourselves but ourselves to the mercy."

TWO THIEVES, NOT APOSTLES.—" Some of Christ's apostles were afterwards crucified, as Peter and Andrew; but none of them were crucified 'with Him,' lest it should have looked as if they had been joint-undertakers with Him in satisfying for man's sin, and joint-purchasers of life and glory; therefore He was crucified between two malefactors, who could not be supposed to contribute anything to the merit of His death."

KINDNESSES.—" If Christ reckons kindnesses to us services to Him, we ought to reckon services to Him kindnesses to us; and to encourage them though done by those who follow not with us."

CHRIST'S PRUDENCE.—" Take these things hence." See His prudence in His zeal. When He drove out the sheep and the oxen, the owners might follow them; when He poured out the money, they might gather it up again; but if He had turned the doves flying, perhaps they could not have been retrieved; therefore to them that sold doves, He said, 'Take these things hence.'"

I come now to III. SAVOURINESS AND QUAINT FELICITIES OF WORDING.—I like the old Puritan word 'savour.' I do not doubt that in it has been one supreme attraction to the readers of the Commentary of Matthew Henry. Not as scent on a pocket-handkerchief, but as fragrance in a flower, is a 'savour' of the Lord Jesus Christ to be found all through the Commentary. However wide his circuit, he leads us back to the Cross. However varied his excursiveness, he remembers Christ. No one who does not love Christ will care for Matthew Henry. No one who cares for Matthew Henry can long fail to love Christ. This being so, it will be perceived that it is less easy to illustrate the 'savour' by examples. Yet I must try. These my closing selections will alternately illustrate his savouriness and quaint felicity of wording.

FAMILY-ALTAR.—"Abram was very rich, and had a

numerous family, was now unsettled and in the midst of enemies; and yet, wherever he pitched his tent, he built an altar. Wherever we go, let us not fail to take our religion along with us."

COMMUNION.—"Communion with God may, at any time, serve to make up the want of conversation with our friends. When our relations are separated from us, yet God is not."

OUR CREATION.—"Let our make and place, as men, mind us of our duty as Christians, which is always to keep heaven in our eye, and the earth under our feet."

UNDER, NOT ABOVE.—"Waters and seas oft in Scripture signify troubles and afflictions (Psalms lxix. 2, 14, 15; xlii. 7). God's own people are not exempted from these in this world, but it is their comfort that they are only 'waters under the heaven,' there are none in heaven; and that they are all in the place that God hath appointed them and within the bounds that He hath set them."

DUST.—"Man was made of the 'dust of the ground,' a very unlikely thing to make a man of; but the same infinite power that made the world of nothing, made man, its masterpiece, of next to nothing. He was made of the dust, the small dust, such as is upon the surface of the earth. He was not made of gold dust, powder of pearl, or diamond dust; but common dust, dust of the ground."

GOD'S CARE.—"He that feeds His birds will not starve His babes."

BREATH.—"Let the soul which God hath breathed into

us, breathe after Him ; and let it be for Him since it is from Him."

FAIR DEALING.—" Those who deal fairly have reason to expect fair dealing."

SAFETY.—" We may comfortably trust God with our safety, while we carefully keep to our duty. If God be our guide, He will be our guard."

DELAYS.—" God's time for the enlargement of His people will appear at last to be the fittest time. If the chief butler had at first used his interest for Joseph's enlargement and had obtained it, it is probable, upon his release, he would have gone back to the land of the Hebrews again, which he spoke of so feelingly (cxl. 15); and then he had neither been so blessed himself, nor such a blessing to his family, as afterwards he proved. But delaying two years longer, and coming out now upon this occasion to interpret the king's dreams, way was made for his great preferment. Those that patiently wait for God shall be paid for waiting, not only principal but interest (Lam. iii. 16)."

CHANGES.—" We cannot judge what men are by what they have been formerly; nor what they will do by what they have done. Age and experience may make men wiser and better. They that had sold Joseph, yet would not now abandon Benjamin. The worst may mend in time."

EXODUS xxiii. 1-9.—"That which we translate, 'Thou shalt not raise,' the margin reads, 'Thou shalt not receive a false report'; for sometimes the receiver, in this case, is as bad as the thief; and a backbiting tongue would not do so much mischief as it doth, if it were not countenanced."

MORNING.—" The morning is perhaps as good a friend to the Graces as it is to the Muses."

GOD.—" God's greatness and goodness illustrate and set off each other. That the tenor of His greatness may not make us afraid, we are told how good He is; and that we may not presume upon His goodness, we are told how great He is."

MERCY.—" The springs of mercy are always full; the streams of mercy always flowing. There is mercy enough in God, enough for all, enough for each, enough for ever."

LAW AND GOSPEL.—" The Law taught the leper to cry, ' Unclean, unclean !' but the Gospel has put another cry into the leper's mouth—(Luke xvii. 12, 13)—where we find ten lepers crying with a loud voice, ' Jesus, Master, have mercy upon us.' The Law only shows us our disease, the Gospel shows us our help in Christ."

CONTEMPT.—" Those are hastening apace to their own ruin who begin to think it below them to be religious. They that begin to despise religion, will come by degrees to loathe it; and mean thoughts of it will ripen into ill thoughts of it: they that turn from it will turn against it."

WAITING.—" There is no time lost, while we are waiting God's time. It is as acceptable a piece of submission to the will of God to sit still contentedly when our lot requires it, as to work for Him when we are called to it."

THE WORLD.—" We are more in danger by the charms

of a smiling world, than by the terrors of a frowning world."

CALLING ON GOD.—"Those that call upon God shall certainly find Him within call."

FLIGHT.—"There is no running from God but by running to Him; no fleeing from His justice but by fleeing to His mercy."

PROPORTION.—"God proportions our trials to our strength and our strength to our trials."

HONOUR.—"Like the shadow [Honour] follows those that flee from it, but flees from those that pursue it."

WISDOM.—"Wisdom is good with an inheritance, but an inheritance is good for little without wisdom."

FALLS.—"Though God may suffer His people to fall into sin, He will not suffer them to lie still in it."

THE GRAVE.—"The grave is a bed soon made. If the grave be ready for us it concerns us to be ready for the grave."

WORLDLINGS.—"Worldlings make gold their God: saints make God their gold; and they that are enriched with His favour and grace, may truly be said to have abundance of the best gold and best laid up."

EXPECTATION.—"We must look up or look out, as he that has shot an arrow looks to see how near it has come to the mark. We lose much of the comfort of our prayers for want of observing the returns of them.'

PRAISE.—"Holy joy is the life of thankful praise, as thankful praise is the language of holy joy: 'I will be glad and rejoice in Thee.'"

FAITH.—"When we want the faith of assurance, we must live by a faith of adherence."

CRIES.—" To cry out, My God, why am I sick? why am I poor? would give cause to suspect discontent and worldliness. But 'Why hast Thou forsaken me?' is the language of a heart binding up its happiness in God's favour."

THE VALLEY OF DEATH.—" It is death indeed that is before us; but 1. It is but the shadow of death; there is no substantial evil in it: the shadow of a serpent will not sting, nor the shadow of a sword kill. 2. It is the valley of the shadow—deep indeed, and dark and dirty; but the valleys are fruitful, and so is death itself fruitful of comforts to God's people. 3. It is but a walk in this valley, a gentle, pleasant walk. The wicked are chased out of the world and their souls are required; but the saints take a walk to another world as cheerfully as they take their leave of this. 4. It is a walk through it, they shall not be lost in this valley, but get safe to the mountains of spices on the other side of it."

PATHS OF RIGHTEOUSNESS.—" In these paths we cannot walk unless God both lead us unto them and lead us in them."

ANSWERS.—" As by the prayer of faith we return answers to God's promises of mercy, so by the promises of mercy, God returns answers to our prayers of faith." Again :—" If we would have God to hear what we say to Him by prayer, we must be ready to hear what He saith to us by His word."

KNOWLEDGE, NOT IGNORANCE.—" Knowledge is the mother of devotion and of all obedience: blind sacrifices will never please a seeing God."

THE SEA.—" We use to say, They that will learn to pray, let them go to sea; I say, They that will go to sea, let them learn to pray."

THREE.—" Solomon compares two together to a threefold cord; for where two are closely joined in holy love and fellowship, Christ will by His Spirit come to them and make a Third, as He joined Himself to the two disciples going to Emmaus."

GOD'S OUTCASTS.—" God owns them when men reject and disown them. They are outcasts, but they are '*Mine* outcasts.'"

HEART-WORK.—" We make nothing of our religion, whatever our profession be, if we do not make heart-work of it."

CONFESSION.—" When we cast our sins behind our back and take no care to repent of them, God sets them before His face and is ready to reckon for them: but when we set them before our face in true repentance, as David did when his sin was ever before him, God casts them behind His back."

GOD'S LOVE.—" God's compassions to His people infinitely exceed those of the tenderest parents towards their children. What are the affections of nature to those of the God of nature?"

FORGIVENESS.—" The sin of sinners is never forgotten till it is forgiven. It is ever before God till by repentance it is 'ever before' us."

THE SABBATH.—" It is a true observation which some have made, that the streams of all religion run either deep or shallow, according as the banks of the Sabbath are kept up or neglected."

THE CHURCH.—"In the Church on earth God dwells with men; in that in Heaven men dwell with God."

OLD AND NEW TESTAMENT.—"The Old Testament begins with the book of the generation of the world; and it is its glory that it doth so. But the glory of the New Testament herein excelleth, that it begins with 'the book of the generation' of Him that made the world."

GOD.—"By the light of Nature we see God as a God *above* us; by the light of the Law we see Him a God *against* us; but by the light of the Gospel we see Him Immanuel, God *with* us, in our own nature, and (which is more) in our interests."

GRADATIONS.—"A wicked man is the worst of creatures; a wicked Christian is the worst of men; and a wicked Minister is the worst of Christians.

MARTYRS.—"As the first Old Testament saint [Abel] so the first New Testament minister [Stephen] died a martyr."

CHRIST POOR.—"Christ went upon the water in a borrowed boat, ate the passover in a borrowed chamber, was buried in a borrowed sepulchre, and He rode on a borrowed ass. Let not Christians scorn to be beholden one to another; and when need is, to go a-borrowing, for our Master did it."

KEY.—"This parable has its key hanging at the door. The drift and design of it is prefixed" (St. Luke xviii. 1-8).

I have thus, with considerable fulness, exemplified those special characteristics of the Commentary of Matthew Henry that have struck myself. I do not question that any hundred others "searching" it, would each find as many noticeable things from their standpoints as I have done from mine. All that I have quoted might be left out of account; and the Commentary still remain an opulent one in everything that belongs to a book designed for the spiritual life of its readers. Surely this one statement — and I make it deliberately — is enough to win attention to the great Commentary from my fellow-ministers and students. Equally does it affirm for Matthew Henry a unique place in THE RELIGIOUS LITERATURE OF CHRISTENDOM, AND AMONG THE SPIRITUAL FORCES THAT HAVE BEEN OPERATIVE SINCE THE COMMENTARY WAS PUBLISHED. I hesitate not to avouch that no estimate of these forces can or has been made—as in your Hunt's 'History of Religious Thought,' or Lecky's books—that leaves this factor out. Far away behind more prominent men and books, this

Commentary of Matthew Henry has been going down with the stillness but also the energizing life of dew or "small rain" on the roots of the spiritual life of England and the English-speaking races. I believe that more and more of the beautifulest and best, the deepest and finest of Christians in all the Churches, have been nurtured on this Commentary than on any other in any language whatever. I have no wish to withdraw either others or myself from study and re-study of the highest criticism available, but I am sure that the sanctified common-sense of Matthew Henry leads us farther into the "secrets" of the Lord, than the most vauntful and most learned exegesis, whether of native growth or foreign. Avowedly Matthew Henry intended his Commentary to be read alongside of 'learned' ones, *e.g.*, Bishop Patrick's and Poole's Synopsis.

I like him, I must add, for his bright, healthy, warm-hearted cheeriness. There is nothing of the morbid from beginning to end. I hold the Commentary finally, to be doubly sacred and venerable as having been born of prayer. Luther's was his watchword, as the Diary fully shows—*Bene orasse est bene studuisse.* I would have us all in this more and more follow in the steps of Matthew Henry.* I find in his imperishable Commentary, and in the beneficent work it has done and continues to do, the fulfilment of our living Laureate's prayer. We may read it :—

> " Mine be the strength of spirit, full and free,
>   Like some broad river rushing down alone,
>   With the self-same impulse wherewith he was thrown
> From his loud fount upon the echoing lea :—
> Which with increasing might doth forward flee
>   By town, and tower, and hill, and cape, and isle,
> And in the middle of the green salt sea
>   Keeps his blue waters fresh for many a mile.

---

* In truthfulness I must notify that his sanctified common-sense sometimes fails him. Homer nods, *e.g.*, on his remarks about Rahab's lie, where he represents her as giving an "ironical direction" to the authorities. So again when in Acts xxiv. 26, he reflects on the disciples for not bribing Felix. These are crucial instances ; but you must search widely for very many more.

> Mine be the power which ever to its sway
> Will win the wise at once, and by degrees
> May into uncongenial spirits flow;
> Ev'n as the warm gulf-stream of Florida
> Floats far away into the Northern seas
> The lavish growths of southern Mexico."

I have thus—however inadequately and beneath my own ideal—delivered the message for TO-DAY from each Life and Life-work of our REPRESENTATIVE NONCONFORMISTS. It were an easy task—a task of love—to multiply "Classic Preachers"—"Masters of Theology"—"Companions for the Devout Life"—Scholars "ripe and good"—Writers of imperishable books—from the ranks of BRITISH NONCONFORMITY, earlier and later, who may be placed man for man, and life for life, and influence for influence, beside the Worthies and Mighties of REPRESENTATIVE CONFORMISTS or Churchmen. I was limited to four; and it was not unnatural that, as being myself a minister of a Presbyterian Church, and giving these Lectures under the auspices of the College Committee of that Church, I should have chosen these from among PRESBYTERIANS. But Independents, Baptists, and Methodists, and other branches of Christ's Church, have representative names comparable with ours and with any. I think it might be beneficial if each Denomination similarly revived the memories and sought to impress the lessons of the Life-work of their respective Worthies.

And NOW I may be permitted, in bringing these Lectures to a close, to recall the CHARACTERISTICS by which I have designated the REPRESENTATIVE NONCONFORMISTS selected, viz.:—

JOHN HOWE : *Intellectual Sanctity.*
RICHARD BAXTER : *Seraphic Fervour.*
SAMUEL RUTHERFORD : *Devout Affection.*
MATTHEW HENRY : *Sanctified Common-sense.*

I have stated, illustrated, and enforced these. Need I say that I have done so throughout, with a thoroughly PRACTICAL AIM? The real truth is, that I shall hold myself to have sadly missed the *motif* of my book if I have failed to stir my Readers to fresh CONSECRATION of themselves to the same Master and to the same service, to which these four venerable and holy men gave themselves. I remember the old pathetic if also accusing message: "Lo, thou art unto them as a very lovely song of one that hath a pleasant voice, and can play well on an instrument: for they hear thy words, *but they do them not*" (Ezekiel xxxiii. 32). I disclaim all assumption of my Lectures having been a 'lovely song,' as all pretence to 'play well.' But it were a spurious modesty not to avouch that I have looked beyond mere pleasing and mere interesting to PERSUASION and QUICKENING of heart and conscience. I shall rejoice and be profoundly thankful, if in any degree these Lectures —whether as spoken or in book-form—be used as helps to my fellow-ministers and fellow-labourers or students or other young men, in efforts to ACTUALIZE the augustness as well as the blessedness, the wonder and also the joyfulness of being "WORKERS *together* with HIM"

(2 Cor. vi. 1). I would summon all of us to catch inspiration from the examples of the Worthies whose Life-work has been re-set before us. The eleventh chapter of the Epistle to the Hebrews warrants such keeping in mind of our forefathers. Nor is it a light matter, that as Presbyterians we have so illustrious an ancestry, and so historically great a place among the 'faithful' Churches of our Land and of Christendom. But, as in hereditary nobility, a great lineage may be a reproach and accusation. That we are a historic indigenous Church,—not a mere transplantation from Scotland, albeit, dear to us are her "very stones and dust,"—the Church of HOWE and BAXTER and HENRY and far beyond them, is indisputable. That —with every deduction—we have been true to our evangelical 'Confession of Faith' and (substantially) wise and noble 'Catechisms,' is equally indisputable. That in the living Present, we have a work of God to do in this England in large-hearted co-operation with our fellow Nonconformists, is being increasingly recognized.

What then? I answer, be it ours—by God's help—to aim high and higher,—be it ours to show absolute, undivided allegiance to the LORD JESUS and to THE BOOK,—be it ours to present the "old old story" of the Gospel as a Divine revelation of God's heart and purpose, in all its fulness and richness and power and simplicity,—be it ours to speak, as accrediting that God the HOLY SPIRIT abides in vigilant and gracious patience of hope, with men,—be it ours to bear forth to our fellow-men EVERYWHERE, and as adapted for universal man, the "good news" of our heavenly Father's everlasting love,—be it ours to be content with nothing less and nothing else than multiplied winning of sinners at home and abroad to the Lord,—be it ours to urge and expect likeness to Christ on earth and exhibition of the Divine peculiarity of conversion and that Divine 'beauty of holiness' that belongs to those who have been "born again,"—be it ours to evidence that to us prayer is a grand reality and the coming of 'The Kingdom' a certainty, —be it ours to 'convince' every observer, even gainsayer, ay the very un-churchers of us as of all Nonconformists, that our Presbyterianism is simply our ecclesiastical Church-form and framework and 'preaching' Christ—Christ crucified once and now enthroned and living—'commending' Christ, 'magnifying' Christ, placing Christ supreme over all else, our charter, our impulse, our *credenda*, our consecration, our song of pilgrimage, our prelibation of heaven. It is a magnificent function that our REPRESENTATIVE WORTHIES filled and that we to-day fill, when we are in any way trying to WITNESS and WORK for Christ. I would have us ennoble, engrandeur our conception of our office and commission. We live in a time when the very oppositions of 'science falsely so-called' that JOHN HOWE and RICHARD BAXTER combated with high-hearted courage and enduring success, are being clamorously and audaciously revived. The signs of the times seem to be declarative of increasing rather than diminished antagonism between Christianity and modern Scientism, Faith and Sense. But spectres of doubt have risen in the

Past, and being gone up to have been shown to be spectres; and so they shall again. Ghosts of dead heresies have had strange resurrection and been laid; and they shall be re-laid. A phantasmagoria of unbeliefs and disbeliefs has come and vanished; and comes and vanishes to-day. Very ancient is the endeavour to degrade man's soul into a finer—if finer—organization of matter as to-day; but in wrath or ruth, in despair or aspiration, the soul has asserted itself and refused to be materialized; and so shall it ever be. I would have each of us play the man, the Christian, in these inevitable conflicts, fearless of the issue—because 'strong' in Him who lives and reigns and abides "God over all blessed for evermore." I would have us recognize that purified and unselfish, noble and beautiful lives lived out before God and men on every day of the week, and with no sorrowful contradictions between our practice and our preaching or teaching, are the supremest and most irrefutable evidence for Christ and Christianity. I would have us understand

that it is obligatory on everyone called upon
to contend for the faith to be well instructed,
widely read, richly cultured, scholarly, thought-
ful, patient, and willing to hear the 'other side;'
and not only so, but ready to discern that your
intellectual Doubter is to be met frankly rather
than suspiciously—as in not a few cases resembling the son in the parable, who, whilst
the other said, 'I go,' and went not, said, 'I
go not,' and went. I would have us copy after
the long, long patience and inviolate silence of
Him Whom the blaspheming and base, the
arrogant and false, the swift-generalising and
insulting, un-deify and assail—still magnanimously causing His sun to shine and His rain
to fall "upon the *evil*" as well as on the good,
when He might lay them dead as ever were
the' invading hosts of Sennacherib. I would
have us rise above our own human weakness, and 'lay hold' of His strength as that
is 'brought near' to us in the Word and in
the historic progress of His Church and 'the
Truth' from age to age until now, as calmly

assured of this, that He Who said of old, "My Father worketh hitherto, and I work," abides the SAME "Yesterday and To-day and For Ever;" and that the ground of assurance of ultimate triumph is not that we are on God's side, but that God is on ours. I would have us realize that 'the Kingdom' of the Lord Jesus comes by conquest—true, indeed, by conquest that wields no weapons of destruction, sheds no blood, perpetrates no atrocities, covets no provinces, yet none the less conquest—conquering love, redeeming grace, transforming mercy, sanctifying power, heart-won allegiance. I would have us apprehend that it is no losing cause on whose behalf we are honoured to be 'called'—any seeming ebb of Christianity here or yonder being but as of the sea, that only ebbs to thunder again on a hundred shores; any delay, the outcome of the Divine order that works slowly because everlastingly, and can wait as foreseeing 'the end from the beginning.' I would have us, while others hang back, say, 'Here am I, send me.' I would have us decide while others hesitate; advance while others argue; stand forth and fast, while others delay; 'come out and be separate' while others conform to the world; leap up to the rallying-cry, 'Who is on the Lord's side?' while others are deaf.

"Who is on the Lord's side?" I would catch up across the centuries, from Ebal and Gerizim, the grand question. I would turn it into our watchword. I would exult in it as our 'call.' I would have it reverberate from every pulpit. I would have it interpreted by every life. I would have it mark off unmistakably and irreversibly the friends and the enemies of "my Lord and my God." "Who is on the Lord's side?" There must be a taking of sides. The time is irrevocably gone for compromise as for lukewarmness, for dallying as for dexterities of diplomacy, for neutrality as for cowardice. It is DEMANDED that we make up our minds FOR or AGAINST. "Who is on *the Lord's* side?" I ask not that men pronounce my shibboleth. If 'sibboleth' come readier, be it sibboleth. I seek no aggrandizement of my own Church at the expense of others, I desire no sectarian increase for her. I denounce rival bigotries and narrownesses. I covet, first and foremost, coming to THE LORD'S side. I un-church none, as I will suffer myself to be un-churched by none. I know that we have the Divine insignia that we are "ministers of religion," and it matters not to me a straw that Episcopacy and Roman Catholicism deny our orders' and succession. But these are merest trivialities and accidents, beside the transcendent differentiating matter, "WHO IS ON THE LORD'S SIDE?" To multiply the number, I pray for the INTELLECTUAL SANCTITY of JOHN HOWE —the SERAPHIC FERVOUR of RICHARD BAXTER—the DEVOUT AFFECTION of SAMUEL RUTHERFORD — the SANCTIFIED COMMON-SENSE of MATTHEW HENRY to be reproduced among us. I seek that we shall enter ourselves heirs to the great historic evangelical Presbyterianism of the Past. But whilst I urge that we shall maintain our individuality and continuity, I do so as longing for the breaking-down of all dividing walls between fellow-servants and fellow-Christians under the same Divine and only possible Head. I mourn over oppositions and divisions, antagonisms and exacerbations, between the Lord's common friends when His enemies, in their deepening hate and opposition, demand that we close our ranks and present a united phalanx. For myself, I do not despair of ultimate recognition and co-operation by and between ALL who believe in and love and serve the One Divine Lord and Saviour Jesus Christ. Whoever dies, He lives on. Whoever and whatever is deposed or changed, he 'reigns.' The Kingdom 'comes.' We believe that by-and-bye Christ Himself shall bulk larger than the Church, the Shepherd than the Folds. Toward this,

> "We want no aid of hurricane
>   To show a front to wrong;
> We have a citadel of truth,
>   More amiable and strong:
> Calm words, great thoughts, unflinching faith,
>   Have never stirred in vain;
> They've won our battles many a time,
>   And so they shall again."

APPENDIX A.

(Lecture on Howe, page 13.)

FROM EDMUND SPENSER'S "HYMN OF BEAUTY."

"How vainely . . . doe ydle wits invent,
　That beautie is nought else but mixture made
　Of colours faire, and goodly temp'rament
　Of pure complexions, that shall quickly fade
　And passe away, like to a sommer's shade ;
　Or that it is but comely composition
　Of parts well measur'd with meet disposition !

"Hath white and red in it such wondrous powre,
　That it can pierce through th' eyes unto the hart,
　And therein stirre such rage and restlesse stowre
　As nought but death can stint his dolour's smart ?
　Or can proportion of the outward part
　Move such affection in the inward mynd,
　That it can rob both sense and reason blynd ?

"Why doe not then the blossomes of the field,
　Which are arayd with much more orient hew,
　And to the sense most daintie odours yield,
　Worke like impression in the looker's vew ?
　Or why doe not faire pictures like powre shew,
　In which oft-times we Nature see of Art
　Excel'd, in perfect limning every part ?

"But ah! beleeve me there is more then so,
That workes such wonders in the minds of men;
I, that have often prov'd, too well it know,
And who so list the like assayes to ken,
Shall find by trial, and confesse it then,
That Beautie is not, as fond men misdeeme,
An outward shew of things that onely seeme.

"For that same goodly hew of white and red,
With which the cheekes are sprinckled, shal decay,
And those sweete rosy leaves, so fairly spred
Upon the lips, shall fade and fall away
To that they were, even to corrupted clay:
That golden wyre, those sparckling stars so bright,
Shall turne to dust, and loose their goodly light.

"But that faire lampe, from whose celestiall ray
That light proceedes, which kindleth lovers' fire,
Shall never be extinguisht nor decay;
But, when the vitall spirits doe expyre,
Unto her native planet shall retyre,
For it is heavenly borne and cannot die,
Being a parcell of the purest skie.

"For when the soule, the which derived was
At first out of the great immortall Spright
By whom all live to love, whilome did pas
Down from the top of purest heaven's hight
To be embodied here, it then tooke light
And lively spirits from the fayrest starre
Which lights the world forth from his firie carre.

" Which powre retayning still, or more or lesse,
  When she in fleshly seede is eft enraced,
  Through every part she doth the same impresse,
  According as the heavens have her graced ;
  And frames her house, in which she will be placed,
  Fit for her selfe, adorning it with spoyle
  Of th' heavenly riches which she rob'd erewhyle.

" Thereof it comes that those faire soules, which have
  The most resemblance of that heavenly light,
  Frame to themselves most beautiful and brave
  Their fleshly bowre, most fit for their delight,
  And the grosse matter by a soveraine might
  Tempers so trim, that it may well be seene
  A pallace fit for such a virgin Queene.

" So every spirit, as it is most pure,
  And hath in it the more of heavenly light,
  So it the fairer body doth procure
  To habit in, and it more fairely dight
  With chearefull grace and amiable sight :
  For of the soule the bodie forme doth take,
  For soule is forme, and doth the bodie make."

The later hymn, on "Heavenly Beautie," only deepens the earlier; for its burden, too, is, "All that's good is beautifull and faire."

APPENDIX B.

(*Lecture on Howe, page* 24).

THOMAS LARKHAM AND HOWE, AND AN EARLIER CONTROVERSY.

IN the very noticeable book "On the Attributes" referred to in the text, Thomas Larkham introduces a curious insertion. After page 91 of Part II., in the Sermon-lecture on "The Justice of God," there is a special address to his readers in reference to the challenge and 'lashing' of John Howe. It is here given *in extenso*. In order to its being understood I first of all quote the words fastened on by Howe :—

"Christ saith (John iv. 34), 'My meat is to do the will of Him that sent Me, and to finish His work.' Here ye see Christ wills and acts under the power of the anointing which He had 'above His fellows,' and 'not by measure.' But Matt. xxvi. 39, where He saith, 'If it be possible let this cup passe from Me: neverthelesse not as I will but as Thou wilt.' There our blessed Saviour, looking to the supream reason, the will of God, though not of inferiour reason, His purely natural will as mere man, under a short conflict of nature, desires the removal of that bitter cup ; yet He stoops to his Father's will, and is quickly called to obedience from that creaturely desire, which proceeding from a principle of self-preservation suddenly seized upon Him : by the power, I say, of this anointing, He submits Himself to God's will. Neither do I find that ever He is said to be obedient in all the New Testament but touching this one thing; but of this we read, Hebrews ix. 8, 'Though He were the Son, yet learned He obedience by the things that He suffered.' (Read Romans v. 19; Phil. ii. 8.) This then was the obedience of effect, to bring His will of nature, by the power of grace, to submit unto the will of God. And doubtless when Christ shared the cup and desired the removal of it, He did not speak these words in faith but in feare, and therefore (whatever ignorant or malitious men may prattle) it was not a desire of grace but of nature. Yet is as void of sin as ever any action of Christ was that ever He did. For though He were made man in all things like other men, yet was He made man void of sin." Then comes the intercalated address thus, *i.e.*, in so far as the dispute itself is concerned, or the personal portions, and only those ; for the vindication of his position is enforced and illustrated from "Mr. Calvin," and Sibbes, and Perkins, and Hayward, and many others beyond our space to give :

"Reader, understand that since I preached upon this attribute, I had occasion to touch upon the same point (by the way) which is last mentioned, on a lecture-day at Tavistock, where among others of my auditors was present one of my young neighbour ministers (I am bold to say young, because I had a gown on my back and Universitie degrees before he could read English long) who, I hope out of ignorance, but fear out of malice (I am sure from one if not from both) hath made a mightie dust in divers places of this countie of Exton, that I had preached blasphemie (as was generally reported by some that it may be made the worst of what he said, as usuallie reports lose nothing in carriage) and that I denied that prayer of the removall of the cupp (which is true I did) to proceed from grace. But this is not all: he so ordered his Master's work that he inveigled many credulous and prejudicial ministers (as I take God to witness hath been related to me by very many) that I should say that at that time Christ had not a jot of grace when He made that prayer; which is a lewd and loud ly. And I must be pardoned that I take it so tenderly as I do. But upon my hunting out of his unworthy carriage, he and some others, *ejusdem savagiur*, have taken much pains to prove, with all the wit they have, that the desire of the removal of the cup proceeded from the same principle that those words did, 'Not My will but Thy will be done.' And they stick not to say that it must needs be so, because of the union of the two natures in Christ's person; and because the Scripture saith, He was full of grace and truth, and because it was a prayer, and because every action in Christ and all men is either gracious or sinfull, and such a deale of odd Divinity as lightly hath not been heard again—all tending much to many dangerous heresies, as of the Monothelites, or Monophysites, of Nestorius or Eutyches manifestly, who denied the flesh of Christ to be like unto ours, and the two distinct natures of the Second Person with their distinct actings. Whereupon I thought it requisite to insert a word or two (though it be not usuall so to do in this manner) to advise our mighty doctors not to be so forward, so peremptory, but to tarry at Jericho till their beards be grown. For forty years have I known what I have preached to be a truth, and never heard it so much as questioned by any alive, until it pleased this minister out of his superabundant knowledge (or pride rather) to begin to prattle about it. . . . Here I might blot more paper with better warrant than my neighbour novices have blotted my good name. But I consider God alone doth all, even when Shimei doth curse David. And I would not have done so much as I have, had it not been pressed upon me as a duty; and I have thought myself bound to keep me from imputations which might make the crosse of Christ of none effect. I am told my neighbour will answer me if I write, etc. I had rather he would have saved me the trouble of this unpleasing task, by seeing his faultinesse and acknowledging his errours. I thank God our ignorant prophane clergie have not power to command magistrates to be their executioners, their Sathans, etc., and hope they never shall. To me it is intollerable that a few weake, blind, unhallowed men, should assume to themselves such power, not only $\alpha\lambda\lambda o\tau\rho\iota o\epsilon\pi\iota\sigma\kappa o\pi\epsilon\hat{\iota}\nu$, but also to forget the old Universitie vulgar phrase (Semonty Freshmen) which is wont to be spoken to impudent youths that forget good manners. If any of my brethren, though by years my children (for I have a sonne of mine own a minister), shall come to me to show me my errours, I hope I shall be able to thank them and to bless God for them. But when they shall wander up and down to reproach, and backbite, and defame; and at their meetings between their cups and tobacco-pipes abuse their brethren and neighbours; this makes them far unlike ministers of Jesus Christ in their behaviour. . . . I think it not meet to spend more words in pursuit of vain and ignorant men. Let them be contented that they are let alone to live by the resources of the Church, which they do but little for (God knoweth), and not begrudge me my pains, and labour, and sufferings in the place in which God hath set me; made much the greater by their ignorance, superstition, formality, and self-ends, shewed in their complying with prophane people in their pollutions of the divine ordinances of Jesus Christ. If any be disposed to take up the controversie, I shall by God's assistance be ready to maintain this truth, that that desire or branch of Christ's prayer, 'Let this cup pass from Me,' did not proceed from grace, but naturale fear and astonishment of spirit, yet without sin."

John Howe, in 1656, was in his twenty-sixth year; Thomas Larkham in his fifty-fifth; so that *prima facie* there was lacking to the elder that respect and reverence due by the younger.

I add concerning good and brave Thomas Larkham—about whom Calamy and Palmer and others have written inaccurately as to the facts of his life—that he was born at Lyme Regis, Dorsetshire, on August 17th, 1601; baptized August 20th—that he must have had a godly home, having, in 1656, for "forty years" known the truth—that he was educated at the University of Cambridge, which he addresses with intense affection in a racy epistle-dedicatory prefixed to Part I. of his "Attributes"—that he married, whereof there is this entry in his "Diary": "1661, I took into consideration that this very day, viz., June 3rd, in Anno. Dom. 1622, I was married at Shobrooke; and have lived in that estate full thirty-nine years; in which time I have seen and enjoyed marvellous providences, vouchsafed to me and mine "—that of this marriage there was issue: Thomas, who died in the East Indies; George, who became parish minister of Cockermouth, and was of "The Ejected"; Patience and Jane—that in 1626 he was settled at Northam, where he seems to have endured "much persecution" for his fidelity in reproof of high-seated wickedness*—that he 'fled,' as all too many of Old England's best had to do, to New England—that he is found again in Tavistock in 1642, as is told in the "Diary": "Nov. 12th, 1656. I call to mind this day, that fourteen years agone, on this day, namely, in the year 1642, I left my home in New England, which was then on a Saturday: now, it is a Wednesday, my lecture-day. For heaps of mercies, I do here set down this remembrance with praise "—that he be-

---

* From the present Incumbent of Northam—which is a village between Appledore and Bideford, in the north of Devon—I learn that the register books of the parish are duly signed by Larkham from 1626 to 1639. In 1640 a Rev. Anthony Downe succeeded him as Vicar.

came an army-chaplain (like Baxter later) to the regiment of Sir Hardress Walker—that he succeeded the Rev. George Hughes, B.D., as Vicar, under the patronage of the Earl of Bedford, who remained his friend to the end—that he left his Church in 1661, constrained to 'resign,' as being less painful than a forcible ejection for his Nonconformity—that in retirement he was pursued with the prevalent persecution of all who remained true to conscience, being again and again imprisoned and "summoned" because he dared not cease to preach—that he became a Congregational minister, meeting in a humble house which is now owned by the Unitarians—that possessed of some property he was also engaged in business—that at last, faithful to the close, he died in 1670—and that, spite of the bigotry of those in local authority, who sought even to deny his body Christian burial, the Earl of Bedford came forward and 'commanded' that the dust of his old friend should take its place in *his* family-vault. There he "sleeps well." No great name, no mighty memory, is that of Thomas Larkham on this hither side; but the Day will declare how fully he was used to do everlasting service for the Master.

Besides his really great book on the "Attributes," whence is fetched our present incident, Larkham published other three lesser, viz., "A Discourse of Paying of Tithes. By T. L., M.A., Pastour of the Church of Christ at Tavistock in Devon. Together with an Appendix by way of Apology for the seasonableness thereof. London, 1656;" and "The Wedding Supper, as it was handled out of the fourteen first verses out of the two and twentieth Chapter of Matthew, in sundry Exercises in Tavistock in Devon" (1652), and another on "Naboth." All are among the rarest of Puritan books. They are in none of our great public libraries, nor in any of various rich Puritan libraries known by us. We had the first two daintily bound in one volume, in our possession by the kindness of their owner, the late Alfred Rooker, Esq., of Plymouth. Unfortunately, the "Wedding Supper" lacks the title-page, and, as shown by a reference in the Errata, an Epistle-dedicatory to the Parliament. The "Discourse of paying of Tithes" maintains the obligation of the Jewish Law, and that "tythes are the Lord's portion, and due *Jure Divino*." The argument is more dexterous than sound, and somewhat diplomatic in meeting objections. The "Wedding Supper" is of a very different stamp, being full of the very marrow of the gospel, and with a good deal of the savouriness of Sibbes and Brooks, if without their felicities of phrase and pungency of appeal. If the "Attributes" shows Thomas Larkham to have had a keen, sinewy, vigorous intellect, the "Wedding Supper" bears witness to a wistful, yearning, loving heart. There are many odd, quaint, out-of-the-way bits, *e.g.* :—

"Now, alas, fear of being gull'd by black coats hath brought a snare upon many; endangered by men whose coats are of another colour .... but I say to all, whiles Christ wooeth 'tis good to be wooen" (pp. 9, 10).

Again :—

"Diligently frequent the places where the word is faithfully preached. Be not so superstitious, or silly, as to think it is nowhere to be had but in a parish-church. Nor so absurd and deluded, as to think it is not there to be had at all" (p. 10).

Once more :—

"Can there any good come out of Galilee? was a question in Christ's time; the answer was, 'Come and see.' I give you that counsell. Come and see, come and hear: forsake no meeting where ye may meet Christ" (p. 10).

Further :—

"They that scoff at God's patience (as 2 Peter iii. 3, etc.) or at the meanness of His worshippers (John vii. 48, 49), and the like, shall find that blue-apron mechanicks shall be too hard at last for scarlet coats" (p. 22).

Again :—

"Our work is to bid you ask; God's work is to enable you to ask. The work of Christ's mouth to Lazarus was to bid him to come forth of the grave. It was the secret work of his Almighty power to make him alive, that he might hear and obey that command" (p. 30).

Once more :—

"This sin [worldliness] is like the disease called the hectick feaver, at first hard to be discerned but easie to be cured; but at last easie to be known (sure enough) when it is grown incurable" (pp. 97, 98).

Finally :—

"I will tell you a dream of one of quality, related to myself, by the dreamer himself. Said he, I dreamed the day of judgement was come and all men appeared before Christ. Some were white, others spotted. Methought (said he) I was all white, saving that I had one black spot upon my breast, which I covered with my hand. Upon the separation of these two sorts, I got among the white on the right hand. Glad was I: but at last a narrow search was made, and one came and plucked away my hand from my breast; then appeared my spot, and I was thrust away among the spotted ones" (pp. 180, 181).

There are applications of the truths drawn out of the parable, passionate in their combined fearlessness and earnestness of entreaty. Local abuses are scathingly exposed, and evidence the preacher to have been bold as ever was John

Knox against the most potent wrong-doers. From Evans' catalogue it is found that Cross engraved the portrait of Larkham. We confess that it should be a great joy to us to recover an impression of it, so as to look on the face of the brave noble old man who, with no less courage than power, met and easily confuted even the supreme Thinker of the "Living Temple." *

By the kindness of my friend, Professor Dowden of Trinity College, Dublin, I have been favoured with an extremely rare book, in which another and earlier glimpse of Howe in controversy is furnished. Its title-page (abbreviated) is as follows :—

"The Churches and Ministery of England, True Churches and true Ministery, Cleared, and proved, in a Sermon preach'd the 4th of May at Wiviliscombe; before a numerous Congregation assembled together to hear the opposition, which had been long threatened to be made that day, by Mr. COLLIER and others of his party, who with the greatest strength the West would afford them, were present at the Sermon. . . . . By Francis Fullwood, Minister of the Gospel at Staple

---

* It is only right to state that the above is mainly taken from a Paper of mine, entitled "An Over-looked Incident in the Life of John Howe," that appeared in *Sunday at Home* for October 1874 (No. 1,067).

Fitzpane in the County of Somerset. Before it there is an Epistle and Preface, shewing the Manner, and a Narrative [subjoynd] shewing the substance of the Dispute after the Sermon (both which lasted nine hours). Set forth by the Ministers that were at the Dispute, and Attested under their hands." London, 1652. 4to.

In the "Preface to the Reader" by Charles Darby, it is stated at page 11, "The third Question (which Mr. Howe held in the affirmative) was, whether the said Ministers of the Church of England be the Ministers of Jesus Christ Exclusively?" Then the narrative continues:—

"This was to be stated and discussed May 4th. It seems that this assertion had as much offended those seduced and turbulent spirits, as that of Infant-baptism. Hereupon swift notice was given to all or the most part of the Sectarians of the West. In the mean time many threatening and insulting speeches were given out by this party; as that no Presbyterian Minister durst show his head there, with much to that purpose. Nor was anything more rife in every man's mouth, than the future dispute at Wiviliscombe."

The words "no Presbyterian Minister" applied to Howe, seem decisive that this was our John Howe, whose Presbyterian ordination was well known. Darby is severe and indeed ribald in his account, and hence must be read critically; but the 'Dispute' must have been a mere wrangle. At page 13 we read:—

"They would not suffer Mr. Howe to state the question intended to have been discussed by the Ministers; they feared belike that he was too well provided for them; but with eager importunity required Mr. Fullwood to maintain what he had delivered. They hoped to have foyled him who had been tyred with a two hours preaching, and came nothing prepared for the dispute, which they intended."

The "Brief Narration of the heads of that long (yet happy) Discourse, betwixt M. Fullwood (assisted Sometimes with M. Wood, M. Howe, etc.) . . . ." is quite dramatic in its dialogue (so-to-say). Pages 57-69 are filled with preliminary debates on Fullwood's sermon, then at p. 69 we read:—

"The Adversaries unwilling to say any more against infant-baptism, were urg'd to return to their first Discourse, touching the Churches; and say what they could against our Ministerie, the thing mainly intended: to which they agreed; but Master Fullwood being overwearied desired respit: it was urged that Master *How*, who had sufficiently provided for it, whose exercise was gladly and thankfully read and transcribed by several Godly Ministers about us, might state the question, touching the Ministerie; which was, whether the present Ministerie of the Churches now in England be the true

Ministerie of Jesus Christ exclusively. Which they refused, pretending that would be too long; but gave way, that Master *How* might bring an argument or two for the Ministerie of England : for which he engaged, and performed as followeth."

As the account is brief and hitherto unknown apparently, I give it here :—

How.—" Those that are instruments in the hands of Christ for the work of Conversion are the Ministers of Christ (1 Corinth. ix. 2). But the Ministers of *England* are Instruments in the *hands of Christ*, for the *work of Conversion* (Rom. x. 11). *Ergo*—again, Those that come in *at the door of the sheepfold* are the true Shepherds. But the present Ministers of *England* came in at the door of the sheepfold ; therefore they are true shepherds."

Coll.—" I deny the Minor."

How.—" Those that come in after *the mind of Christ*, come in at the door of the sheepfold. But we come in after the mind of Christ ; therefore, etc."

Coll.—" I deny the Minor."

How.—" Those that come in an *Apostolical way*, come in after the minde of Christ ; but so we come in."

Coll.—" I deny the Minor."

How.—"Those whose substantialls in point of call, were such as the Apostles acted by in *point of ordination*, came in the Apostolick way. But it was so with us."

Coll.—" I deny the Minor."

How.—" Four things only are required in Scripture, so far as I can find, to make a compleat *Apostolicall ordination*. First, *Examination* for abilities (2 Timoth. ii. 3) ; secondly, the *Savour* of good report from the Church

(*Acts* xvi. 2) ; thirdly, a time of *seeking* for God (*Acts* xiv. 23) ; fourthly, *Imposition* of hands (1 Tim. iv. 14)."
Coll.—" You fail in the *End.*"
How.—" Personal failings do not multiply the *substance* of the act. And I pray you give me a better answer."
Coll.—" You want a lawfull authority, if you have all those particulars. And besides, you are not Ministers of Christ, because *you doe not the work of Christ.*
Master Fullwood step'd up and said,—
Ful.—" Master How, I confesse I shall doe you an unkindnesse ; however be pleased to let me speak with Master Collier a little."
Mr. *How*, having received no satisfactory answer, gladly gave leave.—(pp. 69, 70.)

Howe does not appear again. It will be observed that his name is spelled inter-changeably 'Howe' and 'How.' This was frequent contemporarily. He was then in his twenty-second year only, and so the description of him along with the others, as " three or four *young* despised Ministers, and the whole strength of the adversary," was strictly applicable to him. His uncle Obadiah was too old, and equally so his father. I do not think it probable that there was then another Howe. It is noticeable that John Howe should thus have put himself forward, or been put forward, in so public a disputation in his twenty-second year. Equally noticeable is it, that then he should have 'disputed' for the 'exclusive ministry' of the Church of England.

Rogers and the Biographers have overlooked this. Altogether the Wiviliscombe 'Dispute' links on to the Larkham one four years later; and goes still further to shew that John Howe naturally was all that Larkham represented. The Narrative is "true but short," so that we have none of Howe's retorts or points. Still it is manifest he then held to the 'exclusive' claim of the Church of England. To me the propositions as stated bear the mint-mark of John Howe.

APPENDIX C.

(*Lecture on Rutherford, p.* 204, *foot-note.*)

"*Lex Rex*" had the honour of being ordered to be burnt by the hangman.

Rutherford's theological books found opponents. The following is become singularly rare:—"A Reassertion of Grace or Vindiciæ Evangelii. A Vindication of the Gospel-truths, from the unjust censure and undue assertions of Antinomians. In a modest Reply to Mr. Anth. Burgesse's Vindiciæ Legis, Mr. Rutherford's *Finall and Tryumph of Faith*, etc. By Robert Towne. 1654." Not always perhaps theologically sound, this book has a heart of love in it. In the Preface the saintly author complains pathetically, "It is no sin with them, to bely, disguise us, and with open mouth to declaim against us, as Antinomians, sons of Belial, Seducers, Libertines, disobedient, unholy, profane," etc.

Another separate work by the same author follows:—" Monomachia: or a Single Reply to Mr. Rutherford's Book called Christ's Dying and Drawing of Sinners. Vindicating and clearing onely such Positions and Passages on the Assertion of Grace, as are palpably mistaken and perverted, and so mis-called Anti-nomian. Wherein also it appeareth, that the Adversaries' dealing is neither just nor candid. 1654." He finely says in the Epistle—"If my Adversarie think himself wronged or discredited hereby, I answer I should be sorry to stand guilty of doing that wrong to him, as he hath done against me, and the truth itself." This is a patient and singularly candid reply, objection after objection being stated in Rutherford's words, and briefly answered. A still more noticeable work —seldom to be met with now—is this:—"A Reply to Mr. Rutherford, or "A Defence of the Answer to Reverend Mr. Herles Booke against the Independency of Churches. Wherein such objections and answers, as are returned to sundry passages in the said answer by Mr. Samuel Rutherford, a godly and learned brother of the Church of Scotland, in his Booke entituled The Due Right of Presbytery, are examined and removed, and the answer justified and cleared. By Richard Mather, Teacher to the Church at Dorchester in New England. 1646. 1647 4to." Further:—John Tombes, B.D.— the redoubtable antagonist of Baxter—includes Rutherford in his great roll of enemies on the title-page of his quarto of well-nigh a thousand closely-printed pages "Anti-Pœdobaptism or the Third Part" (1657). In § λxxxvi. we are treated with the following:—"The thirteenth and fourteenth Chapters of Mr. Rutherford's first part of the Covenant, are examined; and found to make nothing for Infant Baptism." Here is the wily as diplomatic description of Rutherford's book "Of the Covenant of Grace" —"I found no more strength than others had brought for it [Infant Baptism], and it is written rather like a Sermon than a Scholastique Dispute, and with so many unproved dictates, such a number of obscure expressions (many of which I cannot discern good sense in, so that they have need rather of construction than refutation), so many incoherences and inconsequences, as that I do not judge it worth while to answer him. Yet because of the name of the man . . . I shall add some animadversions on these two chapters" (pp. 737-8). The self-conceit is superb on the part of a man so every way unformed and inarticulate in his style and so characterized by unwisdom and unreason; but so did he characterise Baxter, Hammond, Fuller, Cobbet, etc., etc.

A more arid logomachy than this section and the entire book, it is scarcely possible to imagine. Still, Rutherford's narrow dogmatism handled by one narrower still, does not come out well, albeit the often-rung changes of "ignorance and impertinency" and 'calumny,' sound grotesquely in such a mouth as this Tombes's. I adduce these details—out of many —to confirm my (reluctant) condemnation of Rutherford's spirit in controversy. I add that his Letters are in living circulation in France in a translation by G. Masson—"Lettres aux Chrétiens persecutés ou affliges," etc. (Paris, 1848). It is a dainty book.

FINIS.

Printed by Hazell, Watson, and Viney, London and Aylesbury.

WORKS PUBLISHED BY
HODDER & STOUGHTON,
27, PATERNOSTER ROW.

BY MARCUS DODS, M.A., D.D.

I.
CHEAPER EDITION.

MOHAMMED, BUDDHA, AND CHRIST.

Third Thousand. Crown 8vo, cloth, 3s. 6d.

"His materials have been carefully collected from the best sources, have been thoroughly digested in his own mind, and are here given forth to his readers in well-arranged, clear, and precise language."—*Scotsman.*

"Its general truth, few reflecting Christians will doubt, and its elevating tendency nobody, Christian or unbeliever, will deny. To us this book is specially welcome, as an evidence, in addition to many others, of a new outburst of earnest religious thought and sentiment."—*Spectator.*

II.

ISRAEL'S IRON AGE;
Sketches from the Period of the Judges.

Third Edition. Crown 8vo, cloth, 5s.

"Rich in lessons for the daily life, both exterior and interior; lessons which are drawn with much ease from the ancient story, and given in pure, quiet, admirable English."—*British and Foreign Evangelical Review.*

"The popularity of this volume is richly deserved. The sketches are bright and forcible, and abound in moral teaching and practical lessons for the golden age of Victoria as well as for the iron age of Israel."—*Evangelical Magazine.*

"Powerful lectures. This is a noble volume, full of strength. Young men especially will find in it a rich storehouse of prevailing incentive to a godly life. Dr. Dods searches with a masterly hand."—*Nonconformist.*

Hodder & Stoughton,

STUDIES ON THE NEW TESTAMENT.
EDITED BY THE HON. AND REV. CANON LYTTELTON, M.A.
Third Edition. Crown 8vo, cloth, 7s. 6d.

"Unquestionably M. Godet is one of the first, if not the very first, of contemporary commentators on the Scripture. His portraits and his description, are projected upon the canvas with the brilliancy of the oxyhydrogen lights as compared with the oil-lamp of ordinary comprehension; and we have no hesitation in advising all students of Scripture to read with careful attention these luminous essays."—*Literary Churchman.*

NINE LECTURES ON PREACHING.
Delivered at Yale, New Haven, Conn.
BY R. W. DALE, M.A., of Birmingham.
Third Edition. Crown 8vo, cloth, price 6s.

"Mr. Dale's volume, conceived in the light of modern requirements and bathed in the atmosphere of modern feeling, characterised moreover by a catholicity that fits them equally for every church in which Christ is preached, will be as useful and suggestive to a young preacher as any manual that has come under our notice. It is a volume of rare richness, manliness, and eloquence."—*British Quarterly Review.*

FROM JERUSALEM TO ANTIOCH.
Sketches of Primitive Church Life.
BY THE REV. J. OSWALD DYKES, D.D.
Second Edition. Crown 8vo, cloth, price 7s. 6d.

"All who have heard Dr. Dykes will expect to find much and clear thought, based on competent knowledge of his theme, expressed in a style of rare finish and beauty, and informed by a devout and refined spirit. Nor will they be disappointed. All these excellent qualities are happily displayed in the volume before us."—*Rev. Samuel Cox in "Expositor."*

TALKING TO THE CHILDREN.
BY ALEXANDER MACLEOD, D.D.
Seventh Edition. Fcap. 8vo, price 3s. 6d.

"An exquisite work. Divine truths are here presented in simple language, illustrated by parable and anecdote at once apt and beautiful."—*Evangelical Magazine.*

27, Paternoster Row.

THE BIBLE AND CRITICISM.
BY THE REV. PRINCIPAL RAINY, D.D.
New College, Edinburgh.

Second Thousand. Crown 8vo, cloth, price 5s.

"On this subject Dr. Rainy has brought to bear the well balanced powers of his comprehensive intellect. He treats his subject not only with power, but also with much popular clearness, and with most apt illustration. The judgment is admirably weighed throughout the book. Principal Rainy's common-sense views of criticism are excellent. As a book of wise and well balanced and searching statement of the general principles of honest, scientific criticism, we would highly commend it."—*Weekly Review.*

THE BATTLE OF UNBELIEF.
BY THE REV. GAVIN CARLYLE, M.A.
In crown 8vo, cloth, price 5s.

"A book which we have much pleasure in commending to the attention of our readers. It deals with a number of subjects which it is extremely desirable that people in these days should make themselves acquainted with, and it is written in a style so clear and interesting and popular, as to be eminently readable."—*Family Treasury.*

THE GREATEST OF THE JUDGES;
Principles of Church Life Illustrated in the History of Gideon.

"The work is very beautiful in a pictorial point of view. A dramatic and poetical interest pervades the whole. Earnest workers in the enterprises, especially the mission enterprises of the Church, cannot read it without much edification and great encouragement. We trust it will be extensively read, and have the effect of arousing energies which, with all our boasted zeal and evangelising labours and successes, are yet very imperfectly developed.'—*Watchman.*

Monthly, price One Shilling.

THE EXPOSITOR.
EDITED BY THE REV. SAMUEL COX.

The First Eight Volumes are now ready, handsomely bound in cloth, 8vo, price 7s. 6d. each.

Cases for Binding Numbers in Half-Yearly Volumes, 1s. each.

"THE EXPOSITOR is a publication of sterling value."—*Spectator.*

"The best results of research are set forth by a company of our best men from all our churches under the leadership of Mr. Samuel Cox, who is an expositor *par excellence*."—*British and Foreign Evangelical Review.*

Hodder & Stoughton, 27, Paternoster Row.

GLIMPSES OF THE INNER LIFE OF OUR LORD.

BY PROFESSOR W. G. BLAIKIE, D.D., LL.D.

Third Thousand. Crown 8vo, cloth, price 3s. 6d.

"A devout, spiritual, and tender little book, reverently seeking to penetrate the religious heart of Jesus in His consecration, temptations, ministerings, sorrows, prayerfulness, peace, joy, cross-bearing, and death. It will be valued as a higher kind of religious reading, in which both mind and heart are ministered to."—*British Quarterly Review.*

THE GLORY OF THE CROSS,
As Manifested by the Last Words of Jesus.

BY A. B. MACKAY.

Second and Cheap Edition. Fcap. 8vo, cloth, price 2s. 6d.

"This is a good volume. With careful pains the author shows us the successive scenes of the crucifixion, and teaches us their meanings. He makes his instructions vivid and bright with well-chosen epithet and illustration, and presses the conscience with energy to receive the gospel of love."—*Dr. Dykes, in the British and Foreign Evangelical Review.*

BY H. K. WOOD, A GLASGOW MERCHANT.

I.
THE HEAVENLY BRIDEGROOM AND HIS BRIDE.

Crown 8vo, cloth, price 3s. 6d.

"Exhibits that power of clear, simple statement, and interesting illustration which characterised his previous works."—*British Messenger.*

II.
THE HIGHWAY OF SALVATION.

Sixth Thousand. Fcap. 8vo, cloth, 1s. 6d.

"Of this emphatically 'good book' it may be truly said, that the farther its reader advances, the more will he enjoy its perusal. An admirable and excellent little work."—*Record.*

III.
HEAVENLY LOVE AND EARTHLY ECHOES.

Fourteenth Thousand. Fcap. 8vo, cloth, 1s. 6d.

"The treatment is most appropriate, winning, and earnest. The various joys and sorrows of life, the vicissitudes, fears, hopes, and victories of Christian experience, furnish many fascinating and impressive illustrations of the triumph of the Father's love."—*General Baptist Magazine.*

www.ingramcontent.com/pod-product-compliance
Lightning Source LLC
Chambersburg PA
CBHW030428300426
44112CB00009B/906